From

The Women's Press Ltd
34 Great Sutton Street, London EC1V 0DX

Carol Jones is a secondary school teacher who as a feminist has campaigned against sexual violence against young women, counselled survivors of sexual abuse, been involved in refuge work and resisted enforced heterosexuality. She facilitates workshops for adults on aspects of sex and power in education.

Pat Mahony lives in South East London and works at Goldsmiths' College, University of London in the Department of Postgraduate Initial Teacher Education. She has two daughters who are mercifully (given the 1988 Education Reform Act) nearing the end of their education in schools. Stubbornly, she still holds a view of education as involving a process through which young people might be enabled to think critically about the world in which they live.

Carol Jones and
Pat Mahony, editors

LEARNING OUR LINES

**Sexuality and Social Control
in Education**

The Women's Press

First published by The Women's Press Limited 1989
A member of the Namara Group
34 Great Sutton Street, London EC1V 0DX

British Library Cataloguing in Publication Data

    Learning our lines: sexuality and social control in
    education.
    1. Great Britain. Education. Equality of opportunity
    I. Jones, Carol   II. Mahony, Pat
    370'.941

    ISBN 0-7043-4199-9

Typeset by MC Typeset Limited, Gillingham, Kent
Printed and bound in Great Britain by Cox & Wyman
Ltd, Reading, Berks

Contents

**Part 2 Denying Realities, Endangering Lives,
Working for Change**

Acknowledgments

We would like to thank all the contributors for their hard work, good humour and friendship. To those women whose work we could not include, thank you for your patience and understanding: we hope you feel present in spirit.

Carol Jones

I would like to thank all my friends, old and new, who have always been excited by this book. In particular thanks to Pat Mahony who during its production has been a source of wit, wisdom and friendship which I know will continue.
Thanks also:
– to Della Gibbins with whom I have bounced ideas every day in our busy classrooms and who covered for me during 'rescue work' with girls in school. To Kate Wilson whose skills as an acupuncturist have enabled me to heal.
– to the London Rape Crisis Centre for their confidentiality and help for myself and other women and girls.
– to Emily and others in the old Incest Survivors Campaign for forcing the issue of sexual abuse into the open.
– to my Mum, Margaret, and my sister, Maria, for their support.
– to Pip Scott for sharing her passionate involvement in education.

Above all thanks to Mary Wynne for the years of sharing, nurturing and pioneering work together – personal as well as political.

Pat Mahony

I would like to thank:
– Catherine and Louise Mahony for their patience, generosity and encouragement.
– Carol Jones in whose friendship I have found a richness which goes way beyond our work as co-editors.
– Barbara Whittington for her support.
– Anne-Mette Kruse who has provided unexpected challenges while continuing to be a source of inspiration.

Introduction

Carol Jones and Pat Mahony

Learning Our Lines is not the book we set out to produce when we first discussed its contents early in 1987. This is because in the last two years there have been major changes in two public spheres in Britain: first, the state education system has been radically restructured, and second we have witnessed a shift in ideology which was subsequently encoded in law, in the area of sexuality.

In our early discussions it emerged that from within our very different work contexts, we were both becoming increasingly concerned about local education authority (LEA) policy and implementation of equal opportunities (gender) work. From a feminist perspective we wanted to evaluate the achievements and limitations of the work so far, and to raise for debate the fundamental assumptions underpinning various initiatives. More specifically, we were both becoming increasingly critical and alarmed about the ways in which different LEAs were responding (or not) to issues of equal opportunities (sexuality) and the limited ways in which these were apparently being defined. Our discussions fell into three main areas.

First, some LEAs, from our perspective as feminists, had not adequately understood the links between equal opportunities (gender) and issues of sexuality, and without such understanding we felt that many initiatives were either doomed to failure or could at best achieve only superficial change. Furthermore, since such links do exist we felt it important that they be made explicit and thus open to public debate. Each of us could give many examples where failure to understand the connections and what at times seemed like wilful refusal to explore them, meant that many initiatives fell short of their full potential. Time and time again, even on the most uncontentious principle of attempting to widen the employment opportunities of both sexes, it became obvious that a lurking fear in many people's minds (parents, teachers, governors and young people themselves) was that such initiatives would 'turn kids queer' (parent at a parents' meeting).

Sometimes the fear was more subtly expressed: 'While applauding the school's attempts to encourage girls into science and technology, we have to be careful not to give the impression that we're wanting to turn out a lot of butch engineers' (school governor at a governors' meeting).

Sometimes it was more politely put: 'I really wanted to retrain to teach Home Economics but I got so much hassle, I dropped it. Everyone thought I'd gone gay' (male teacher).

Just from these three quotes alone, the connections between equal work opportunities and sexuality are obvious. Embedded in attitudes to what constitutes proper work for women and men are notions about what counts as being a proper woman or man, and fundamental to those concepts are questions which are ultimately about sexuality.

Second, as we discussed the issues concerning the politics of sexuality we became aware of the evidence which was beginning to emerge about the experiences of gay teenagers in school (Trenchard and Warren, 1984). It was shocking. We learnt that the attempted suicide rate amongst the London Gay Teenage Group was one in five. We became even more convinced that issues of sexuality had to be addressed and that for some young people it was already too late. They had killed themselves for not being heterosexual.

Finally we became alarmed when some LEAs did begin to address issues of sexuality as part of their equal opportunities policy. It seemed to us that some, in a flush of liberal tolerance, were in danger of supporting anything 'gay' just because it was gay. As feminists this was not our standpoint. We wanted to explore the links between male power, male sexuality and the sexploitation of women and children in education and from this point of view there is nothing sacred about 'gay' sexuality. It was in this context that while some LEAs apparently condoned the book *Jenny Lives With Eric and Martin* (which was later to become a *cause celèbre*), feminists were critical of the images it contained of a young girl in bed with her father and his male lover. The objection was not that the men were gay and the point was made that Jenny was no more at risk than if she were in bed with two heterosexual men. Rather, feminists argued, in a world full of women and girl survivors of sexual abuse, the particular image in question had especially painful connotations. We wanted to warn at that stage against an 'anything goes because it's gay' policy which we believed would be an indefensible position.

But we were too late. Even as the first draft of the book was being written, a substantial section of which contained these discussions of LEA policy and practice, the general election of 1987 got under way. In the run-up to the election the Conservative Government and its press had a field day. *Jenny Lives With Eric and Martin* figured as one of the main characters in what became a charade of Labour-controlled LEA bashing. The facts of what some LEAs were trying to do (reduce the number of teenage suicides?) became fictions in which, according to the gutter press, five-year-old children were taught gay sex. The concern for equal opportunities which in reality involves a commitment to eradicate prejudice and discrimination (and has done so for the last 2000 years) was defined as the sudden and latest invention of the loony Left, intent as they supposedly were on withholding a proper education from children. Perhaps most frightening of all was the bare-faced admission by the Prime Minister that her attack on 'anti-racist mathematics whatever that is' was delivered from a position of complete ignorance.

We had passed the point of rational debate, and with the

Labour Party unable to produce a properly argued and reasoned defence the Conservative Party was voted into its third term of office with an endorsement from the electorate to remove education from LEA control.

It was a bad moment for many of us in education as we assessed the likely effects of the measures about to be imposed on the state system. There was a particular irony for those of us involved in the book, which at that first draft stage was critical of LEAs for not doing enough in a context in which by now at least one (the Inner London Education Authority) was to be abolished under the guise of having done too much.

We had barely begun to grasp this before once more the situation began to change rapidly. Two pieces of legislation had special relevance for the issues we were discussing. The first was the 1986 Education (No. 2) Act, parts of which began to be implemented after the 1987 election. This Act gives responsibility to headteachers and school governing bodies for the overall management of their schools (though it remains to be seen how far this apparent power is an illusion). In particular it lays a duty on the governing body to devise whole school policy on sex education, within the parameters however, of encouraging pupils to have: 'due regard to moral considerations and the value of family life' (Section 46, Education (No. 2) Act 1986).

The second piece of legislation of direct relevance is Section 28 of the Local Government Act 1988, which makes it illegal for a local authority to 'intentionally promote homosexuality' or to 'promote the teaching in any maintained school of the acceptability of homosexuality as a pretended family relationship' (Local Government Act 1988).

We decided that since the issues we had wanted to raise had been brought into the arena of public attention in a way which ruled out the possibility of careful and sensitive discussion, we would try to produce a book which drew out the implications in this wider context: that since the government is promoting a highly laundered and mythologised version of heterosexuality, we would produce evidence that concentrated on and emphasised the other side of the story. We have tried to meet fire with fire in deliberately producing a strongly argued case. We have omitted discussion of LEA policy and concentrated on what we see as the main issue. This is the state's control of sexuality through education. In particular what is at issue is the promotion of a model of heterosexuality in which masculinity (central to which is sexual violence) and femininity (as it is stereotypically understood) go unchallenged. The effect of this is the increased social control of all women and girls.

As we have tried to clarify for ourselves the links between male power, sexual violence, masculinity and femininity, and sexuality, defined, structured and expressed as they are in a racist, classist society, we have generated more questions than answers. Not least has been the problem of separating at a theoretical level the concepts or stereotypes of 'masculinity' and 'femininity' from the diverse and some-times contradictory ways in which human beings express their gendered identities. Also, in focusing on the way in which the institution of heterosexuality is organised in this society we were aware of the importance of not collapsing discussion about the nature of a political institution into one in which, at the level of lived experience, we were claiming the same for all women. This is particularly important since our aim was not to produce a book on how women in different ethnic and social class groups survive or resist differently but how the institution works. But if the motiva-tion to separate the concepts or the institution from the individuals inhabiting them was generated by an attempt to avoid crude analysis, then on the other hand, we concluded, there must be some relationship between the two, and a significant one at that. How else could the system be maintained?

For example, there are limits on how far 'masculinity' and 'femininity' can be stretched and still be regarded as 'normal' definitions. So too, there are limits on male and female behaviour such that the individuals expressing it continue to be regarded as 'normal' men or women. A boy exhibiting many of the characteristics along the continuum of sexual violence (from wolf whistling at girls to boasting of his prowess in coercing them sexually) would be regarded as 'a bit of a lad'. In other words, 'normal'. A soft gentle sexually non-aggressive boy begins to challenge the conventional view of masculinity, and if this boy shows no sexual interest at all in girls but is attracted to other boys, then he shows none of the characteristics of 'normal masculinity'. Similarly, it is easy to think of the concept of 'femininity' as comfortably embracing the helpless, simpering female forever seeking approval from the male eye: it becomes less easy to accommodate within the concept the girl who asserts herself with boys and at the point where she actively rejects the sexual attentions of boys by both her behaviour and her appearance and seeks a sexual relationship with another girl, she is no longer 'properly feminine'. Thus, we concluded, central to both the concepts and the constructions of masculinity and femininity is heterosexuality.

But on this model of heterosexuality, masculinity and femininity are unequal. Central to the construction of masculinity in young boys is what Julian Wood has described as a 'pressure to be a sort of Tarzan-cum-Ripper' (Wood, 1982). Masculinity, structured by sexually aggressive attitudes and behaviour towards women, finds its counterpart in the construction of femininity where the need for protection is the mark of the vulnerable, the weak and the powerless. In short, the point is that masculinity is constructed as both heterosexual and sexually violent and therefore the 'truly feminine' woman is both heterosexual and in need of protection from this violence. Backed by the threat of violence the institution of heterosexuality is organised according to a power imbalance. A short diversion into the politics of the marriage ceremony seems to demonstrate this. The woman is 'given away' by one man to another whereupon she drops her father's name and takes on her husband's. From that point on she cannot by law in England bring a case of rape against her husband. Even out of marriage, sexuality and social control are intimately linked:

> The minute a lady takes part in a sexual act, other than by force, she loses the right to control what happens to her body. (Dicks, 1988)

The reason that *Learning Our Lines*, a book about sexuality and education, contains so much material on male sexual violence is that this is central to the maintenance of male power by being structured into a model of masculinity which schools have done little to challenge. But if we are seriously committed to equality, then we have to make rather fewer curriculum analyses of girls studying physics and boys parentcraft and spend rather more time addressing these much more difficult issues.

We begin, in Part One, with an historical perspective on the promotion of heterosexuality in education in Britain this century.

Margaret Jackson, in 'Sexuality and Struggle: Feminism, Sexology and the Social Construction of Sexuality', explores the way in which a model of heterosexuality which legitimises male domination and women's subordination and which served to undermine feminist work was actively promoted at the beginning of this century through the rise of the 'science' of sexology. Annabel Faraday in 'Lessoning Lesbians: Girls' Schools, Coeducation and Anti-lesbianism Between the Wars', explores the ways in which alternatives to heterosexuality were challenged both directly through the attack on girls' schools and the promotion of coeducation, and indirectly through schoolgirl fiction. Davina Cooper, in 'Positive Images in Haringey: A Struggle for Identity', brings us into the 1980s with a record of a local authority's attempt to intervene in the heterosexist state education system in Haringey, north London, by providing 'positive images' of lesbians and gays. Sue Sanders and Gill Spraggs, in 'Section 28 and Education', record the stages of this direct state intervention, its intended effects on education and the powerful public resistance that followed its journey to the statute books.

Part Two links the historical and state promotion of heterosexuality with the realities of that institution for children and in particular girls in education today.

Liz Kelly begins Part Two with 'Our Issues, Our Analysis: Two Decades of Work on Sexual Violence'. In documenting recent feminist campaigns against male violence and some of the literature which explores the links between sexual violence and male sexuality, she clarifies the continuum of male violence. Pat Mahony, in 'Sexual Violence and Mixed Schools', explores the connections between sexual violence, masculinity and the social control of girls and women teachers in schools, and discusses the strategies which some schools have begun to develop. Carol Jones, in 'Asking the Wrong Question: Schools' Responses to the Sexual Abuse of Children', argues that in failing to ask why men abuse and in failing to challenge 'normal' masculine behaviour, schools will continue to provide an inadequate response to disclosures of sexual abuse, despite a public outcry on the issue. She goes on to make recommendations for change. Julie Melia, in 'Sex Education in Schools: Keeping to the "Norm"', looks critically at the organisation of sex education in schools and at the implications of recent government initiatives that attempt to control the curriculum and promote a particular model of (hetero)sexuality. Jane Dixon, Gilly Salvat and Jane Skeates, in 'North London Young Lesbian Group: Specialist Work within the Youth Service', record the experiences of young women of different ages, classes and races and show how they find strategies of resistance and strength with each other. Finally, Pip Scott, in 'Challenging Heterosexism in the Curriculum: Roles for Teachers, Governors and Parents', describes the limitations of most young people's education as well as the difficulties for lesbian mothers and their children, but offers an optimistic way forward using the very legislation passed by the government – the powers of school governing bodies. We are reminded that not all parents are heterosexual and that many who are, want their children to make informed choices through a balanced education which includes challenging heterosexism.

What unites all of us who have contributed to this book is our commitment to opening up opportunities for young people, to exposing the lack of safety for girls in many of our schools and to placing the often neglected story of sexuality and the social control of women and girls in education, on the map. How far the patriarchal state is prepared to go in attempting to exercise control over sexuality remains to be seen. This book is just one more example of how women throughout the world have resisted and will continue to resist 'Learning Our Lines'.

References

Dicks, Terry (MP), 'Quotes of 88', *Spare Rib* 197, 1988.
Trenchard, Lorraine and Warren, Hugh, *Something to Tell You*, London Gay Teenage Group, London, 1984.
Wood, Julian, 'Boys Will be Boys', *New Socialist* 5, 1982.

Part 1
The Promotion of Heterosexuality in Education: an Historical Background

1 Sexuality and Struggle: Feminism, Sexology and the Social Construction of Sexuality

Margaret Jackson

Sexuality, like any other area of social interaction, has a history. Sexual beliefs and behaviour change over time, often as a result of power struggles between opposing groups, who may attempt to define and control sexuality in their own interests, or resist changes which pose a threat to their power. This chapter is concerned with some of the historical and political factors which have influenced the social construction of sexuality in twentieth-century Britain, and which still to a large extent shape current sexual ideologies and practices.[1]

Feminists have always been interested in the relationship between sexuality and male power, though we often disagree about the centrality of sexuality in the social relations of the sexes, and how those relations – of both sexuality and power – can be changed. An understanding of feminist history is crucial in this process; from it we can learn valuable lessons which should enable us to intervene more effectively in the struggle for change and to use our energies more constructively. Unfortunately patriarchal interests have all too often ensured that our history has been either distorted or erased. The enemy knows only too well that cutting off our links with our past is a very effective weapon in stemming the tide of feminism. It forces us to waste our energies by fighting the same battles all over again, with outcomes which a better understanding of our history would probably have enabled us to predict and perhaps avoid.

Most of us who are currently engaged in campaigning against male violence against women, or the sexual abuse of children, or the right to define and control our own sexuality, were until recently quite unaware that similar campaigns had been fought during the last wave of feminism in Britain (and in many other countries as well). All that most of us knew about Victorian and Edwardian feminism could probably have been written on the proverbial postage stamp. We had probably heard of Mrs Pankhurst and the suffragettes who demanded the vote by chaining themselves to railings, setting fire to pillar boxes, and going on hunger strike. We might have heard vaguely of women's campaigns for access to higher education and the medical profession, or – much less likely – of some of the struggles of working-class women. But how many of us knew that there was a campaign, sustained for more than fifty years, to break what feminists called the 'conspiracy of silence' which surrounded the sexual abuse of girls? How many of us had heard of the campaign to expose what feminists called the 'real facts of life' about the buying and selling of women and girls for the trade in prostitution? Or the campaigns against rape in marriage, and sexual harassment in the streets? Why did we not know that Victorian and Edwardian feminists demanded, not merely political and economic independence, but *sexual* independence from men?

It is bad enough that most women are deliberately kept in ignorance about our history; but the lies and distortions which compound it are even more dangerous. How many of us were brought up to believe that most Victorian feminists were prudes and puritans? That the twentieth century – first in the 1920s and then in the 1960s – ushered in the 'sexual revolution'? And that women's liberation is synonymous with what *men* mean by 'sexual liberation'? It is no accident that such misleading beliefs are so widely held today, sometimes even by women who consider themselves feminists. The prevalence of an ideology of sexual liberation, based on male sexual values and practices, as opposed to the feminist ideal of sexual autonomy, based on the right to define and control our sexuality independently from men, can be traced back to a struggle which took place around the turn of the century.

It is this struggle which is the main focus of this chapter. We now have considerable evidence that central to Victorian and Edwardian feminism was a challenge to the specifically *sexual* aspects of women's oppression; in particular to the use of male violence and male sexuality as weapons of male power and as a means of keeping women in their place. So significant was this challenge, that by the turn of the century it posed a serious threat to the heterosexual social structure. After World War I, feminism, especially its more radical aspects, went into decline and the ideology and practice of sexual 'liberation' began to take over. A key factor in this process was the development of a new 'science' known as sexology: the scientific study of sexuality and sexual behaviour. Sexologists substituted their own 'facts of life' for the realities of male violence and male sexuality which feminists had campaigned to expose and change. What feminists insisted was *political* sexologists asserted was *natural*, and therefore could *not* be changed; and because sexologists came to be accepted as the 'experts' in matters of sexuality, the male sexual values and practices which they defined and promoted became almost impossible to challenge.

The influence of sexology can still be clearly seen today: you only have to look at any sex manual, or sex education literature, or articles about sex in women's magazines, or 'Agony Aunt' columns, to find evidence of the way it continues to shape both the way people think about sex and their sexual behaviour. What makes sexology such a powerful ideological tool is its scientific status, its claims to be objective, neutral, value-free – purely 'factual'. One of the aims of this chapter is to expose the ideological nature of sexology and the way that it has been used to control women in the interests of maintaining male power.

From Female Sexual Slavery to Female Sexual Autonomy: the Feminist Challenge to Compulsory Heterosexuality

> In sexual matters it would appear that the whole trend and tendency of man's relation to woman has been to make refusal impossible and to cut off every avenue of escape from the gratification of his desire. (Hamilton, 1909)

The new science of sexology emerged at an extremely critical point in history, in terms of the changing power relations between women and men. Throughout the nineteenth century feminists were attacking male supremacy on many fronts – political, economic, legal, educational and sexual – and by the turn of the century many significant gains had been made. From 1905 to 1914 there was a quite unprecedented wave of feminist militancy, which was directed chiefly at securing votes for women. The vote was seen, not as an end in itself, but as an important weapon in the fight for women's emancipation, and highly symbolic of the ultimate aim of freedom and equality with men. The feminist challenge to the patriarchal definition and control of sexuality, which was integral to the wider struggle against male power, was complex and multi-faceted, and is difficult to summarise without over-simplifying.[2] In essence it was a struggle to emancipate women from what feminists called 'female sexual slavery' – from all forms of sexual exploitation and abuse by men, inside and outside marriage.[3] There were three main aspects to this struggle, all of which were interrelated and directed towards a common goal: female sexual autonomy.

1. Campaigns Against Male Sexuality

From the 1860s to World War I there was a series of campaigns against the whole spectrum of male sexual violence, abuse and exploitation of women, including organised prostitution, the trafficking in women and children, the sexual abuse of children, and all forms of sexual coercion and harassment inside and outside the home. The most well known of these is probably Josephine Butler's campaign in the late nineteenth century to repeal the Contagious Diseases Acts, which were an attempt to prevent the spread of venereal disease amongst men by the compulsory medical examination of prostitutes – what Butler called 'instrumental rape'. There was also a protracted campaign to raise the age of consent, in order to protect young girls from sexual abuse inside and outside the home, and to curb the procuring of young girls for use in British and foreign brothels. There were many other campaigns against various forms of sexual harassment, such as male soliciting of women on the streets, and sending obscene letters – the equivalent of today's obscene telephone calls.

Although these campaigns were partially successful, the inherent male bias in legislation, and male hostility to feminism, meant that throughout the Edwardian period and World War I it was necessary to keep remounting the campaigns in different forms. In addition, militant feminists worked hard to raise public awareness of the ways in which the male bias of the police and the judiciary operated to protect the identities of men suspected of sexual violence and abuse. Newspapers such as *The Vote, Votes for Women* and the *Suffragette* published comparisons between the extreme leniency of the sentences for such crimes, and the severe penalties meted out to suffragettes for civil disobedience or crimes against property, and to any woman who defended herself against male violence or sexual assault.

All these campaigns had two principal aims in common. One was to break the conspiracy of silence which protected male sexual behaviour from critical scrutiny and challenge, and to expose what feminists called 'the real facts of life'. The other was to challenge the double standard of sexual morality which legitimated male sexuality: the assumption that men are driven by powerful sexual urges over which they have no control, and that sexual self-control is possible only for women. Feminists refused to accept that it was men's biological 'needs' which drove them to exploit and abuse women's bodies for sexual gratification. They argued that what rape, sexual abuse and exploitation were really about was power and control: that men were using their sexuality to exert power over women and keep them in their place. The feminists' refusal to accept the myth that male sexuality was natural and uncontrollable was in political terms extremely significant, because it enabled them to insist that male sexual behaviour could be changed, and to demand that men take responsibility for changing it. Emmeline Pankhurst made this very clear when she declared:

> If it is true – I do not believe it for one moment – that men have less power of self-control than women have . . . then I say as a woman, representing thousands of women all over the world, men must find some way of supplying the needs of their sex which does not include the degradation of ours. (*Suffragette*, 29 August 1913)

In order to force men to change, some feminists, such as Lucy Re-Bartlett, even advocated a 'sex-strike':

> In the hearts of many women today is rising a cry somewhat like this: I will know no man, and bear no child until this apathy is broken through – these wrongs be righted . . . It is the 'silent strike' and it is going on all over the world. (Re-Bartlett, 1912)

2. The Critique of 'Normal' Heterosexual Sex

The campaigns to transform male sexuality were based on the concept of the right of women to control their own bodies, not only outside but inside marriage. Some feminists extended this challenge by attacking the concept of 'conjugal rights', which in effect legalised rape within marriage (which to this day is still not a crime). They asserted that women should have the right to decide not only whether or not to have children, but also when and how heterosexual activity should take place. Elizabeth Wolstenholme Elmy encapsulated this sentiment in a line from a poem in which she expressed her hope that woman would be able to live 'Free from all uninvited touch of man'. Feminists insisted that no man should have the right to use a woman's body for his own sexual gratification and that no woman should be pressurised or coerced into responding to her husband's sexual demands.

They also argued that many women disliked sexual intercourse: that apart from the risk of pregnancy it was the cause of many diseases and disorders of the reproductive system, and that it was perfectly possible to have a fulfilling sexual relationship based on other forms of lovemaking.

In Sheila Jeffreys' words what these feminists were attempting to do was 'to articulate their discontents' with male-defined sexuality 'and to explore what a woman-centred sexuality might consist of' (Jeffreys, 1985). Elizabeth Blackwell, the first woman to qualify as a doctor, and the first woman to write about sexuality from a scientific as well as a feminist perspective, stood the patriarchal concept of sexuality on its head. She argued that sexual passion was equally strong in both sexes, but that the essence of being human was the capacity to guide and control instinct by means of reason and the power of the will. She drew on evidence from physiology to show that there was absolutely no scientific justification for the double standard, arguing that not only was it possible for both men and women to exercise self-control, but that it was *failure* to do so which was *unnatural*.[4]

What Blackwell and other feminist sexual theorists were pointing to was a radically new way of conceptualising sexuality, based not on the assumption of men's imperious sexual nature, but on the recognition of female sexual autonomy. This was potentially revolutionary in its implications for the relations between women and men, since it implied a major shift in the balance of power within heterosexual relationships. If women were able to define their own sexual needs and desires, rather than having them defined by men, and being forced to service male sexual 'needs', one of the main obstacles to women's liberation might have been overcome.

3. The Rise of the Spinster

Throughout the Victorian and Edwardian periods feminists consistently attacked the institution of marriage, which they regarded as little more than legalised prostitution – a form of institutionalised sexual slavery, in which a woman exchanged her body for the means of subsistence. Some campaigned for

7

the reform of marriage, for example by securing the right of married women to own their own property. Others chose to resist marriage and celebrate spinsterhood, explicitly rejecting the doctrine that woman's one true vocation was marriage and motherhood, and that a woman without a man was sexually incomplete. By the turn of the century it was already clear that the achievements of feminism were making it possible for more and more middle-class women to be economically independent of men, and that many were positively choosing to remain single – exercising what Cicely Hamilton (1909) called their 'power of refusal'.

This was extremely threatening to the patriarchal social structure and provoked a vicious backlash.[5] Vitriolic anti-spinster tracts were published, in which extreme solutions to the problem of 'redundant' or 'superfluous' women were proposed: polygamy, compulsory deportation to the colonies, and female infanticide were all specifically mentioned. One eminent scientist referred to spinsters as 'the waste products of our civilisation' (Heape, 1913). Cicely Hamilton's explanation for the 'active and savage dislike' of the spinster hit the nail squarely on the head: she suggested that it must have originated, 'in the consciousness that the perpetual virgin was a witness, however reluctantly, to the unpalatable fact that sexual intercourse was not for every woman an absolute necessity' (Hamilton, 1909).

The politics of spinsterhood were very much in the foreground in the years immediately before World War I when militant feminism, and the campaigns against male sexuality, were at their height. Lucy Re-Bartlett's statement about the 'silent strike' left little room for doubt that the refusal to engage in sexual relationships with men was a deliberate political choice: a form of resistance to male power. Christabel Pankhurst, one of the leaders of the Women's Social and Political Union, 60 per cent of whom were spinsters (and most of the rest widows!) expressed it unequivocally:

There can be no mating between the spiritually developed women of this new day and men who in thought and conduct with regard to sex matters are their inferiors.

(Pankhurst, 1913)

This very brief outline is intended to show that the Women's Movement of the nineteenth and early twentieth centuries posed a threat, not merely to the general system of male power, but specifically to the *sexual* basis of that power. The increasing militancy and success of the movement;[6] the challenge to male sexuality and the double standard; the critiques of marriage and heterosexual sex; the rise of the economically and sexually independent middle-class spinster – all these together constituted a threat to the system of compulsory heterosexuality through which male power is constituted.[7] The campaign for votes for women may have begun as a single-issue reformist campaign; but by the pre-war years the vote had become a symbol of the liberation for which women were fighting, rather than an end in itself. As Christabel Pankhurst pointed out, the opposition was well aware of the potential implications of votes for women for heterosexual relationships:

> The opposition argues thus: if women are to become politically free they will become spiritually strong and economically independent, and thus they will not any longer give or sell themselves to be the playthings of men. That, in a nutshell, is the case against votes for women. (Pankhurst, 1913)

Unfortunately, despite the partial enfranchisement of women in 1918, and full enfranchisement in 1928, these implications were not to be realised. One of the main reasons for this has to do with the development of sexology, and the promotion of an ideology of sexual liberation, which subverted the feminist threat to the patriarchal definition and control of sexuality, and made a significant contribution to the decline of the women's movement.

Sexology and the Construction of Heterosexuality: Eroticising Women's Oppression

To be aroused by a man means acknowledging oneself as

conquered. (Stekel, 1926)

The nineteenth-century women's movement and the feminist debates and campaigns around sexuality described in the last section played an important role in structuring the social context in which men like Havelock Ellis, the 'founding father' of Western sexology, developed their theories of sexuality. Ellis was married to Edith Lees, a feminist and lesbian, had close relationships with the feminists Margaret Sanger and Olive Schreiner, and had many other feminist friends, and there is considerable evidence in his writings that he was influenced by the sexual politics of the period. He regarded himself (and is still regarded by many today) as a champion of women's rights, though his attitude to the more radical aspects of feminism was extremely critical, and more than once he accused feminists of turning women away from 'the laws of their own nature'.[8]

Sexologists have a significant place in the history of sexualtiy because they were the first to construct a *science* of sexuality. Although their theories and evidence were regarded from the beginning as controversial, and it was a long time before sexology acquired scientific status, the basic outlines of the model of sexuality which they constructed soon gained acceptance and were promoted as the 'facts of life'. As we shall see, the sexologists' facts were in direct opposition to the facts which feminists had tried to expose and place on the sexual–political agenda. The scientific model of sexuality which the new breed of male experts constructed subverted the feminist challenge by depoliticising sexuality and placing it firmly in the realm of 'the natural'.

The principal characteristics of the sexological model of sexuality may be summarised briefly as follows:

1. Male sexuality, the *political* nature of which feminists had struggled so hard to expose and challenge, was alleged to be *natural*. Havelock Ellis argued that male sexuality was inherently aggressive and violent because it was rooted in a biological urge to conquer and capture the female. The political implications of this supposedly scientific fact are

clear: an instinct which is biologically determined cannot be changed, and feminists who demand that men change are wasting their time – men just cannot help their sexuality being the way it is. As Ellis put it: 'to exert power . . . is one of our most primary impulses, and it always tends to be manifested in the attitude of a man towards the woman he loves' (Ellis, 1913).

2. Female sexuality was defined in terms of the desire to surrender to the male; this, according to Ellis, was what women *really* needed and enjoyed and any resistance was merely pretence, designed by nature to increase male arousal, and intended by nature to be overcome:

> The sexual impulse in woman is fettered by an inhibition which has to be conquered . . . her wooer in every act of courtship has the enjoyment of conquering afresh an oft-won woman . . .

> the normal manifestations of a woman's sexual pleasure are exceedingly like pain. (ibid.)

3. Thus male dominance and female submission were structured into heterosexual relations and defined as natural, inevitable and essential not only to male but also to female sexual pleasure. Ellis conceded that women might find some difficulty in accommodating themselves to this state of affairs and declared that the task of the husband was to cultivate 'the art of love', in order to arouse in the wife 'an emotional condition which leads her to surrender'. In the end, though, it was simply a matter of women getting *used* to sexual intercourse. Comparing penis and vagina to a key entering a lock he said: 'a lock not only requires a key to fit it, but should be entered only at the right moment, and, under the best conditions, may only be adjusted to the key by considerable use.' (ibid.)

By arguing that male dominance and female submission were biologically determined and intrinsic to 'normal' heterosexual sex the sexologists gave scientific legitimation to precisely the model of sexuality that feminists were attempting to challenge. Male dominance and female sub-

11

mission, far from being abolished, were to be sexualised in the interests of sexual 'liberation' and women's 'erotic rights' – concepts which had nothing to do with female sexual autonomy, and everything to do with re-establishing male right of sexual access to women. This may have been liberating for men; for women it would be more accurate to say that it represented a sexual counter-revolution. Instead of having to 'grit your teeth and think of England, dear', they were now expected to enjoy an activity designed not to diminish but to enhance male power. In other words, women were now to be enthusiastic participants in the eroticisation of their oppression. Sexology was thus instrumental, not only in constructing a form of heterosexual relationship designed to maintain and reconstitute male power, but also in reasserting patriarchal social control.[9]

The Facts of Life: Teaching Women What to Feel

During the 1920s and 1930s there was a sustained propaganda campaign, conducted mainly by means of marriage manuals and other sex education literature, to popularise the new science and teach 'the facts of life' to 'ordinary' people. Marriage manuals were written mainly by doctors, and their explicit aim was to teach married women – in some cases to teach *husbands* to teach their wives – how to enjoy heterosexual sex. In essence what this meant was teaching women to accept male sexual demands, to consent to be conquered, and to participate enthusiastically in their sexual submission to men. In the words of Van de Velde, whose *Ideal Marriage* became the 'bible' of sex manuals: 'the wife must be *taught*, not only how to behave in coitus, but, above all, how and what to feel in this unique act'! (Van de Velde, 1928, emphasis in original).

– and he left his readers in absolutely no doubt as to *what* should be felt:

> What both man and woman, driven by obscure primitive urges, wish to feel in the sexual act, is the essential force of *maleness*, which expresses itself in a sort of violent and absolute *possession* of the woman. And so both of them can and do exult in a certain degree of male aggression

and dominance – whether actual or apparent – which proclaims this essential force. (ibid, emphasis in original)

Quite a few marriage manuals were written by women, and it is indicative of the strength and influence of the new sexual ideology that most of the female authors adopted it quite uncritically. Even the feminist Margaret Sanger, who is famous for her campaign for birth control, seemed intent on promoting this essentially anti-feminist message: 'Nature and tradition have decreed that man shall be the wooer, the pursuer, the huntsman. Man is the aggressor . . . adventurous, primitive man does not value highly an easy capture' (Sanger, 1926).

All the marriage manuals conceded that mutual sexual adjustment between husband and wife would be difficult to achieve. The main problem lay with the woman: she was more often than not 'slow' to arouse and needed to be made 'ready' for intercourse. On the basis of Ellis' concept of the 'art of love' the practice of 'foreplay' was advocated with the specific intention of overcoming the woman's lack of readiness. No one seems to have asked: if she really *desires* heterosexual intercourse, why does she need to be *made* ready? To have asked such a question would have been to acknowledge what the marriage manuals had already subtly ruled out: a woman's right to sexual self-determination – to define her own needs and desires. Even when faced directly with evidence that many women did *not* desire or enjoy heterosexual intercourse the experts persisted in their efforts to cure their 'maladjustment'. Helena Wright, for instance, a gynaecologist who worked in one of the early birth control clinics, frequently quoted one of her patients who complained: 'Doctor, have I got to put up with this? I can't bear it [penis] pumping in and out!'[10] Wright's response to this was to write two books explaining how the clitoris could be 'used' to 'educate' the vagina, emphasising the importance of 'practice' and 'maintaining an optimistic attitude'! (Wright, 1930; 1947).

Despite the tremendous efforts expended by the experts to educate women – and their vaginas – many of them obstinately refused to be 'wooed into compliance', as Van de Velde wished. By the late 1920s there was apparently such a widespread epidemic of 'frigidity' that whole tomes had to be written on the subject. Walter Gallichan's definition of and prescription for frigidity speaks for itself: 'The hysterical frigide must be taught to face the realities of Nature, and to abandon the false perceptions of the "horridness" of sexuality' (Gallichan, 1927). The concept of the frigid woman was often used as a term of abuse synonymous with 'prude'. The experts recognised that frigidity was a form of refusal or resistance to male control – a way of saying 'I will not' – and used it as a weapon to discredit spinsters and any lingering feminist protest about male sexuality: 'the cold natured woman is often an active supporter of reformative organizations, female emancipation crusades, purity campaigns, and societies for the suppression of vice . . . (she is) lacking understanding of the fundamental facts of life'. (ibid)

The fact that this was 'science' made it much harder for feminists to challenge, especially if they also happened to be spinsters. Sexology played a key role in fuelling the anti-spinster backlash which had occurred at the height of militant feminism. There was now a 'scientific' reason why celibate spinsters were so bitter and twisted: they were sex-starved. For some sexologists sex-starvation was not simply a synonym for sexual frustration. They meant it *literally*. Marie Stopes, for example, claimed that women deprived of regular heterosexual intercourse lacked the chemical substances supplied by male secretions, and recommended that sex-starved women take a daily dose of capsules containing prostatic extracts! (Stopes, 1928). Spinsters, with their 'thwarted instincts', were accused of 'defying Nature' and spinster schoolteachers were targeted as especially dangerous, because they were allegedly in a position to exercise such great influence over the young. It was also strongly implied, and sometimes explicitly asserted, that they were lesbian.

Divide and Rule: Anti-feminism and Anti-lesbianism

It will come as no surprise to today's feminists to learn that the word lesbian was used to smear feminists, especially those who did not have sexual relationships with men. There are, of course, good political reasons why there should be a strong relationship between lesbianism and feminism, but the point here is that the label 'lesbian' was used as means of discrediting not only feminists but *any* woman who was sexually independent of men, and *any* form of love and solidarity between women, irrespective of whether it actually involved a *sexual* relationship. Before World War I many feminists had openly expressed their feelings of love and solidarity towards their sister feminists, which had naturally strengthened as a result of their common experiences and aims in the women's movement. Several feminist historians have also shown that during the nineteenth century it was regarded as quite normal and acceptable for women, single or married, to develop intensely emotional, and often passionate and sensual, bonds with other women, and for these to be openly expressed. Lillian Faderman (1981) has also traced the key role of sexology in what she calls the 'morbidification' of love between women; in other words the definition of such relationships as abnormal, sick and perverted, whether or not they actually involved physical sexual expression.

The social construction of lesbianism and the social construction of heterosexuality are two sides of the same coin, and the one cannot be fully understood without the other. Space does not permit a detailed discussion of the construction of lesbianism here, but it is important to be aware that the process of stigmatising love between women began to take place at a time (in the late nineteenth century) when feminism and women's increasing independence became a serious threat to the patriarchal – and heterosexual – social order. The construction of 'the lesbian' as a *scientific* category was part of a system of social control designed to conscript women into heterosexuality. As Faderman says: 'If they gained all the freedom that feminists agitated for, what

15

would attract them to marriage?' Or, in Nancy Sahli's words:

> one way to control these sexless termites, hermaphroditic spinsters, or whatever one might call them, was to condemn their love relationships – the one aspect of their behaviour, which, regardless of their other social, political, or economic activities, posed a basic threat to a system where the fundamental expression of power was that of one sex over another. (Sahli, 1979)

It is also important to be aware that sexologists made a distinction between the 'real' lesbian (who was 'born that way') and 'spurious imitations', or 'pseudo-lesbians'. The model of the 'real' lesbian was based on the stereotype of male fantasy and pornography: the masculine woman, a sort of man-without-a-penis, butch, hairy, aggressive, predatory, and *dangerous*; dangerous because she/he was liable to seduce 'normal', feminine, heterosexual – in other words 'real' – women away from men. It is not difficult to see how this distinction could be used to fuel anti-feminism: the women's movement was seen as all the more dangerous because it encouraged the spread of 'pseudo-lesbianism'.[11]

Anti-lesbianism was – and still is – a weapon designed to subvert and undermine feminism by dividing women. 'Real' lesbians were marginalised by being defined as a special breed of 'invert' – members of a 'third sex' – and modelled on a stereotype so horrific and alienating that few women would be able to identify with it and would be likely to reject the possibility of loving women sexually.[12] Other spinster–feminists were 'tainted with lesbianism' but 'redeemable' if only they would stop trying to deny the 'laws of nature' and recognise that what the 'real' woman 'really' needs is a man – and regular heterosexual intercourse. This technique is commonly known as 'divide and rule'. It constitutes an attempt to divide women from each other in two ways: first, by placing us into one of two categories, (a) heterosexual and normal, or (b) lesbian and abnormal or deviant – the latter being a tiny perverted minority and thus of no serious account; second, by constructing a *form* of heterosexuality which institutionalises and sexualises male power and female submission, thus harnessing women's bodies to the service of men's needs and placing them under male control.

Naturalism and the Anti-feminist Backlash

The struggle over sexuality which I have tried to describe here is only one aspect of a complex, multi-faceted and continuing process of constructing and challenging male power. A key factor in this process is the struggle over what is *natural*. One question which the evidence I have presented immediately raises is: if it is so natural for women to desire only men, to enjoy servicing male sexual needs, to find pleasure in sexual submission, why has it taken such a huge and sustained effort to structure women into heterosexuality? Put simply, if heterosexuality is natural why does it need to be *compulsory*, and why does it need to be *taught*? Why is lesbianism such a threat? Why is it apparently so dangerous for women to be allowed to define and control our own sexuality?

The power to define what is natural has always been absolutely crucial to the maintenance of any system of power relations. The allegedly 'natural' inferiority of Black people, for instance, was used as a major justification for slavery, colonialism and imperialism, and still operates today to legitimate apartheid as well as less blatant forms of racism. In the nineteenth century the principal justification for denying women political, economic, educational and legal equality with men was their 'natural' inferiority, physical and intellectual – a notion which persists even today, albeit in more subtle disguises. The very existence of the nineteenth-century women's movement, and the increasing achievements of women in various fields, such as education and medicine, posed a threat to patriarchal definitions of the natural differences between the sexes. The most common masculine response was to denounce women who refused to accept their place in the patriarchal order as 'unnatural'. As we have seen, the charge of defying nature was directed with particular vehemence towards those who resisted female sexual slavery and struggled for female sexual autonomy.

17

One lesson which it seems to me we can learn from this period of history is how formidable a weapon the ideology of naturalism can be in the hands of anti-feminists, especially at a time of crisis in the power relations between the sexes. As soon as some barriers to women's liberation are torn down, and some naturalist myths are exploded, others are erected or reinforced. It was no accident that marriage manuals teaching the joys of heterosexual sex began to appear at a time when more and more women were choosing not to marry, feminism was at its most militant, and the divorce rate was beginning to soar. Indeed, the explicit rationale of the marriage manual during the inter-war years was to restore stability to the institution of marriage by eliminating sexual disharmony between husband and wife.

This attempt to shore up the institutions of marriage and heterosexuality was part of a broader drive to push women back into the home, which was also a central element in the Fascist ideology – *Kinder, Küche, Kirche* – which began to take root in Western Europe during the 1930s. There are some disturbing parallels with the ideological shift to the Right which has been taking place in this country during the 1980s. The Conservative Government's recent and unprecedented attempts to intervene in sex education in schools can be seen as a response to the challenge to the institution of heterosexuality which has been developing during the current phase of feminism.[13] It is symptomatic, not merely of a general resurgence of right-wing ideology, but also of a specifically anti-feminist-lesbian backlash, expressed through the ideology of naturalism. Cloaked in pious rhetoric about the value of family life, it represents in essence an attempt to regulate and control sexuality by reasserting patriarchal and heterosexist definitions of what is natural and normal in sexual relations. The intention can only be to maintain and reinforce the patriarchal, heterosexual social structure and thus to undermine the struggle of lesbians and feminists for female sexual autonomy. This makes it all the more imperative that we reassert the feminist challenge to naturalism in all its forms, and especially in the sphere of sexuality.

Notes

1. Although most of the sources used in this chapter are British, both feminism and sexology were international movements, in terms of their membership and their influence, though sexology had a particularly strong base in Western Europe.

2. The most comprehensive account to date of the feminist challenge to the patriarchal definition and control of sexuality during the late nineteenth and early twentieth centuries is Jeffreys (1985). For a more concise account see also her contribution to Coveney *et al*. (1984). For a useful collection of primary source material see Jeffreys (1987).

3. Many early feminists or their families had been involved in the movement for the abolition of slavery and readily made the analogy between the trade in African slaves and the trade in women's bodies. The term applied specifically to prostitution and international trafficking, but also more generally to any form of sexual exploitation of women, including within marriage. In the early twentieth century the term 'white slavery' became common, though some feminists were uneasy about its racist connotations and took care to point out that the trade or traffic in women involved women of all colours.

4. Blackwell's significance for a feminist history of sexuality has been vastly underrated. My own assessment of her contribution will be presented as part of my PhD thesis, Birmingham. Most of her writings were published between 1850 and 1900, and were reprinted as a two-volume collection in 1902.

5. Although there were also large numbers of working-class spinsters they were not regarded as such a threat, probably because they could be easily absorbed into the system as domestic servants, for whom there was a big demand in the late nineteenth and early twentieth centuries.

6. The increasing success of the women's movement may be measured by a number of legal and educational reforms, including the Married Women's Property Acts, the repeal of the Contagious Diseases Acts, the admission of women to higher education and the medical profession.

7. The phrase 'compulsory heterosexuality' is borrowed from

Rich (1981), but it is evident from the quotations used in this chapter that the concept itself predates her use of it.

8. The main body of Ellis' work on sexuality was published at the turn of the century. For accounts of his life and work see especially Robinson (1976); Rowbotham and Weeks (1977); Weeks (1977; 1981).

9. For a more detailed analysis of the sexual ideology of Havelock Ellis, marriage manuals between the two world wars, and the later work of Kinsey and Masters and Johnson, see Jackson (1983; 1984; 1987).

10. Personal interview with the late Helena Wright, 5 January 1982.

11. For a more detailed analysis of women's friendships and lesbianism see Smith Rosenberg (1975); Sahli (1979); Faderman (1981); Jeffreys (1985).

12. The best known examples of such stereotypes may be found in Radclyffe Hall's novel *The Well of Loneliness*, first published in 1928, with an introduction by Havelock Ellis.

13. I am referring to the various DES publications on sex education in schools, as well as Section 28 of the Local Government Act 1988. See Chapters 4 and 8 of this book.

References

Blackwell, E., *Essays in Medical Sociology*, Ernest Bell, London, 1902.

Caplan, P. (ed.), *The Cultural Construction of Sexuality*, Tavistock, London, 1987.

Coveney, L., Jackson, M., Jeffreys, S., Kaye, L., and Mahony, P., *The Sexuality Papers: Male Sexuality and the Social Control of Women*, Hutchinson, London, 1984.

Ellis, H., *Studies in the Psychology of Sex*, F.A. Davis, Philadelphia, 1913.

Faderman, L., *Surpassing the Love of Men: Romantic Friendship and Love Between Women from the Renaissance to the Present*, Junction Books, London, 1981.

Gallichan, W., *Sexual Apathy and Coldness in Women*, T. Werner Laurie, London, 1927.

Hall, R., *The Well of Loneliness*, Virago, London, 1982 (1st edn 1928).

Hamilton, C., *Marriage as a Trade*, Chapman and Hall, London, 1909.

Heape, W., *Sex Antagonism*, Constable, London, 1913.

Jackson, M., 'Sexual liberation or social control?' *Women's Studies International Forum* 6(1), 1983; reprinted in Coveney et al., 1984.

'Sex research and the construction of sexuality: a tool of male supremacy?' *Women's Studies International Forum* 7(1), 1984; reprinted in Coveney et al., 1984.

'Facts of life or the eroticisation of women's oppression? Sexology and the social construction of sexuality', in Caplan (1987).

Jeffreys, S., *The Spinster and Her Enemies*, Pandora Press, London, 1985.

(ed.) *The Sexuality Debates*, Routledge & Kegan Paul, London, 1987.

Pankhurst, C., *The Great Scourge and How to End It*, Women's Social and Political Union, London, 1913.

Re-Bartlett, L., *Sex and Sanctity*, Longman, London, 1912.

Rich, A., *Compulsory Heterosexuality and Lesbian Existence*, Onlywomen Press, London, 1981.

Robinson, P., *The Modernisation of Sex: Havelock Ellis, Alfred Kinsey, William Masters and Virginia Johnson*, Harper & Row, New York, 1976.

Rowbotham, S., and Weeks, J., *Socialism and the New Life: the Personal and Sexual Politics of Edward Carpenter and Havelock Ellis*, Pluto Press, London, 1977.

Sahli, N., 'Smashing: women's relationships before the Fall', *Chrysalis*, 8 (Summer 1979).

Sanger, M., *Happiness in Marriage*, Brentano, New York, 1926.

Smith Rosenberg, C., 'The female world of love and ritual: relations between women in 19th century America', *Signs* 1 (1), 1975.

Stekel, W., *Frigidity in Woman in Relation to her Love Life*, Livewright, New York, 1926.

Stopes, M., *Enduring Passion*, Putnam, London, 1928.

Van de Velde, T., *Ideal Marriage: its Physiology and Technique*, Heinemann, London, 1928.

Weeks, J., *Coming Out: Homosexual Politics in Britain*

from the 19th Century to the Present, Quartet, London, 1977.

Sex, Politics and Society: the Regulation of Sexuality since 1800, Longman, London, 1981.

Wright, H., *The Sex Factor in Marriage*, Williams & Northgate, London, 1930.

More About the Sex Factor in Marriage, Williams & Northgate, London, 1947.

2 Lessoning Lesbians: Girls' Schools, Coeducation and Anti-lesbianism Between the Wars

Annabel Faraday

In England, before 1944, secondary and higher education for girls had traditionally been separate. Girls and boys in the nineteenth century were rarely taught in the same schools beyond elementary level. This meant that both public and private secondary schools and colleges provided their largely middle-class intake of girls with an all-female community in which to develop, and women teachers in positions of leadership providing positive examples of female power. Moreover, separate education enabled girls to study in freedom from the competition and domination of males or the invidious effects of sexual stereotyping and comparison. As girls' schools grew in size and number while the century progressed, educationalists became aware of the potential of such a community for nurturing lesbianism in its members; as such they posed a potential threat to the maintenance of male power in both the family and the educational system.

It was not until the early decades of this century that a strong lobby in favour of coeducation became audible. In the postwar atmosphere of the twenties and thirties, with the anti-feminist backlash and expanding ideologies of heterosexual need and the 'natural' woman, arguments against single-sex schooling for girls were fired by an ever-growing fear, the independent and 'unnatural' woman – the lesbian. The education of girls and boys together came to be seen by many 'progressive' educationalists as the only solution to 'sex antagonism' and the only insurance against the intransigence of postwar feminism. It was openly promoted as the most radical method of ending the sex war, and what I propose to show in this chapter is that far from aiming to meet the demands of feminists or to enable women to have more control over their own lives, the coeducationalists sought to create conditions whereby women would not question their own subordinate position or the right of men to positions of power and privilege.

I shall broadly trace the history of girls' education before World War II and examine the roots of coeducational support which began in those early decades and which fed on the fears of lesbianism and women's autonomy.

Schooling for Girls: the Legacy of Separate Provision

In the last decades of the nineteenth century in England, education was mainly mixed and elementary. Board schools, set up by the Elementary Education Act of 1870, provided schooling for all children not already catered for by the voluntary, church sector. Such schools were intended for children of the poor and were usually the only type of formal education those children would receive. It was not until 1880 that schooling up to the age of 13 was made compulsory, but for the majority of working-class children this included no grammar school education. Schooling was 'mixed' in the sense that girls and boys were taught in the same classrooms but were usually separated within the classrooms and had separate school entrances and playgrounds. This 'mixing' was for economic rather than ideological reasons, and coexisted with Victorian values stressing sharp sexual division maintained by doctrines of biologically determined sex differences.

For most of the nineteenth century, schooling beyond elementary level remained the prerogative of boys from the middle and upper classes. But small pockets of provision for girls' secondary education had started in the late eighteenth century, with academies for young 'ladies'. For decades, these remained the only form of education for middle- and upper-class girls, unless parents could afford the services of a private governess, services beyond the resources of any working-class family.

From the ranks of those governesses rose the pioneers of secondary education for girls in the 1850s – Miss Buss, who founded the North London Collegiate School, and Miss Beale, the first Principal of Cheltenham Ladies College. The contrasting ideologies embodied in their educational approaches have formed the bases of girls' education ever since, the former believing in equal education for both sexes as training for the world outside the home, the latter tending to emphasise different and 'complementary' needs by preparing girls for more domestic and maternal careers (Lavigeur, 1980). It was however, Miss Buss' philosophy, of similar need, which was to have greater influence in shaping girls' secondary education in grammar schools.

1872 saw the founding of the Girls' Public Day School Company, modelled on the North London Collegiate School; by 1900 it had provided more than 7000 largely middle-class girls with secondary education equal to that which boys then received. Working-class girls' education tended, however, to remain confined to the elementary school system, half the elementary schools in England and Wales being mixed by 1900 and the proportion increasing with the years. Separate elementary schooling was not always considered economically viable, especially in rural areas with fewer pupils.

Throughout the second half of the nineteenth century, higher education for women was steadily gaining ground. Colleges for women opened in the 1870s and 1880s in London, Oxford and Cambridge, creating places to train university educated teachers for the growing number of girls' grammar schools. Again the movement for higher education was divided by contrasting ideologies. Miss Emily Davies and Miss A.J. Clough pioneered the movement to make colleges in the older universities open to women, and their approaches coincided broadly with those taken by Miss Buss and Miss Beale. Miss Davies founded Girton at Hitchin in 1869, and in 1873 the college moved to Cambridge. Newnham was founded as a women's college by Miss Clough in 1880.

Whether the ideology was of similar or of separate need for girls and boys, girls' secondary and higher education began as a separate movement. Towards the end of the nineteenth century, however, support for coeducation began to emerge. In 1895 a Royal Commission on secondary education, the Bryce Commission, recommended secondary coeducation very strongly, largely because it was deemed 'successful' in other countries. The Commission cited mixed schools in England – the public elementary schools, the higher grade schools which had developed out of them, and a few endowed grammar schools – and claimed that 'the mixed system in them seems to have worked well' (Bryce, 1895, p.159). This 'mixing' ranged from dual systems, where boys and girls met only for certain subjects, to completely free association of the sexes, largely confined to a few schools in the private system. The report also recommended the creation of a central authority for education, and in 1899 the Board of Education was formed.

A number of other recommendations from Bryce were implemented in the 1902 Education Act. Under this legislation, elementary and secondary education were brought together within the province of newly created local education authorities (LEAs). Although the Bryce support for coeducation was not enacted, the recommendations can be said to mark the start of the movement against separatist schooling and the gradual erosion of girls' educational autonomy which continued throughout the earlier decades of this century. What the 1902 Act did was to allow local education authorities to provide what secondary education they thought desirable, whilst secondary schools run by voluntary bodies were able, following the Act, to receive grants from local authorities and the Board of Education. Overall, the next ten years saw the building up of the secondary school system and the introduction of the free place system. The number of grant-aided secondary schools more than doubled during this time, whilst the number of pupils in schools virtually trebled (Lawson and Silver, 1973, p.139). Under the free place system, schools received grants if more than a quarter of their intake came from elementary schools.

Whilst elementary schools tended to remain mixed, secondary schools were mainly sex segregated; in 1905, less than a quarter of the 500 or so secondary schools recognised by the Board of Education were mixed (Kamm, 1965, p.231), but the curriculum tended to remain sex-specific.

During the inter-war years the major educational changes were in terms of growth in school size and in the phasing out of elementary schools. School expansion was on a massive scale and the Education Act of 1914 raised the compulsory school leaving age to 14. By 1936 the number of secondary school places for girls had nearly trebled in just over a decade (Kamm, 1965, p.233), but even so, these places were far outnumbered by the provision for boys.

Of the recommendations issued by the Board of Education during the inter-war years, only the 1923 report raised coeducation as an issue. Of a number of teachers from mixed and coeducational schools who gave evidence, only two women supported the system unequivocally, whilst men on the whole felt that girls would benefit from coeducation more than would boys (Kamm, 1965, p.232) Not the least of the reasons women gave for their opposition to coeducation was their anticipation of harassment by adolescent boy pupils (ibid., p.233). The underlying message of the 1923 report, whose committee consisted of a four to one ratio of men to women, was that feminism had 'gone too far' in shaping the academic tradition in girls' schools. The committee argued that 'the individuality of womanhood had been sacrificed upon the austere altar of sex equality' (Dyhouse, 1978, p.305). The report generally recommended a protective policy towards girls who, it claimed, required a less demanding and more domesticated education than boys. In the postwar opposition to women's widening employment, this ideology of girls' vulnerability served to reinforce the growing 'back-to-the-home' movement and provided fuel for traditional male hostility to women working (ibid., p.307).

Within this context, local education authorities' restrictions on the employment of married women teachers, introduced in the 1920s, was another factor in the backlash directed at girls' education. Many authorities automatically dismissed married women teachers, and most women were required to resign at marriage. By 1926, three-quarters of all LEAs, which were overwhelmingly male in composition, operated some sort of marriage bar (Oram, 1983, p.147).

The next major government report on education, the Hadow Report of 1927, simply made passing reference to its opposition to coeducation beyond primary school age (Hadow, 1927, p.91), and the issue was not discussed by the Spens Committee whose report on secondary education was made in 1938. Despite the Bryce recommendations, coeducation was never officially encouraged by the Board of Education during the inter-war years. During this period, however, elementary schools became increasingly coeducational, whilst secondary schools in England and Wales tended on the whole to be single-sex.

As the growth of both state and public secondary education accelerated at a faster rate than the elementary sector, education for teenage girls was, then, largely separate during the pre- and inter-war years of the twentieth century. With this in mind, and remembering the potential of girls' schools for developing and maintaining female autonomy, I shall now look more closely at the coeducation lobby, where it originated and what it aimed to achieve.

Coeducation and its Early Supporters

It was during the century's first twenty years that the main arguments in favour of coeducation, which are still recognisable today, were formulated. Those coed secondary schools that did exist were mixed for economic rather than ideological reasons and were largely set in more rural areas, where separate schooling was decreed economically unviable (King, 1929, p.93). The experience gained from these, plus the theories from the progressive school movement, helped to fire the coeducation lobby. It was largely in the private sector, with its boarding schools and its freedom from intervention, that an ideology for coeducation developed since private education allowed greater scope for experimentation.

Kevin Brehony points out that the progressive educationalists, many of whose schools were well established by 1920, came to be seen as the 'experts' on coeducation and so helped to construct a 'semi-official ideology of coeducation' (Brehony, 1984, p.7). This ideology saw coeducation as the major vehicle for social change, and aimed at 'the perfection of the relations between man and woman'. This 'perfection' would be reached by claims to either 'nature' or 'nurture' depending on what the situation called for.

Resistance to coeducation came, inevitably, from women teachers in girls' schools and they appeared to voice many of the concerns which recent feminist research has proved well founded; girls' reduced assertiveness and lower self-image and women teachers' pay reduction and loss of control were among their forecasts. One of these women teachers, Alice Zimmern, wrote in 1898:

> The attempts recently made in some schools aided by public money to economise by teaching boys and girls together, abolishing the headmistress and putting a headmaster over boys and girls alike, while arranging the curriculum and timetable to meet the needs of the boys and letting the girls do the best they can with it, is only a revival, under a new guise, of the old idea, that girls are not entitled to the same consideration as boys. Our modern reformers will not find their occupation gone while they have this old prejudice to combat. It is unjust to the teachers as well as to the taught. (Zimmern, 1898, p.244)

The well-founded fear of such women teachers was to be perpetuated in the following decades by the strength of the sexologists' influence on theories of both 'natural' femininity and the role of education in promoting these 'natural' functions. These theories provided the impetus for a groundswell in anti-lesbianism directed at 'educated' women and the single-sex school in which they taught.

The Spinster Teacher and the Shaping of a Stereotype

It was in the late nineteenth century that day and boarding schools, with trained women teachers, began to replace the governess system of education for middle-class girls. Women had fought for and entered higher education against massive opposition which preached dire threats and dealt harsh punishments; learning would make women infertile and sickly, and 'bluestockings' would remain old maids not through choice but by default since men would inevitably come to see them as 'intolerable monsters' (Burstyn, 1980, p.42). The threat of the 'educated' woman resulted in stereotypes which were to persist in various forms for decades to follow, with the notion of spinsterhood as a sacrifice or misfortune rather than positive choice being constantly reinvoked (Beddoe, 1983, p.55).

These stereotypes had already surfaced earlier in the century in relation to governesses in both the school and the home. Vicious caricatures of irresponsible 'old hags' in dame schools circulated in a period when women had great control over education; the contempt which they received at the hands of male reformers helped to discredit and undermine women's educational initiatives and to permanently erode the educational power which they had held in the first half of the nineteenth century (Beddoe, 1983, pp.51,52; Burstyn, 1980, p.3). Whilst the governess of the early nineteenth century presented no organised feminist challenge within the educational system, unlike her 'educated' sisters later in the century, her position within the middle-class family as a single woman in charge of children was a constant threat to the familial status quo. The ideal woman for the job would not threaten to compete with the wife and mother for the attentions and adulation of husband or child; she would therefore tend to be, in her ideal type, somewhat severe and 'masculine'. Indeed, it was the threatened encroachment on maternal rights and roles, and fears of exploiting naive girlish dependence, affection and trust which continued to underlie the twentieth-century lesbian threat of the spinster teacher.

This threat became a panic as women's education left the home and as the movement to found girls' day and boarding schools was formed. Daughters no longer remained entirely under the watchful surveillance of the mother or tied to the domestic concerns of the family. As women teachers also achieved a greater measure of autonomy and financial independence behind school walls, their potential for subverting the nation's daughters from the course of femininity began to be recognised. Additionally, both feminist struggles and male demands in wartime enabled women to escape being 'given away', and their numbers, increasingly outweighing those of men, could mean there was no one to give them to anyway.

This exodus of education from the home was very gradual, however, and the governess system coexisted with secondary education well into the 1920s. The vampire governess still lurked in the novels of the inter-war years, her threat perhaps enhanced because now she had a university degree to prove her unfemininity. A study by Katherine West demonstrates how vindictively most fictional governesses were portrayed during this time, as 'villainess' on the domestic scene (West, 1949). A particularly poignant example, strangely ignored by West, comes in Virginia Woolf's novel *Mrs Dalloway* (1925), the eponymous heroine being locked in constant battle with her daughter's tutor, Miss Kilman, who is both ugliness and corruption personified in her 'unlovable' body, her bald, egg-like forehead and her base determination to 'steal' her pupil from her mother's influence.

The caricature of the perverse and perverting spinster teacher contrasted strongly with the woman-as-nurturant-mother image which came to the fore in the early twentieth century. The emergence of the ideology of motherhood as a response to 'national need' has been thoroughly documented by Anna Davin. As the century turned, the role of mother became elevated to an unprecedented position. The nineteenth-century ideology of woman-as-wife gradually gave way to the twentieth-century one of woman-as-mother, and 'good motherhood' became the duty of all classes of women (Davin, 1978).

The teachings of sexology provided an ideological buttress by claiming that woman's greatest function was reproduction and that her psychology was determined by that capacity; Havelock Ellis maintained that

> In order to live a humanly complete life, every healthy woman should have, not sexual relationships only, but the exercise at least once in her life of the supreme function of maternity, and the possession of those experiences which only maternity can give. (Ellis, 1922, pp.65-6)

Women teachers managed to resist 'deviant' self-images as non-mothers partly through support networks (Vicinus, 1982) and partly because the division between 'mother' and 'teacher' was reinforced in the 1920s with the introduction of the marriage bar. Introduced by local education authorities throughout the country, this meant that women could be automatically dismissed at marriage. Its justification was that such a measure would reduce the unemployment rate of young, qualified teachers and help to cut public expenditure during the postwar economic crisis (Oram, 1983, p.135). Moreover, 'motherhood' in this context implied self-sacrifice for the sake of the nation; contrasted with women teachers' aims and aspirations of professional status, the two roles of 'mother' and 'teacher' could hardly be confused. Additionally, the 'new woman' who resisted domesticity was considered inferior breeding stock. She was deemed by the medical profession largely to have developed her intellectual and athletic skills at the expense of her reproductive capacities; this was either through her own volition, and by implication her own fault (Davin, 1978, p.21), or through the dictates of her biology, whereby she could claim no responsibility for her achievements.

So the unmarried woman teacher was placed in a position of conflict and contradiction. The teaching of children had traditionally been seen as 'women's work' and hence low status work, as long as it involved 'caring' and socialisation. The 'educated woman' who had been through higher education posed a double threat; she potentially challenged the mother's authority over the child – a position of authority which she was expected to abuse since she could not outshine 'real' biological motherhood – and she was seen to usurp the male prerogative to intellectual and academic success. Popular advice to mothers often warned of predatory mistresses forming 'unwholesome' alliances and of the young innocent falling prey to her educated hero.

Fiction again played its part in the propaganda; whilst lesbian writer Christa Winsloe provided a rare glimpse of the potential worth and warmth of such a match in the 1934 novel, *The Child Manuela*, more common was the motherless victim of the vampire teacher such as the tragic Louise in Clemence Dane's *Regiment of Women* of 1917, and Bella the one-time lackey of her embittered feminist headmistress in Brett Young's *White Ladies* of 1935. The setting of such novels was invariably the single-sex school, where the 'sour' spinster reigned supreme, and where the sexologists thrust the main weight of their anti-lesbian assaults.

Sexology, Separate Schooling and the Lesbian Threat

One of the earliest sexologists in England to warn against sexual segregation in schools was Havelock Ellis himself, in his 1897 study *Sexual Inversion*. Ellis believed that crushes, or 'rudimentary homosexual relationships' were more common among schoolgirls than among boys, for several reasons. Firstly, he felt that girls in general have a stronger need for affection than do boys – a belief which tied in with his notions of innate masculinity and femininity and his doctrine of female dependency. Secondly, he argued that girls are shielded from both sexual knowledge and male company and so do not often understand or recognise the sexual side of 'crushes' nor are they allowed as much free expression for their overtly sexual feelings. Finally, Ellis maintained, conventions allow girls more physical contact than boys (aided no doubt by beliefs such as Ellis' own that girls need more affection) and so lesbian passions can flourish freely under the guise of feminine friendship. Ellis remained convinced that single-sex schools created homosexuality, was certain that school authorities did their best to conceal the facts, and was adamant that the only salvation lay in coeducation. But the rationale for this was not that both sexes should receive the same type of education. Ellis argued that 'co-education does not necessarily involve identity of education for both sexes' (1913); coeducation would, he claimed, 'train the sexual emotions' towards heterosexuality in the direction deemed appropriate for each sex.

Ellis' support for coeducation was echoed by many other sex reformers of the day. In his 1908 study *The Intermediate Sex*, Edward Carpenter dedicated an entire chapter to 'Affection in Education', which eulogised male bonding in ancient Greece and contrasted it with contemporary boys' schools. The difference between these two situations, for Carpenter, was that whereas in Greek culture affection between youths and men was openly encouraged and institutionalised, in British public schools it was repressed and stifled, resulting in furtive sexual contact and stunted emotional growth. Carpenter's assumption was evidently that such contact was inevitable: the driving force of sex needed constant outlet. Carpenter's entire concern was with boys, except to mention in conclusion that the opposite problem arose in girls' schools. Here relationships were equally unhealthy but for reasons of over-indulgence rather than repression, and he claimed that friendships amongst girls were weak and sentimental. Carpenter's enthusiasm for coeducation seemed to stem from the belief that boys' 'natural' feelings would be less repressed and that girls would benefit from the more 'healthy' example which boys set. In short, what he was arguing was that boys' standards would and should set the tone for both sexes – a position entirely consistent with his extolment of manly love.

Writing in 1917, Stella Browne, who was greatly influenced by Ellis and Carpenter, also argued for coeducation as a remedy to what she saw as the 'unhealthy sexual conditions' prevalent at the time. Browne was a socialist–feminist campaigner for birth control and abortion rights and a leading sex reformer, helping to found the British Society for the Study of Sex Psychology in 1914. She viewed the

34

conflict between the sexes during this period of heightened feminist agitation largely as the result of sexual segregation in childhood:

> Much of the unhealthiness of sexual conditions at present is due to the habit of segregating the sexes in childhood and partly in later life, and making them into 'alien enemies' to one another. Some measure of co-education and a much wider professional and administrative co-operation will clarify our views and induce a more generous and human tone. (Browne, 1977, p.95)

As mentioned above, one of the earliest warnings about the 'sexual' and dangerous nature of schoolgirl crushes came from Ellis. His information about English girls' schools came from an unmarried 'lady' who told, from personal experience, of 'raving' and 'spooning' in 'one of the largest and best English colleges'. Already, at the turn of the century, such attachments were seen to stem from 'unhealthy' and 'morbid' feelings, and she claimed that the school had been organised to minimise and discourage their development. Despite such measures, which included encouraging outdoor games and separate bedrooms for older girls, raves on other students and teachers were the rule rather than the exception, 'hardly any being free from it', she reported: 'any fresh student would soon fall a victim to the fashion, which rather points to the fact that it is infectious' (Ellis, 1913, p.252).

Bernard Hollander, writing in 1922 of his 25 years practice as a medical psychologist at the Maudesley Hospital, warned of the grave dangers awaiting girls at the hands of lesbian teachers. 'Unsuspecting parents are little aware how common homosexuality is among women,' he announced, 'and how many little girls get seduced to the practice'. This could unfold even at the hands of their own teachers, and Hollander claimed to have known of a fashionable girls' school in London which was closed down on the discovery 'of the degrading and criminal habits of the headmistress who for years had seduced one girl after another' (Hollander, 1922, p.144). As a reassurance, he advised that there was hope for the many lesbian perverts thus produced if they would only volunteer for treatment, but his declaration undoubtedly served to reinforce the paranoia surrounding girls' schools.

Warning the general reader of the 'unwholesomeness' of all-girl settings, Helena Powell wrote in the early 1920s from her experiences as principal of St Mary's College, Paddington. She emphasised that the optimum balance of influence for adolescent girls was one where the effect of the single-sex day school was counterpoised by family life and contact with brothers, father and 'the call of the nursery' (Powell, 1924, p.106). This set of influences would prevent girls becoming too absorbed in themselves or developing 'undesirable intimacies', Powell claimed, especially since the mother would be able to keep in close touch with her daughter's companions. In school itself, a teacher may become a confidante in times of need, but a mother must ensure that such hero worship remains 'wholesome' and that the teacher herself could be trusted and respected. Without referring directly to the dangers which could ensue if the 'heroine' were not to be trusted, Helena Powell, with her forty years' experience of teaching adolescent girls, could intimate the catalogue of horrors, detailed elsewhere in advice manuals and novels, to which daughters could fall prey at the hands of unscrupulous teachers.

The phantom of the rampant and predatory lesbian teacher haunted Marie Stopes in her crusade for sex reform and universal heterosexuality. In 1918, at the age of 38, Stopes had risen to fame with the publication of *Married Love*. A biologist and botanist by training, she turned to studying and writing about sex education and birth control after three years of unconsummated marriage, and in 1921, with her second husband, she opened the first ever birth control clinic, in north London.

Stopes' anti-lesbian crusade was fuelled by the work of American biologist Maurice Bigelow, who had warned in his lectures on *Sex Education* (1916) against teachers who were themselves 'victims of sexual abnormality'. Such people should not, Bigelow preached, undertake to teach about sexual hygiene or morality:

Certain neurotic and hysterical men and women who lack thorough physiological training and whose sexual disturbances have led them to devour omnivorously and unscientifically the psychopathological literature of sex by such authors as Havelock Ellis, Krafft-Ebing and Freud, are probably unsafe teachers of sex-hygiene. (Bigelow, 1916, p.116)

How such individuals were to be recognised was not made clear, but Bigelow reinforced his point by adding that, regardless of whether the teachers themselves were 'abnormal', information about 'perverted life' was a grave danger to young people: 'The less that people without professional use for knowledge of sexual pathology know concerning it, the better it will be for their peace of mind and possibly for their morals' (ibid., p.118).

Writing ten years later, in 1926, Marie Stopes used Bigelow's arguments to reinforce her own warnings against spinster, and especially lesbian, teachers. Marie Stopes' criticism of the marriage bar stemmed not from any sense of injustice against women's claims for financial independence; what outraged Stopes was that girls should be taught by unmarried women teachers at all. Any school with a high proportion of unmarried women teachers would do great harm to the developing child's mental health and sexual development. Stopes argued that such dangers may be caused by teachers who are 'under-sexed' and hence unaware of children's need for guidance, and by those whose bitterness at not having succeeded in marriage makes them unbalanced and inadequate. Moreover, children are not the only victims of spinster teachers. Married women teachers, according to Stopes, also come in for a considerable degree of invective. Jealousy of their married colleagues who have combined career with heterosexual 'fulfilment' leads spinster teachers into vindictive postures and 'sheer spitefulness' towards them.

Such was the situation where only a proportion of the staff were unmarried, Stopes claimed. She argued that legislation should ensure that at least half the staff were married to prevent them from being in a weak minority position. Such a situation would be harmful enough, but where the entire staff was unmarried, Stopes warned of a hotbed of corruption, of homosexual 'rages' spreading to deform fresh young lives. According to her observations, lesbian teachers came in varying degrees of unwholesomeness, from the 'slightly erotic and almost hysterically affectionate' through to those 'indulging in intense and repeated physical experiences with a member of their own sex'.

Whilst Stopes' lesbian angst tended to focus more on the individual than the institution – suggesting that she favoured psychological rather than sociological theories – she did later suggest that single-sex schools were themselves the cradle of much emotional imbalance (Stopes, 1928, p.17).

Criticising coeducation as 'education for boys of which girls are permitted – or forced – to partake', in 1937 the headmistress of Manchester High School, M.G. Clarke, nevertheless felt it important to sing the praises of male teachers in girls' schools, who, she argued, would have a 'bracing' effect on adolescent girls. In addition, the stultifying influence of unmarried women teachers should be avoided by employing married women, who, by contrast, have a 'fuller and often more satisfying experience of life' (Clarke, 1937, p.66).

In the world of fiction, girls' schools were frequently the site of lesbian practices in both teachers and pupils, the more so at boarding schools where the family could not provide a counterbalancing influence. In Ivy Compton-Burnett's *More Women than Men* (1933), masculine and cynical Miss Rosetti, whose 'happiness depends on women' is the intimate friend of Miss Luke, both of whom are on the senior staff of the girls' boarding school. Love between pupils was often an autobiographical theme; Henry Handel Richardson's account of her own school crush in *The Getting of Wisdom* (1910) was found so offensive that the school authorities prevented her from revisiting (Richardson, 1964, p.70).

Testaments of the menace of lesbianism in education, from sexologists, psychologists, authors and pupils between the wars inspired the crusade of the coeducation lobby, of which the progressive theorists formed the vanguard.

Heterosexism and the Progressives

By the 1920s, sexology had helped to build a notion of the 'heterosexual ideal' to which the progressive school movement wholly subscribed and which it aimed to achieve through its ethos and its coeducational system.

In the inter-war years advocates of coeducation argued that mixed schools would make girls more adjusted to the demands of heterosexuality, rather than arguing that girls would receive a more 'equal' education. This was as true for those representatives of the so-called 'progressive' school movement as it was for the arch-traditionalists, both of whom placed primacy on complete heterosexual development. Summerhill, Dartington Hall and Frensham Heights were all creations of the 1920s, but progressive schools had started as early as the 1890s when Leighton Park, Bedales and King Alfred's were founded.

In general, the ethos behind the progressive school movement was one of *laissez-faire* liberalism. The emphasis was on allowing the child to grow in as 'natural' and unfettered an environment as possible. Stress was laid on developing the personality through personal decision making and goal formation rather than on gaining academic qualifications. After World War I, Freudian notions of the dangers of repression and the power of the unconscious mind served to reinforce this approach and to give it 'scientific' weight. The emphasis on 'naturalism' inevitably extended to ideas about sex. The majority of progressive schools were coeducational because this was considered the most natural setting for boys and girls, in contrast to the 'artificiality' of single-sex schools (Jacks, 1962, pp.35,39).

Ostensibly concerned with equality of the sexes, the underlying belief in women's 'natural' place never veered sharply from traditional views of the inevitability and desirability of wifehood and motherhood. In this respect, coeducation was seen as an important mechanism in avoiding homosexual development in either sex and thus in construct-

39

ing heterosexuality. Writing in 1935, the joint head of King Alfred's School, V.A. Hyett, warned that girls' schools encouraged homosexual development and argued that this could only be avoided by mixed schools:

> There is . . . a definitely pathological consequence of segregated education, most noticeable, perhaps, in boarding school life. The biological tendency to compensate for absent factors shows itself in social as well as in individual life. Just as the blind man develops an acuter sense of touch, so a community from which one sex is excluded tends to develop in certain members the characteristics of the missing sex. The boyish type of girl becomes more boyish, and her psychic development is pushed in the direction of homosexuality by the influence of her fellows who need the boy contact as a normal part of their lives. No one who has worked in girls' boarding schools can remain blind to the truth of this, and I am told that its counterpart is a perpetual problem in boys' schools. (Hyett, 1935, p.33)

Comparing seven years' teaching experience in a girls' school with 13 years in a coeducational school, Hyett claimed that the girls' school limited experience and activities, whilst the mixed setting ensured the greater happiness of children.

The headmaster of Summerhill since it was founded in 1921, A.S. Neill, wrote some twenty years later of what he saw as the iniquity of girls' schools; they either produce girls who are totally unselective in their choice of men, or they create frigid latent, if not overt, homosexuals:

> It is comparatively easy for a girl, lately come from a girls' boarding school, to fall for the first man who pays her any marked attention. She has no standard by which to compare men, and her knowledge of sex is confined to half-truths learned from other ignorant girls. The segregated school is fundamentally a funk hole made by parents and teachers who fear sex and too often hate it. They are ready to face the evil that youthful sex, when denied a natural outlet, tends to become homosexual, apparently

thinking that, of the two, homosexuality is less objectional than heterosexuality. The conspiracy of silence about homosexual practices at public schools is a well-preserved one, and only a fraction of public school products will admit that homosexual affairs took place in their school-days. Just as silent is the conspiracy to hide the fact that boarding-school girls get passions on bigger girls and mistresses, a fact that must throw some light on the prevalence of frigidity among many middle- and upper-class women. If a woman is unconsciously seeking love from a schoolmistress, she cannot be much of a wife or mistress to a mere man. (Neill, 1945, pp.78-9)

L.B. Pekin addressed the most common criticisms of coeducation in the 1930s. It had been argued that boys may develop a sense of inferiority at inevitably being 'outshone' by girls. Pekin reassured that 'co-educationalists do not posit the same, but complementary, capacities in the two sexes; they emphatically do not prescribe identical training' (Pekin, 1939, p.54). There would be no danger of boys being held back, since girls would be encouraged in the domestic realm and would thus not pose a threat. There was no question, for Pekin, that girls might develop a sense of inferiority in such a setting, and he emphasised that the goal of coeducation was 'true masculinity for the male and true femininity for the female, which, it may be held, can only be attained by either sex through the companionship and the help of the other' (ibid., p.55).

Discussing public school teachers, Pekin also attacked unmarried staff, and hailed the day when universal coeducation would 'see the last of these sour old bachelors and sour old maids who at present disfigure boys' and girls' schools of the segregated type' (Pekin, 1932, p.161).

Far from espousing ideals about equality, the unfettered development of the individual which the progressive educationalists had in mind was limited by stereotyped images of heterosexual development. Their female pupils were destined to be the next generation of wives and mothers.

41

Conclusion

Most single-sex girls' schools have been closed at an accelerating rate this century. In contrast to the inter-war years, state run girls' schools are now the exception rather than the rule. Clearly the normal development which sexologists and early progressive educationalists had in mind as an aim of co-education duplicated the imbalances in power and status between women and men in the world outside school. The lynchpin of this normal development was heterosexuality. Girls' schools threatened to prevent or reverse the subserviant image of femininity by engendering a sense of self worth. This could extend to girls and women making choices about sexuality instead of passively acceding to the male demands for female devotion.

The campaign towards co-education was greatly rooted in a loathing of lesbians, but especially of the lesbian spinster teacher. She personified the threat that women might not choose heterosexuality when left to their own devices. The phasing out of girls' schools was one way of making a lesbian existence seem impossible and unthinkable. It was a basic and crucial strategy in the reinforcement of heterosexist ideology in the inter-war years. The concept of femininity defined by heterosexuality continues to limit and distort the potential of girls and women and this historical legacy is no less iniquitous within girls' education today than it was fifty years ago.

References

Beddoe, Deirdre, *Discovering Women's History*, Pandora Press, London, 1983.

Bigelow, Maurice A., *Sex Education*, MacMillan, New York, 1916.

Board of Education, *The Differentiation of Curricula Between the Sexes in Secondary Schools*, HMSO, London, 1923.

Brehony, Kevin, 'Co-education: perspectives and debates in the early twentieth century', in *Co-education Reconsidered*, Rosemary Deem (ed.), Open University Press, Milton Keynes, 1984.

Browne, Stella, 'The sexual variety and variability among

women and their bearing upon social reconstruction', in *A New World for Women*, Sheila Rowbotham, Pluto, London, 1977.

Bryce Commission, *The Royal Commission on Secondary Education*, HMSO, London, 1895.

Burstyn, Joan, *Victorian Education and the Ideal of Womanhood*, Croom Helm, London, 1980.

Byrne, Eileen, *Women and Education*, Tavistock, London, 1978.

Carpenter, Edward, *The Intermediate Sex*, Allen & Unwin, London, 1908.

Clarke, M.G., 'Feminine challenge in education', in *The Head Mistress Speaks* (preface by Eleanor Addison Phillips), Kegan Paul, London 1937.

Clarricoates, Katherine, 'Dinosaurs in the classroom: a re-examination of some aspects of the hidden curriculum in primary schools', in *Women's Studies International Quarterly*, 1 (4), 1978.

Compton-Burnett, Ivy, *More Women Than Men*, Heinemann, London, 1933.

Dane, Clemence, *Regiment of Women*, Heinemann, London, 1917.

Davin, Anna, 'Imperialism and motherhood', *History Workshop Journal* 5 (Spring), 1978.

Deem, Rosemary, *Women and Schooling*, Routledge & Kegan Paul, London, 1978.

Dyhouse, Carol, 'Towards a "feminine" curriculum for English schoolgirls: the demands of ideology 1870-1963', *Women's Studies International Quarterly* 1 (4), 1978.

Ellis, Havelock, *Sexual Inversion*, F.A. Davis, Philadelphia, 1913.

The Task of Social Hygiene, Constable, London, 1922.

Hadow Committee, *Report of the Consultative Committee on the Education of the Adolescent*, HMSO, London, 1927.

Hollander, Bernard, *The Psychology of Misconduct, Vice and Crime*, Allen & Unwin, London, 1922.

Howe, Florence, 'The education of women', in *And Jill Came Tumbling After: Sexism in American Education*, Judith Stacey et al. (eds), Dell, New York, 1974.

Hyett, V.A., 'Social life in school and its bearing on sex deve-

lopment', in *Experiments in Sex Education*, Federation of
Progressive Societies and Individuals, London, 1935.

Jacks, H.B., 'Bedales School', in *The Independent Progressive
School*, H.A.T. Child (ed.), Hutchinson, London, 1962.

Kamm, Josephine, *Hope Deferred: Girls' Education in English
History*, Methuen, London, 1965.

Katz, Jonathan, *Gay/Lesbian Almanac*, Harper, New York,
1983.

Keane, Molly, *Full House*, Collins, London, 1935.

King, Bolton, *Schools of Today*, Dent, London, 1929.

Lavigeur, Jill, 'Co-education and the tradition of separate
needs', in *Learning to Lose*, Dale Spender and Elizabeth
Sarah (eds), The Women's Press, London, 1980.

Lawson, J. and Silver, H., *A Social History of Education in
England*, Methuen, London, 1973.

Mahony, Pat, *Schools for the Boys?: Co-education Reassessed*,
Hutchinson, London, 1985.

Neill, A.S., *Hearts Not Heads in the School*, Herbert Jenkins,
London, 1945.

Oram, Alison, 'Serving two masters: the introduction of a
marriage bar in teaching in the 1920s', in *The Sexual
Dynamics of History*, Feminist History Group, Pluto,
London, 1983.

Pekin, L.B., *Public Schools: Their Failure and Their Reform*,
Hogarth Press, London, 1932.

Co-Education in its Historical and Theoretical Setting,
Hogarth Press, London, 1939.

Powell, Helena, 'The problem of the adolescent girl', in *Sexual
Problems Today*, Mary Scharlieb (ed.), Williams &
Northgate, London, 1924.

Richardson, Henry Handel, [Ethel Florence Lindesay] *The
Getting of Wisdom*, Heinemann, London, 1910.

Myself When Young, Heinemann, London, 1964.

Sarah, Elizabeth, Scott, Marion and Spender, Dale, 'The
education of feminists: the case for single-sex schools', in
Learning to Lose: Sexism and Education, Dale Spender
and Elizabeth Sarah (eds), The Women's Press, London,
1980.

Shaw, Jenny, 'Education and the individual: schooling for girls,
or mixed schooling – a mixed blessing', in *Schooling for*

Women's Work, Rosemary Deem (ed.), Routledge & Kegan Paul, London, 1980.

Stopes, Marie, *Sex and the Young*, Gill Publishing Co., London, 1926.

Enduring Passion, G.P. Putnam's Sons, London, 1926.

Vicinus, Martha, 'One life to stand beside me: emotional conflicts of first generation college women', *Feminist Studies*, 8 (3), 1982.

West, Kathleen, *Chapter of Governesses: A Study of the Governess in English Fiction 1800-1949*, London, 1949.

Whitehorn, Katharine, 'All girls together', *The Observer*, 1 December 1986.

Winsloe, Christa, *The Child Manuela*, Chapman and Hall, 1934.

Woolf, Virginia, *Mrs Dalloway*, Hogarth Press, London, 1925.

Young, Francis Brett, *White Ladies*, Heinemann, London, 1935.

Zimmern, Alice, *Renaissance in Girls' Education*, Innes & Co., London, 1898.

3 Positive Images in Haringey: a Struggle for Identity

Davina Cooper

> There was a time, in the dawn of the permissive society,
> when enlightened liberals campaigned for an end to the
> laws which made homosexuality illegal – on the grounds
> that they were a vicious discrimination against a minority.
> But by a law of human nature, once this reasonable
> concession was granted, some homosexuals could not stop
> there. Next they wanted homosexuality to be regarded as
> socially quite acceptable. Then they wanted actually to
> crusade for it, by having it taught in schools and written
> about in books for children as something quite admirable.
> (*Today*, 2 September 1986)

Haringey Council – the media's darling, a place where fantasy is presented as truth and reality denounced as pitiful
fiction. Many know the list of press stories where anti-racist,
pro-gay policies are taken to incredible extremes – pink bin-
liners; compulsory enlistment of homosexual teachers sport-
ing gay pride badges; 'baa baa green sheep' and the banning
of bananas on council premises. Some also appreciate the
reality – a London borough where sections of the community
experience discrimination, prejudice, violence and ridicule.

To understand more fully the conflict over Haringey's
lesbian and gay rights policy it needs to be placed within the
context of Haringey's recent history. We need to return to
the autumn of 1985 when a council estate in Haringey,

pushed to its limit by economic deprivation, racism and police harassment, fought back.[1] State agencies responded by occupying Broadwater Farm and restricting the activities of its residents, in a manner which showed a total disregard for the rights of Black and working-class people over their environment. Questions are raised regarding the privacy and integrity of the family home, when residents can be arrested at any time in their flats, taken away for interrogation, and held in cells for several days without being charged. The media echoed their own outrage as press reports became increasingly distended, but it did not concern police treatment or parental rights to be informed of their children's arrest. Instead they focused their attack on the council and its leader, Bernie Grant, and condemned Haringey's anti-racist policies.

A year later right-wing forces were mobilising again, this time around a different issue, urging people to organise in order to protect traditional values now under attack – the family, home environment and parental rights. Haringey residents were called upon to obstruct and render impossible their council's latest plans. For Haringey Council was embarking on a policy which became known as 'positive images': to eradicate the discrimination facing lesbians and gay men, by means of its education provision.

This chapter attempts to document the pursuit of and resistance to positive images in Haringey, between the summers of 1986 and 1988. It focuses on the process of mobilisation – how different groups became involved – and the way in which interpretations and meanings attributed to positive images were constructed and struggled over. My involvement was both as a member of the groups that formed to support positive images and as a Haringey Councillor. I will start by providing an outline of the main issues positive images was intended to address, and then go on to discuss the events surrounding the policy between the council elections of May 1986 and the general election in June 1987. The third section considers the impact of Section 28 of the Local Government Act 1988 on Haringey's policy of positive images and, finally, I consider what positive images meant to the various groupings involved and why it precipitated such an intense response.

Positive Images – a Definition

'Positive images' is not a term specific to lesbians and gay men. Rather it refers to the need for role models for all sections of the community who internalise societal prejudice and derogatory stereotypes about themselves. Underlying this perceived educational need are principles of meritocracy and the self-fulfilling prophecy: that if adults and society in general project a negative image of certain young people, they will not succeed to the full extent of their capabilities. This has been shown to explain why Black, working-class students and young women often underachieve in non-traditional areas of study.

> It is held that of the main causes of underachievement and lack of confidence in the learning process some of the more important are situations in which many people have to cope with the effects of low expectations, severe stereotyping and institutionalised prejudice.[2] (*Mirrors Round the Walls*, 1988)

'Positive images' of lesbians and gay men refers less to educational expectations than to the general assumptions of social and sexual development. Although links can be made between a low sexual self-image and academic attainment, Haringey Council's policy was predicated on a broader understanding of education regarding both the knowledge and ideas to be communicated and a positive instrumentalist approach aimed at ensuring the next generation of adults would be more tolerant and appreciative of diversity. Yet this conscious attempt to redefine the remit and parameters of education unleashed considerable fear and raised an important question for public debate – which unfortunately became hidden in the debacle of Section 28 – 'What is the purpose and function of schooling and who has the right to determine the direction taken and issues encompassed?'

In the next section of this chapter I will discuss how the policy of positive images for lesbians and gay men developed in Haringey. An outline of some of the main objectives is contained in a leaflet produced by the council in March 1987, *What Every Parent Needs to Know about Lesbian and Gay Issues*. These objectives can be summarised as follows: (1) staff in schools should prevent name calling; (2) support for 'out' lesbian/gay staff; (3) ensuring that all staff receive training on this issue; (4) not avoiding mention of lesbians and gay men where relevant, e.g. in sex education; (5) teaching students about the contribution of lesbians/gay men to cultural, social and political life (i.e. positive images); (6) placing useful information in schools; and (7) not assuming that everyone is heterosexual unless they state otherwise.

The Struggle for Positive Images, 1986-7
Part 1

> *Lord Monson*:
> 'My Lords I beg leave to ask . . . Her Majesty's Government whether they approve of Haringey Borough Council's plans for compulsory lessons intended to promote "positive images" of homosexuality in nursery, primary and secondary schools in the borough . . .?' (House of Lords, 28 July 1986)

In Haringey at the present time, there are few 'positive images' let alone 'compulsory lessons'. Demands though on local authorities to end the discrimination facing lesbians and gay men go back well before 1986. In 1981, the leadership of the GLC committed themselves to working towards this end. They set up a working party which included many London activists and provided funding for lesbian and gay organisations such as counselling services, social amenities and oral history projects.[3]

In 1983, Haringey Council initiated a consultation process which incorporated both service committees and the community. Large public meetings were held for lesbians and gay men, and from these meetings emanated demands for a unit. This was in preference to a centre, as it would enable officers to be employed within the council to work on the issues that affected lesbians and gay men. In the autumn of 1984, two council employees were seconded to begin developmental work. (A year later, Camden Council appointed two workers to investigate and report on the needs of lesbians and gay men in their borough.) In the spring of 1986 Haringey's lesbian and gay unit was established, and after the local municipal elections in June 1986, the subcommittee followed.

We fought the 1986 local elections with a campaign and manifesto that prioritised equal opportunity policies (EOPs). Contained within the manifesto was a section on lesbian and gay rights. The paragraph relating to education was short and somewhat vague. It made the following points: support lesbian and gay educational workers to be 'out'; give support to students realising their own gayness; and ensure such issues are treated positively within the curriculum.

The manifesto was formally agreed by the full council after the May elections, and became the council's programme for the forthcoming four years. However, recommendations as to how the equal opportunities policy for lesbian and gay men would be implemented had still to be agreed by the appropriate standing committees and council, before any programme could be put into effect. Consequently, even though equal opportunities for lesbians and gay men in education had been agreed in principle, when the lesbian and gay unit wrote to head teachers during the summer months of 1986 to remind them of this commitment, the storm which had been slowly gathering momentum, burst. The letter sent by the unit was leaked to the local press and the government. As schools stood closed and empty, fearful parents read their morning newspapers and panicked about the new teaching that would greet them in the autumn.

The council had now to validate the unit's actions quickly. On 30 September 1986, the Education Committee heard deputations from both sides and formally agreed to initiate a policy of positive images. The recommendations were very preliminary – setting up a working party to develop educational resource materials, and establishing a forum for consultation with parents and the lesbian and gay communities as to how best to implement the policy. On 20 October 1986 the full council debated the issue and agreed the Education Committee's proposals. Almost 1000 people flooded into the civic centre to hear the debate. The majority – including lesbians and gay men from all over the country – came to support positive images.

Although the night of 20 October felt like a victory, over the following eight months many lesbians and gay men became dissatisfied. They felt the council was moving too slowly and feared the policy would get lost in bureaucracy, never to re-emerge. Teachers who had come out during the intense early autumn months, trusting the council's statements, started to feel let down, exposed and vulnerable. A number faced truculent, unsupportive heads, who clamped down on any positive work, justifying delay in anticipation of the Education Service's guidelines.

So as various sections of the community attempted to seize the initiative in defining positive images and began to mobilise, the arena of activity shifted away from the council. And although pressure groups tried to pin it down, particularly those on the Left who wanted to know the practical effects of the policy, Haringey, like a hydrogen balloon, drifted further away, far from anyone's reach.

Part 2

The government responded quickly on hearing of Haringey Council's plans. A debate was held in the House of Lords (28 July 1986), and Education Secretary, Kenneth Baker, launched an inquiry into the matter, nominating Tory councillor Ron Bell as the government 'watchdog' on positive images. In tandem the Parents Rights Group (PRG) was being formed. Ostensibly a local organisation not affiliated to any political party (unlike the Tottenham Conservative Association election campaign for Normal Family Life), PRG provided the enticing bait for a campaign which would culminate in the 1987 general election. The aim – explicit as the general election drew nearer – was to induce terror at the prospect of a Labour government. The Committee for a Free Britain, an apparently 'independent' organisation, spent more than £110,000 during the 1987 general election on full-page advertisements in a number of national newspapers, including one with a photograph of a woman and the following words underneath:

> 'My name is Betty Sheridan. I live in Haringey. I'm married with two children. *And I'm scared.*
>
> If you vote LABOUR they'll go on teaching my kids about GAYS AND LESBIANS instead of giving them proper lessons.' Signed E. Sheridan.

During the wet summer of 1986, the PRG organised a march from Tottenham town hall to the Education Service's offices in Wood Green. Only 50 'parents' turned up, but more than 1500 had signed the 'mum's' petition. The strategy adopted by the opponents to the policy was clear – Haringey Council was placing families and family values in jeopardy; moreover, it was acting undemocratically by not consulting parents or allowing them to voice their protests.

> Cllr. Diane Harwood, who has two children aged four and six said this week: 'We have nothing against homosexual people as such, but it is not something the average mother will allow their [sic] children to be taught.' (The *Independent*, 31 July 1986)

Focusing on the rights of parents, particularly mothers, was a crude attempt both to win over the sympathy of a nation and to unite people around a role and ideology they could most easily identify with.[4] Parenthood was used repeatedly by the Right and the media to validate and give legitimacy to wide-ranging statements. Parents had a moral authority emanating from their nurturing, selfless role, with which lesbians and gay men (perceived as decadent and sexually indulgent) could not compete. All normal families are under attack, screamed the press, Conservative Party and PRG; everyone must join in the struggle to protect their 'way of life'. How many times have such headlines been used, urging people to forget their differences and fight a common enemy? In the past, the war was physical, joining the army to defend the British way of life. Here we were engaged in ideological warfare, but the tactics and goal posts were the same. Lesbians and gay men were held out by the gathering right-wing forces as 'the other', the 'enemy within', who aimed to destroy all that was sacred. The family, in contrast, was presented as a place of innocence and stability, nurturing wholesome traditional values. Clearly, this necessitated ignoring many features of the family: the existence of lesbian and gay parents on the one hand and, on the other, sexual abuse and marital violence; as well as the rejection, hostility and non-communication which often exists between parents and children.

The contradictions in the PRG stand were brought home in the uproar over *Jenny Lives With Eric and Martin*.[5] The book was a photostory of a very young girl staying with her father and his boyfriend. Published in this country by Gay Men's Press, the book had been available in shops for some time. However, in September 1986 it was brought to the attention of Education Secretary Kenneth Baker as being stocked by the ILEA and available in Haringey libraries: 'Mr Baker felt as a parent he could not stand by while County Hall allowed the book's distribution' (The *Standard*, 16 September 1986).

The response of the PRG was equally hostile, although their interest caused sales of the book to rocket, and requests to borrow it from lending libraries flooded in. '"We won't rest until we have publicly burnt every copy of that book that is available to our children", said Mrs Pat Head, leader of the Haringey Rights Group (PRG) in North London' (The *Mail*, 17 September 1986).

The book was described by its opponents as promotional material aimed at children in their formative years. Yet, at the same time, local authorities who withdrew racist and sexist literature from their stocks were attacked for heavy-handed censorship. Even Frances Morrell, Labour leader of the ILEA, stated that *Jenny Lives With Eric and Martin* would only be used 'in exceptional circumstances'. Neither she, nor critics of the book who claimed its presentation of homosexuality was one-sided, responded in a similar fashion to stories of heterosexual parenting. Clearly, the book's opponents were not arguing for a neutral presentation of the facts, as their criticisms might have implied, but rather that there should be a clear heterosexual bias in which the dominant perspective is equated with neutrality.

Across the media, the views of the PRG attracted considerable interest and support. Haringey was portrayed as the 'looney, out of touch' council, opposed by a responsible, concerned community. Consequently, many people remained oblivious to the local groups which mobilised to support the policy. The first to come together was Positive Images, formed in September 1986 as a broad based left-wing opposition to the PRG. It was initiated primarily by Tottenham Communist Party and Haringey Campaign for Lesbian and Gay Rights, but members of the Labour Party, SWP and other organisations joined, as well as individuals who wanted the educational proposals implemented in the borough's schools.

> 'I was one of the many local lesbians and gay men who were glad when the council finally came around to raising the issue of lesbian and gay rights in schools. When trouble started over it, and bigots began making a fuss, it was important the council didn't retreat and the community kept up pressure on the council and also helped explain to other people what the policy was about.' (Member of Positive Images)

Positive Images maintained a high profile over the year; organising pickets and demonstrations; producing leaflets and giving talks to various groups including sessions for local school governors. Meanwhile, the PRG splintered and reformed, a consequence of diverse political views, particularly in relation to homosexuality. One of the most inspiring aspects of Positive Images (PI) for myself, was the working alliances formed by the various left-wing organisations involved. At times though, friction arose as when party allegiances took precedence and heterosexual political activists were deemed to be monopolising the organisation's decision making. There was also some disagreement as to whether PI should be a single-issue pressure group or an organisation for socialism, 'with lesbian and gay politics high on the agenda'. 'But it was a campaign not a political party . . . It needed to think about how it could be most effective in winning support for positive images' (Member of Positive Images).

The formation of Positive Images brought to the PRG the realisation they had to contend with another community based group who also claimed to represent a significant section of local residents. In the early autumn of 1986 PRG began to change tack, by emphasising how they spoke on behalf of all Haringey's minority ethnic communities. They and Haringey Conservative Party hoped to mobilise Black people, especially religious, traditional leaders, against the council, thereby undermining Haringey's anti-racist image and winning the support of people perceived as traditionally loyal to Labour. 'Their strategy was based on the stock racist stereotype that if they could win the support of what they saw as the leadership, the rest of the Black communities would follow' (Member of Haringey Black Action).

Although such a strategy could not succeed, the relentless presentation of the council's policies as implicitly racist because they supposedly conflicted with the values and lifestyles of Black and minority ethnic communities, put many people in an invidious position, as did the portrayal of a borough no longer concerned about racism because of its obsession with lesbian and gay rights. It is ironic, but not surprising, that this confusion was initiated by those same people who a year earlier were whipping up racist feeling among the white community, claiming the council only serviced the needs of Black residents in the borough. Yet for many Black people statements that their council was aiming to destroy and fragment their families held a more serious threat than for their white neighbours.

'I think there was a mistrust of local authorities among Black people which was justified . . . and this was seen as a council attempt to bring in something from out of the blue . . . and to divert attention from racism in schools.' (Outreach

Worker, Black Lesbian and Gay Centre)

In the winter months of 1986-7, Haringey Black Action (HBA) was formed. It came together to oppose attempts to win over the Black community against positive images, and to challenge the overt racism that was surfacing in connection with the policy. Unlike the organisation PI, the aim of HBA was not necessarily to support the council, which was seen as a part of the repressive state, but to oppose oppression at the level of grass-roots activity.

HBA appreciated that lesbian and gay rights could not be demanded in isolation. For although oppressions operate differently – a point EOPs have often failed to realise – the people affected may be the same, and furthermore oppressions interact in complex ways with each other. The Right used racism to reinforce homophobia. On the Left attempts at solidarity (often shaky) were made, illustrated in the 'Smash the Backlash' demonstration – 'Fight Bigotry, Fight Racism'. On 2 May 1986, the march wended its way through Wood Green with little sign of the Far Right. For many people the march was symbolic – reclaiming the streets which had been filled for months by opponents collecting signatures, speaking out against lesbians and gay men, and attempting to mobilise passers by.

The PRG, meanwhile, was aiming for the moral monopoly. From the beginning it had purported to represent dutiful parents. Later it explicitly drew to its side sections of the Christian church. Although many church members, including the Gay Christian Movement, were sympathetic to Haringey's educational policy, the public face marketed by the media and right-wing forces was of an institution horrified at being expected to condone the teaching of sin. Christian fundamentalists and others wrote letters, attended councillors' surgeries and held meetings to raise a number of issues with the council. First, we were exploiting our position as an education authority, to inculcate the young with our 'extremist' views. Claims by the Education Service that we were merely attempting to eradicate prejudice became translated into interfering in an area which was none of our business. Morality and ethics, it was argued, were the responsibility of families, and schools should not teach children in a way that might conflict with values learnt at home. Repeatedly, supporters of positive images argued that education already presented a biased picture of family life and that homosexuality was a vital issue for many young people, irrespective of what their parents believed.

Second, and more fundamentally, sections of the church argued that homosexuality was itself highly immoral, and that schools had a social responsibility to discourage it. The PRG, on the other hand, were careful to say publicly that they had no objections to lesbians and gay men themselves; it was just the promotion of homosexuality they objected to.

> . . . whilst believing in the freedom of the individual to choose his or her own sexual orientation, we demand that Haringey Labour Party withdraws their policy of promoting positive images of homosexuality . . . (Conservative Party petition)

One might doubt the honesty of a position which in any event appears contradictory, but the distinction drawn is interesting. What the PRG and Conservatives perceived as a threat was not the existence of lesbians and gay men, but the acknowledgement of homosexuality as acceptable, an implicit challenge to the ideology of compulsory heterosexuality. A press statement from Tottenham Conservative Party described Haringey's lesbian and gay unit as 'a greater threat to family life than Adolf Hitler' (quoted in *Hampstead and Highgate Express*).

Since June 1986, the church in Haringey had been at odds with the Education Committee. For many years their representative had taken one of the co-opted places on the committee, but after the 1986 municipal elections the Education Committee decided to co-opt instead a representative from the Haringey Disablement Association. Church members saw this as a challenge to their authority, both in running many of the borough's schools and in providing the moral flavour to policies formulated by the committee.

For the first time since the borough was constituted twenty-one years ago no church representative was co-opted on to the council. And this is an area where one in four of the children are in a church school. No wonder a leading voice among the Catholics of Haringey . . . said: 'This Labour council is anti-church'. And their gullibility makes them receptive and impressionable to the persuasive voices in the homosexual lobby. (*Westminster Record*, November 1986)

So the church, already mobilising its forces, joined with the PRG against a 'dangerous' council, which believed it could undermine the establishment and put a new set of values in its place.

Involvement came not only from traditional quarters of the church. Others, including the New Patriotic Movement (NPM), also joined in the attack on left-wing policies – chanting and praying outside Wood Green civic centre; while other members of the NPM demonstrated in Manchester to show support for the Chief Constable in his mission of 'carrying out the word of God' by ridding society of 'sin'. In January 1987 the Reverend Rushworth-Smith began his fast, which he vowed would last until death, unless the council reversed its lesbian and gay policies. 'Mr Rushworth-Smith said: "Haringey council want to equate homosexuality with heterosexuality, if they carry this through they will destroy society as we know it"' (The *Standard*, 10 December 1986).

Now a new moral weight was flung around Haringey Council's neck. If we did not reverse our policy a 'man of God' would die. Rushworth-Smith, however, did not die. When he decided no more mileage could be gained from his weight loss, he ceased fasting (an incident which few of the newspapers that had followed his fast so assiduously decided to report). Although Rushworth-Smith focused his attack on positive images, the broader political purpose of his actions was soon made apparent. In an interview with the *Independent*, shortly after the 1987 general election, he claimed that Mrs Thatcher was the only leader who could save us from 'shocking sinfulness', and that 'the Lord has raised her up during these past years for that very purpose . . . The Labour Party was going to let people have sex with animals.'

I have highlighted in this section the strategy of the policy's opponents, because to a considerable extent they set the terms within which the struggle for positive images took place. The various sections of the Left were often placed on the defensive, responding to the Right's arguments.

> 'We were in a weak position because we seemed only able to use rational arguments. Most of the debate wasn't conducted very rationally at all, and that was the strength of groups like PRG, they could tap hidden fears . . .' (Member of Positive Images and Haringey Campaign for Lesbian and Gay Rights)

Later on, the balance seemed to change. During the period of Lesbian Strength and Gay Pride, 1987, a number of successful events were organised by community groups and the council. A cross-section of Haringey residents attended the celebrations, which renewed the confidence of some, and allayed the fears of others.

Section 28 – Promotion of Homosexuality Banned

It was a whimper in the early hours of a December morning that heralded an amendment to the Local Government Bill, soon to symbolise internationally Britain's unrelenting progression towards repressive centralism.[6] All year in Haringey, we had waited for the legislative response to positive images, eschewing the earlier false starts. The shock though, when it came, was in realising how many other areas of council activity were included within the amendment which aimed to prohibit the promotion of homosexuality by Local Authorities (see Chapter 4). Would the legislation affect council licensing powers? What did 'promote' mean in this context? And who had ever encountered a 'pretended family relationship'?

Although locally the council and community groups considered with mounting disquiet the implications of what was to become Section 28, Local Government Act 1988, the effect of the legislative proposal was to shift the locus of political activity. National attention was deflected from the validity or otherwise of Haringey Council's education policy on to the meaning and purpose of central government plans. Positive images had brought together in its wake a constellation of right-wing forces; Section 28 was to achieve the converse. A wide range of groups and individuals became active in a campaign which aimed principally to raise public awareness and create a massive lobbying force. As well as many high profile actions, sections of the workforce mobilised their unions; liberal, middle-class theatre goers signed petitions and wrote letters opposing increased censorship, and various groups opposing Section 28 (or clause 27/28/29 as it was then) were formed, for example within the Jewish community, to demonstrate solidarity against the clause and to increase consciousness within the community about the oppression facing lesbians and gay men. Although, not surprisingly, the majority of activity against Section 28 came from lesbians and gay men, heterosexuals were seen publicly to be giving their support, such as through the very successful arts lobby.[7] This countered the media view of positive images as a minority, fringe sexuality supported by an ultra-leftist local council out of touch with normal, heterosexual, mainstream society.

The spring of 1988 witnessed the lesbian and gay movement 'out', public and on the streets, in some of the largest gay demonstrations held in Western Europe. Meanwhile Conservative ministers, peers and backbenchers got on with the task of processing the clause through its various readings, avoiding the wrecking amendments – which they claimed were unnecessary – as the day of the Royal Assent drew nearer. In Haringey the Conservative minority on the council did not wait for the provision to come into force before using it to threaten organisations and projects which had a link, however tenuous, with lesbians and gay men.

On 25 April several Conservative councillors requisitioned a council meeting to agree a motion submitted in the name of Cllr Murphy (by this time the Tories were seriously divided in their response to homosexuality and Section 28).[8] It called on the council to close the lesbian and gay unit, abolish the curriculum working party, cease all measures to promote homosexuality in schools, abolish all references to homosexuality as contained in the Labour Party manifesto, now council policy, and to cease all grant aid to Reading Matters (a local progressive bookshop) and any other homosexual group [*sic*].

The motion was not carried. Instead the Labour majority on the council reiterated their opposition to Clause 28 [*sic*] and continuing support for lesbian and gay policies. Outside the civic centre, several hundred people had gathered; the 'revolutionary' Left with their placards and newspapers jostled with representatives of lesbian and gay organisations. But the mood was different to that eighteen months earlier when lesbians and gay men had left the council chamber in triumph. Tonight the council, with its in-built Labour majority, could agree a statement of support and solidarity, but what concrete opposition could it realistically provide against the wishes and intentions of central government? For in between the two mass council demonstrations, Haringey had been 'forced' as a result of Central Government financial controls to cut its expenditure by over 25 per cent, causing severe hardship to local people dependent on its services. This was the council which had committed itself to 'NO CUTS IN SERVICES AND NO LOSS OF JOBS' (Haringey Labour Party's Manifesto, 1986). Yet when it had come to a choice between being surcharged and ejected from local government or agreeing a legally balanced but reduced budget, the majority on the Labour group had voted for the latter.

Local activists were therefore well aware of the unlikelihood of a strategy of non-compliance with Section 28 by their council, even if this was promised by some councillors. If the section once in force was to be defeated, particularly its educational provisions, resistance needed to come from outside the formal political structures – from trade unions, community groups and front-line staff. In the case of schools, neither teachers nor governing bodies were directly affected by the legislation, although there might be an obligation on local authorities to act, if a teacher appeared to be consistently flouting the terms of the prohibition. These bodies therefore seemed to offer more chance of effectively implementing positive images than the local educational department.

Unfortunately the large, centralised bureaucracy of the council seemed unable to make the necessary adjustments to encourage a dispersal of initiative and policy development. Their emphasis remained on what the council itself would do, and the council politically was paralysed by the ongoing debate amongst Labour councillors as to whether breaking the law in any circumstances was justified and, if so, what those circumstances might be.

Section 28 provoked several different positions within the Council Labour group. The leadership, at various public and private meetings, argued that Haringey had in fact always operated within the parameters set by Section 28, because the promotion of homosexuality was a ludicrous impossibility, and to attempt it would be a gross misuse of our educational powers. Left-wing councillors claimed that the legislation was offensive, treating lesbians and gay men as second-class citizens. Most avoided the question of whether or not promotion was possible, considering this a red herring in relation to their basic position of non-compliance with the law. However, since the Left's position had consistently been rejected by a majority of the Labour group, positive images would have had more chance of moving forward if alternative, imaginative solutions had been considered. Instead, the Left relentlessly struggled to persuade moderate Labour councillors to adopt a confrontational strategy. They failed.

Whilst events surrounding Section 28 quickened their pace and the civic centre remained caught in a seemingly unresolvable impasse, down the road from Wood Green's town hall the curiculum working party, set up in the autumn of 1986, continued to meet. Their remit had been to assist the development of equal opportunities within the education service, with particular reference to curriculum provision, recognising the rights and responsibilities of lesbians and gay men and examining ways an environment could be created to overcome discrimination and prejudice.[9]

On 19 April 1988 the working party presented a draft copy of their report to the Education Committee, with barely any public opposition or controversy, compared to that shown in the preceding two years whenever the subject of positive images had been raised. The report was warmly welcomed by the majority of the meeting. At over 100 pages in length it provided a thorough consideration of primary and secondary education as well as youth provision, with many suggestions of good practice and recommendations for adaptions to the curricula. Once discussed and initially agreed by the Education Committee, *Mirrors Round the Wall* and an abbreviated version were distributed for consultation. It was unclear what would follow. Would it be left to schools to decide for themselves what aspects of the policy, if any, they would choose to implement? What monitoring mechanisms would the education authority use? And what could they do if schools rejected the ethos of lesbians and gay rights altogether, not only refusing to implement positive initiatives, but refusing even to intervene when clear acts of abuse, prejudice or discrimination took place?

Sexual Politics – Whose Identity?

For two years Haringey Council navigated its way through a growing sea of legislation and circulars,[10] slowed down by attempts to appease anxious parents and communities. Yet, however much the council toned down positive images, Conservative councillors continued to claim that it was 'a Marxist plot to destabilise society'. The Revd Rushworth-Smith said about council plans:

'They are set on destroying family life in Haringey. They don't care about men and women marrying and having children. This is (not) just politics, it is an attack on the cosmos.' (*Hampstead and Highgate Express*, 23 January 1987)

Although the cosmos still remains out of reach, how radical and far-reaching was 'positive images'? In discussing this question, several points need to be borne in mind. First, that what is actually meant by positive images is itself uncertain – a detailed description of the policy did not surface until April 1988 – and many groupings exploited this ambiguity to transform the policy into something that favoured their own position. Second, any implications or consequences of positive images cannot be assumed to reflect what was intended. Haringey Council may have underestimated the potential impact on the status quo of policies concerning sexuality, by conceiving sexual orientation as principally a matter of private choice. This raises a third issue of where ownership and responsibility for positive images lies. Although ostensibly a local authority policy, is this really the case? Or does positive images also belong to the many voices in the debate who were significant in determining its purpose and parameters? Fourth, any analysis of the effects and implications of a progressive lesbian and gay strategy will depend on the relationship believed to exist between sexuality and (1) patriarchy and capitalism, or (2) matters of morality and religion, if these are considered more fundamental. Fifth, positive images became a party political issue; exploited by the Conservative Party to discourage people from voting Labour, it was assiduously avoided as an electoral liability by the Labour Party leadership, who throughout the positive images debate and for most of the campaigning against Section 28, distanced themselves from the lesbian and gay movement and from taking any clear position on gay rights or sexual politics.

Elements Within a Discourse

The publicity and attention that surrounded positive images and later Section 28 popularised the terms and concepts prevalent within the discourse of sexual politics to an extent previously unimaginable. It would have been impossible to have ascertained in advance the specific form that the debate would take. Diverse elements came together to create perspectives that interwove, sometimes united, sometimes opposed, in a struggle embracing many issues. Around positive images two broad positions stood out; others also existed, but their proponents either remained outside the debate or chose a compromise in supporting one or other of the more dominant perspectives. On the Left was the meritocratic model of equal opportunities sharpened by local government's practical and ideological constraints; whilst the Right organised around their favoured themes of family, social stability, parental rights, and 'night watchman' state.

Such themes both reflected the interests of groups already part of the campaign against positive images and laid the groundwork for attracting new ones – local working-class residents 'who used to vote Labour', elements within the church and other organised religious groupings, some members of the different (minority and majority) ethnic communities, the media, 'parents' and peers of the realm. But even now it is hard to gauge the extent to which the claims made by right-wing activists were actually believed either by themselves or by others.[11]

> 'I think there were a variety of motives to why people opposed positive images. Some opposed it on grounds of bigotry . . . some saw it as part of a broader attack on all those forces undermining the way of life they believed in . . . Communists, travellers [caravan dwellers], lesbians and gay men, black people . . . amongst the leadership there were members of the far-right, people seeking to manipulate . . . stir up trouble for a Labour local authority, particularly one with a Black leader [Bernie Grant].' (Outreach Worker, Black Lesbian and Gay Centre)

Many of those responsible for whipping up anti-gay resentment, particularly the Conservative councillors and MPs involved, knew that Haringey Council was unlikely to be either intending or able to initiate a policy of the magnitude suggested. But confusing the council's broad claims for positive images with radical statements of sexual politics, and orally inflating the power of local government, created an impression of a council (a) desirous and (b) capable of achieving anything. While the council was quick to reject the former assumption, its negation of the latter was more tardy.

Consequently, groupings on both sides had an exaggerated view of what was possible for a Labour local authority to achieve.[12]

Mirrors Round The Walls, the policy document eventually produced, aimed to set out Haringey Council's aims and objectives. The predominant themes were equality of opportunity, pluralism, rights and diversity. Labour councillors argued that lesbians and gay men had as much right to equal opportunities as any other section of the community. But what does equal opportunities mean in this context?

A Haringey Education Service leaflet on equal opportunities for lesbians and gay men described it as 'allowing them to choose to be open about themselves without fear'. How meaningful is such an approach to challenging discrimination and oppression? Can lesbians and gay men be treated as a discrete section of the community with the potential for liberation, within our present environment? The council's implicit response to both questions was in the affirmative. Based on a liberal vision of a market place of values and lifestyles from which people can freely choose, its analysis does not conceive of structural constraints operating within society that make the achievement of equality for any section of the community impossible without wide ranging fundamental changes.

In any case, what is equality? So often this is interpreted to mean parity with the values and lifestyle of the dominant class or group. To argue that it can never meaningfully be discussed while we live in an unequal society is unhelpful; but the concept of equality does need to be considered within the context of an articulated set of social values – hegemonic or otherwise. The following extracts from the journal *Education* (1986) illustrate what can otherwise result:

> The main issue confronting the Educational Welfare Officer (EWO) is usually one of helping the lesbian couple present themselves as acceptable parents to the world in general and school in particular . . . discussing difficulties in role allocation involved in a woman taking on

> fathering roles or mothering roles . . . As a couple
> become more secure in their family arrangements, they
> tend to emerge from the gay subculture and try to fit in
> with the school life of the neighbourhood . . . potentially
> well motivated parents, usually ensuring any boy children
> are involved in masculine activities. (Eric Blyth and
> Judith Millero, *Education*, 22 August 1986)

Although Haringey Council has clearly stated 'it is not the
business of any of the partners in the Education Service . . .
to attempt to force on to others their own opinions and
views, no matter how strongly they may be held',[13] nevertheless, it has stressed certain values, namely, pluralistic notions
of acceptance and difference, emphasising the enrichment
diversity offers.

> 'The curriculum is recognised also as a vital means by
> which positively to develop understanding of and respect
> for individuals and groups whose cultural and linguistic
> heritage, religious beliefs or whose sexuality might be
> different.'[14]

It is unclear though what degree of respect is considered
necessary for the sexual norm and whether 'sexual difference' encompasses anything other than homosexuality.
    The above quotation illustrates that Haringey Council
treated sexual orientation as another aspect of the borough's
cultural diversity: a fixed immutable characteristic. PRG
predictions of the catastrophic impact that would follow
were consequently considered by the council to be ridicu-
lous, unscrupulous exaggerations. The policy would in no
way undermine the lives of Haringey's heterosexual majority. Steve King, whilst deputy leader of the council, echoed
this view in defence of positive images:

> 'Nobody can be taught to be lesbian or gay . . . [we want]
> to work towards an understanding that lesbians and gay
> men exist and lead fulfilled lives . . .' (*Haringey Indepen-
> dent*, 7 August 1986)

Although many people in Haringey would question the

presumption of a true, permanent sexuality that simply needs the opportunity to 'come out' and express itself, the practical effect of Section 28 has been to force councils to reassert this presumption every time they do anything which could otherwise be considered promotion. The legal advice given to Haringey's lesbian and gay sub-committee, when it met on 22 November 1988, was that before agreeing recommendations which might involve the council in incurring expenditure, it should ask itself whether it was thereby intending to promote homosexuality and ensure that reasons advanced by the committee for not so intending were minuted. (Such action is necessary in case a decision of the council is challenged in the courts.)

The combination of repressive legislative constraints and liberal ideology has turned positive images into a paradox. On the one hand it attempts to offer young people the freedom to express their sexuality as they desire; on the other, it claims emphatically that sexual orientation is not a matter of choice, but is preconditioned by factors which cannot be socially undone. 'No one can control their sexual orientation' (*Mirrors Round the Walls*, op.cit., para. 9.18). The paradox resolves itself by offering homosexuality solely as an option for homosexuals. 'There are forces at work in our society which seek directly to limit personal growth and the option of free choice for lesbians and gay youth' (ibid., para. 9.17). Heterosexual students, though, will also benefit from being able to appreciate their community of diverse lifestyles and experiences.

Can homosexuality be discussed in schools in isolation from questions concerning the social construction of heterosexuality? The majority of heterosexual socialists seemed to consider their own orientation and sexual practice as a matter neither of educational interest nor of political concern. In Haringey the most sympathetic of them tended to see their role as supporting their 'gay comrades', in similar fashion to the support men frequently offer women fighting sexual harassment and job discrimination, not perceiving their own gender to be of any relevance in the matter.

Within Haringey politics between 1986 and 1988, to be gay or lesbian was to have an identity which was a matter of legitimate public interest and concern, whereas heterosexuality implied an impartial nature, an orientation still private and personal with no bearing on the rest of one's identity.

How progressive or helpful is a sexual politics which places everyone in well defined categories, thereby treating as different and other that which appears neither the majority nor the norm? In the early days of the modern gay liberation movement, many radical activists argued we should be destroying, from within, the artificial categories of sexual orientation; and that since we were all potentially bisexual, the focus of our attraction could change according to time, place and interest:

> (S)exuality is not a drive that is simply oppressed and confined by society and which can therefore be liberated to achieve some natural form. It is a socially constructed category whose definition, regulation and meanings change historically.

> The push in the Anglo-Saxon world for protection from discrimination is in effect an attempt to redefine homosexuals as a legitimate minority group. Such a redefinition for all the immediate benefits it may produce, also has the effect of reinforcing the popular prejudice that homosexuals are a distinct and recognisable group, rather than the realisation of a potential open to all.[15]

Yet perhaps the early aims of left-wing gay activists were too premature for a society where sexual identities remain unequal. Rejection of the homosexual/heterosexual dichotomy would probably have little impact on the majority heterosexual lifestyle, while at the same time it would undermine the ability of lesbians and gay men to create communities of their own based on a common – however 'artificial' – characteristic. EOPs such as positive images are predicated on the importance of this latter occurence – the construction of a strong, alternative, though not oppositional, identity –

so that minority groups do not become assimilated into the majority culture, as frequently occurs, when 'mixing bowl' philosophies are applied to cultures whose material conditions and place within the dominant ideology are very unequal. Again we come back to the question of whether sexuality can be approached in the same way as other forms of oppression. Are we trying to create an equality amongst people of differing sexual 'preferences', or to achieve something else, and is that something else rendered impossible while we continue to treat lesbians and gay men as falling within a specific sexual category?

Lesbian feminism has provided a certain resolution of such dilemmas, by arguing that lesbianism is an important political identity in a movement which aims to achieve significantly more than sexual equality between straight and gay women. A radical feminist perspective, which considers heterosexuality to be both socially compulsory and institutionalised to protect and support male/patriarchal power, perceives all lesbianism as having nascent feminist content since its very existence poses a challenge to heterosexuality's monopoly on 'normality' and removes a section of the female population from consenting to unpaid work servicing male partners and the nuclear family. However for lesbian existence to realise this content in an ultimately liberating form, it must deepen and expand into conscious woman-identification.[16] Is positive images then a first step in achieving such 'woman-identification', by demonstrating that lesbianism is an acceptable way of life for young women? To what extent can it challenge or overcome the fear of being labelled 'dyke' or 'butch', accusations that have been used to police women's behaviour for a long time?

Within the confines of Haringey municipal politics, little has been heard from a lesbian feminist perspective. In part this has been a product of the alliances operating between lesbians and gay men, which has meant that the dominant political strategy has focused on the similarities experienced, rather than the differences. But such similarities may be deceptive. Many lesbians have argued that coalition work with gay men generally leads to issues taking precedence that focus on questions of rights and sexual freedom, but that ignore many of the constraints that impede women's ability to exercise such freedom.[17]

The local authority structure with its women's committees, units, and lesbian and gay equivalents, has provided lesbians with various options for alliances.[18] By 1986, coalitions with gay men appeared to have attained greater profile and impact than work with heterosexual women perhaps in part because women's committees depended on the availability of large-scale resources, which by 1986 had disappeared, to be effective in the areas they had prioritised – transport, child care provision, safety, better housing, social services etc. But perhaps also because, however controversial they appeared to be, lesbian and gay rights were more compatible with the progressive liberalism of socialist-led councils than a feminist politics would have been.

After more than two years of debate over positive images, I feel a radical feminist approach would have provided us with a more successful strategy for dealing with sexual politics in our schools and in offering a coherent challenge to the general set of values pervading them. Rights, freedom and choice alone offer everything and nothing. It is not surprising that positive images could be so easily manipulated, because the language and concepts used within the policy documents and debate have little intrinsic meaning outside a specific social and political context; nor do they adequately contribute to an understanding of what it is lesbians and gay men experience, and why. The council perceived the primary problem as ignorance and so the logical solution was education. But it seems highly likely that even with a better education system prejudice and discrimination would continue and no reasons for this have been forthcoming. What guidelines will positive images provide for teachers trying to educate young people about the causes of lesbian and gay oppression?

Losses and Gains

Finishing this chapter in the early hours of 1989, with the attention of public and media turned to reminiscences of last year's events, I want to finally sum up what I consider the Left and lesbian and gay communities gained and lost in the struggle for positive images.

For me there were three major omissions. First, we allowed 'sin' and 'human nature' to divert us from the debate we should have had on the ideological functions of the education system. Positive images began to challenge notions of neutrality, by demonstrating how schools currently favour and promote certain interests, for example heterosexual families as the normative ideal. But we needed to take this further, in order to understand how best to develop a counter-hegemonic practice that would lead to a disidentification with status quo ideology, and – equally important – how to respond to the opposition such activity would generate.

Second, although positive images focused on the right (of a section of our community) to make choices, the 25 per cent of Haringey residents at the centre of the policy were asked neither for their opinions nor to join in the struggle. Instead of being given the opportunity to function as subjects, they became the objects in a battle to determine their future.

> 'Various ways were used to project adults' own needs and desires on to children . . . Ageism has been an important factor in the whole issue. The attitude "they're our children, what are you doing with our children? And if I want to teach my children that the world is flat, who is anyone to contradict me!"' (Outreach Worker, Black Lesbian and Gay Centre)

Third, the emphasis placed on sexual orientation as a discrete issue, meant the values underlying positive images became marginalised. In the concluding paragraphs of *Mirrors Round The Walls* an attempt is made to draw these two elements together.

> We believe it is part of the task of the Education Service, in partnership with parents, to encourage young people to develop the confidence to manage their relationships with integrity, to establish friendships and other relationships

which have equality and respect as their basis, and which are not exploitative. (op.cit., para. 11.8)

These are the values we need to be promoting in schools,[19] potentially much more challenging than teaching tolerance of gay relationships, which can themselves involve eroticising power and the enactment of gender stereotypes. What we need are positive images of relationships – both sexual and platonic – thereby challenging at the same time the social construction of masculine and feminine socio-sexual identities. Such an approach would, I think, have been harder to oppose legitimately; have provided a firmer base for a pro-gay policy, and would have been more likely to win the support of genuinely concerned conventional communities.

Yet, in spite of these omissions, the struggle for positive images had many positive qualities. Numerous examples of good practice can be found in Haringey schools, and also elsewhere, as committed teaching staff incorporate positive images and suggestions for curricula development into their work.

Saturation media coverage, however hostile in intent, has helped homosexuality to lose some of its invisibility and stigma. A major part of heterosexuality's hegemony has been in pretending lesbians and gay men do not exist, except occasionally as pathological specimens. The media's obsession with Haringey's educational policy dented that hegemony. Lesbians and gay men were there – in the newspapers, as stark facts – to be read and digested over breakfast, lunch or tea. We may have been portrayed as extreme or politically esoteric, but we were treated as too much of a 'menace' to remain the sorrowful, pathetic creatures of a twilight world.

For the many lesbians and gay men, particularly students and youths, the policy and campaign were additional evidence that their feelings were not unique, but experienced by a large and vocal section of the community. Even if they could not come to Haringey and be part of events, they could gain strength from knowing activists (at all levels) were mobilising on their behalf.

During an era when the politics of Thatcherism was gaining increasing legitimacy, and when right-wing values became so entrenched that they were no longer considered new or different, initiatives like Haringey's are an important example that even in a period of reaction we can still attempt to realise our ideals.

'So that young child and the thousands upon thousands like that child know there is hope for a better world, hope for a better tomorrow. Without hope, not only gays, but those Blacks and the Asians, disabled and seniors – the us's – without hope the us's give up. I know you cannot live on hope alone, but without it life is not worth living. And you and you and you, have got to give them hope.'[20]

I would like to thank the friends, relatives and comrades who discussed with me the issues raised in this chapter, and in particular Kitty Cooper, for giving up part of her winter vacation to comment on this chapter.

Notes

1. On disturbances of Broadwater Farm, 6-7 October 1985, and subsequent trials, see the report of The National Council for Civil Liberties on the trials; *The Broadwater Farm Inquiry*, report of inquiry chaired by A. Gifford, QC, 1986 and *Broadwater Farm Revisited*, second report of inquiry, 1988.
2. *Mirrors Round the Walls – Respecting Diversity*, first report of the curriculum working party on lesbian and gay issues in education, Haringey Education Service, April 1988.
3. See *Changing the World; A London Charter for Gay and Lesbian Rights*, produced by GLC in conjunction with GLC Gay Working Party.
4. The PRG and Tory opponents of positive images stressed in their arguments that childhood was a time of innocence, equated with lack of sexual knowledge, which the policy's implementation would destroy. The prevalence of heterosexual relations and their impact on child development were ignored.

5. *Jenny Lives With Eric and Martin*: When PRG began their well publicised junking of the book, the Left responded with a show of support. Many feminists however were concerned about this unquestioning acceptance of the book's validity by sections of the Left and gay men. They argued that the imagery of a young girl in bed with two men was provocative, negating the existence of child sexual abuse and the inequalities of power extant between adult men and young girls. In *Mirrors Round the Walls*, the working party also rejected *Jenny Lives With Eric and Martin* for use in schools, although on different grounds to those articulated by lesbian feminists. They stated that the book was an inadequate educational resource because of its lack of awareness of language development and its unattractive and inconsistent presentation.

6. See the *Guardian* 8 April 1988. Jill Knight asked the Prime Minister to introduce legislation to protect children and the concept of the family. The PM said she wanted to see the legislation initiated by a backbencher.

7. The arts lobby organised well publicised PR events at which famous heterosexuals, as well as lesbians and gay men, pledged their opposition to the amendment.

8. See *Capital Gay* 14 April 1988. Tories distanced themselves from Cllr Murphy's motion. An alternative petition was initiated by Ron Aitken, prominent gay member of the local Conservative Association, calling on Haringey to abide by the law, but not to use Section 28 to attack lesbians and gay men.

9. The terms of reference of this working party are set out in *Mirrors Round the Walls*, (op.cit., para. 2.4 i).

10. For the legal framework see Appendix pp.76-78.

11. *Hornsey Journal* 14 April 1988. Ron Aitken is quoted as saying that Clause 28 [*sic*] wouldn't have come about if the cross-party consensus on social issues hadn't been broken by the Left of the Labour Party.

12. For example, B. Campbell in *Marxism Today*, February 1987: 'The local state has replaced the political party within civil society as the agency of regeneration.' However since autumn 1987 when left-wing Labour councils across London introduced large-scale cuts in expenditure, disillusion-

ment in the potential of local government has increased considerably and people are searching for a politically innovatory force elsewhere.

13. Haringey Council, *Equal Opportunities – The Lesbian and Gay Perspective*, 1988.
14. Haringey Council Education Service, *Equal Opportunities Policy Statement*, Section 142, November 1985.
15. Keith Birch, Dennis Altman, in *Homosexuality: Power and Politics*, ed. Gay Left Collective, Allison & Busby, 1980.
16. See Adrienne Rich, 'Compulsory Heterosexuality and Lesbian Existence', *Signs* 5 (4), 1980.
17. See MacKinnon, *Feminism, Marxism, Method and the State: An Agenda for Theory*; and Ferguson, Zita and Addelson, 'On Compulsory Heterosexuality and Lesbian Existence: Defining the Issues'; in *Feminist Theory*, eds Keohane, Rosaldo and Gelpi, Harvester Press, Sussex; 1982.
18. Many lesbians have also formed their primary alliances/ coalitions around issues of race, disability, age and class. Several Labour councils have race equality committees and a few have strategic committees dealing with youth or disability policy development.
19. Such values need to be extended even further to incorporate all relationships which currently involve inequalities of power, particularly those already existing within the education system. Haringey's education policy is based on the notion of partnership, yet the hierarchical structure with young people and manual education workers at the bottom remains.
20. Harvey Milk – 'out', gay, supervisor on San Francisco City Council, who was killed by fellow supervisor Dan White; quoted in the film *The Life and Times of Harvey Milk*, directed by Robert Epstein and Richard Schmiechen, USA, 1984.

Appendix

Outline of the developing legal framework that faces authorities attempting to implement a policy of positive images or similar at the time of writing (December 1988).

Education Act 1944

S.7 places a duty on the LEA (Local Education Authority) to secure sufficient education to meet the needs of the population of their area.

S.68: the Secretary of State for Education may intervene if satisfied the LEA or school governors are acting unreasonably.

Education (No. 2) Act 1986

S.17(1): LEAs have a duty to determine and keep under review their policy regarding secular curriculum of schools maintained by them.

S.18(2): Responsibility on governing bodies for determining whether sex education should form part of the secular curriculum.

S.46: LEAs, governing bodies and headteachers are responsible for ensuring that where sex education is given, pupils are encouraged to have due regard to moral considerations and the value of family life.

Local Government Act 1988

S.28: A local authority shall not intentionally promote homosexuality, nor within maintained schools, the acceptability of homosexuality as a pretended family relationship.

Circular 11/87 Sex Education at Schools

Circulars are interpretations by government of their statutes or an explanation of how they should be implemented; they do not themselves have statutory force.

Para.2: Some parents may not feel able to discuss sexual matters freely with their children. Because of this, the school has a clear role to ensure pupils are adequately prepared for adult life.

Para.19: Pupils should be helped to appreciate the benefits of stable married and family life.

Para.21: Schools cannot generally avoid controversial sexual matters and should offer balanced factual information, acknowledging major ethical issues involved.

Para.22: There is no place in any school for teaching which advocates homosexuality or presents it as the norm.

Circular 12/88
Section 28, Local Government Act 1988, does not affect the activities of school governors or of teachers; nor does it prevent the objective discussion of homosexuality, nor the counselling of pupils about their sexuality.

See also *European Convention on Human Rights* and relevant case law, particularly that laying down principles of administrative law.

The legal framework, and in particular the DES Circulars, show a large number of inconsistencies in how homosexuality is to be treated, thus leaving responsibility with the courts to set down the parameters of the law in this area, and to provide 'authoritative' definitions of the relevant terms.

4 Section 28 and Education

Sue Sanders and Gill Spraggs

During the last few years the presentation of lesbian and gay issues has become inextricably entwined in the public mind with party politics, a tendency which came to a head in the campaign surrounding the notorious Clause 28 of the Local Government Bill 1988. During the same time, the field of education, and especially school-based education, has become established as a key site of conflict and confusion. How has this come about?

In the late 1970s and early 1980s the impact of feminist critiques of patriarchy, coupled with the rise of Black consciousness, did much to challenge and enrich socialism, especially in local government. As a result, councils began to look at both their own employment practices and at the services they provided to see just how these affected minority and disadvantaged groups within their area. Among other matters there was a recognition that local government employees appointed to serve the local population failed to reflect the composition of that population in terms of gender or race, while services such as housing, arts and leisure, and social services often did not recognise the needs of particular groups. To rectify this, many authorities, to very varying degrees, began to implement forms of equal opportunity and positive discrimination policies.

This movement naturally influenced the education service, where many feminists were already agitating and attempting at grass-roots level to put into practice projects and programmes designed to challenge the white male middle-class dominance of the curriculum. It seems to us no accident that much of this work was carried out by lesbians, who had both the personal experience of marginalisation and the developing political analysis of the realities of discrimination in its many forms. However, initially, lesbian and gay issues were not, in general, tackled directly.

There were good reasons for this. National legislation on race relations and sex discrimination, passed in response to widespread agitation and growing public awareness of the importance of these issues, offered a background of legitimation to local initiatives. In contrast, there was no such widespread recognition of the discrimination and disadvantage experienced by lesbians and gay men. The one significant piece of legislation of recent years, the 1967 Sexual Offences Act, studiedly declined to reverse Victorian legislation prohibiting male homosexual acts, merely decriminalising certain limited forms of sexual behaviour between men (that is, broadly speaking, sex in private between two men over the age of 21). In the context of the prejudice against homosexuals which was widely voiced even by the Bill's supporters, there was absolutely no question of steps to outlaw discrimination, so that although the Act undeniably contributed to a more liberated atmosphere, it endorsed rather than challenged public hostility towards gay people.[1]

An important aspect here is the question of visibility. Until very recently, lesbians and gays have been perceived as constituting an imperceptibly tiny minority in our society. Virtually all lesbians and gays can, and commonly do, 'pass' for at least part of the time – at work, for instance – as heterosexuals, whereas women and Blacks are readily identifiable. This has affected both our ability to organise politically – in the sense that, very often, we have literally been unable to identify each other – and the public recognition of our existence and experience. (There are some analogies here with the position of people with disabilities, whose concealment, however, springs rather from their restricted access to the public environment. They, too, have had to fight longer than either women or Blacks for a recognition of their needs and rights.)

The women's movement, which initiated political groupings around issues such as abortion, rape and violence and the setting up of women's centres had, since the early 1970s, provided the political and geographical space for women to meet, and to discover that many who were agitating most strongly for women's rights were lesbians. The discrimination and prejudice in society were reflected in the women's movement, and much work had to be done to raise consciousness around race, class, lesbianism and disability. However, with members of all the oppressed groups active in the movement, these issues did receive varying degrees of attention. It must, of course, be recognised that the battle is still not won on any of them.

Analyses developed within the movement were then taken outside and used as the basis for work in social institutions of wider society. Trade unions, local political parties and, to a certain extent, the national Labour Party all recognised the membership and voting potential of the newly organising groupings, particularly of women and ethnic minorities, and tentatively began to listen to their demands. It is worth noticing that at a local level Conservative politicians in search of votes were often prepared to go along with the rhetoric and in some cases the practice of equal opportunities and minority rights. At national level the Conservative Party was at best ambiguous: lip service was paid to 'equal opportunities' at the same time as policies on immigration betrayed the most pernicious racism and the steady dismantling of the welfare state placed particularly heavy burdens upon many women.

It was in the context of the newly fashionable interest in the rights of marginalised groups that attempts began to be made, notably by the now defunct Greater London Council (GLC), to woo the pink vote. Politicians who had cut their teeth on feminism and race began to pay attention to the demands of feminist lesbians and of lesbians and gay men from the mixed gay movement which had grown up since the law reform of the late 1960s, and which had received much of its momentum from the parallel movement which had developed in America following the Stonewall riots. Some important preliminary work was carried out. In the field of education we might notice, for instance, the research conducted by the London Gay Teenage Group, which gave an invaluable picture of the lives and experiences of young lesbians and gays,[2] or the pioneering curriculum development work of the Inner London Education Authority (ILEA) 'Relationships and Sexuality' project.

However, it soon became very clear that many local councillors were extremely superficial in their analysis of sexuality politics and insufficiently prepared for the political costs of pursuing the pink vote. When their opponents showed themselves fully inclined to make adroit use of anti-gay prejudice as a means of scoring party points, our self-appointed cavalry too often retreated in disarray, pursued by the triumphant catcalls of the Tory press. Too often, controversial policies were presented without sufficient discussion, either with the lesbian and gay communities or with the public at large, and then, when these policies came under attack, their proponents fell suddenly silent. This was particularly the case with initiatives in education; in more than one authority, ill-thought-out promises of action on heterosexism in schools were then left unexplained and undefended in the face of accusations that councillors were seeking to encourage children to grow up gay.

Similarly, work undertaken in less harried years was frozen or at least put under restrictions when the climate began to change. A good example of this was the ILEA 'Relationships and Sexuality' project, whose excellent pair of videos, 'A Different Story', finished in 1986 and intended for use with young people, were promptly put on ice by nervous officialdom.[3] Ultimately, the real brunt of this kind of behaviour was borne by lesbians and gays, whose position in the community began in many ways to be publicly undermined, at first by growing prejudice, eagerly encouraged by Tory politicians and the right-wing press, and latterly by a significant loss of civil liberties, in the shape of Section 28 of the Local Government Act 1988. This legislation makes it an offence for local authorities to 'promote sexuality' and is intended to inhibit them from responding appropriately to the needs and concerns of the lesbian and gay communities.

The debate on Clause (now Section) 28 and its forerunner, the Earl of Halsbury's Private Member's Bill of 1986, occupies many columns of Hansard. But the keynote message from the supporters of the legislation, so far as lesbians are concerned, was delivered right at the start by the Earl of Halsbury in December 1986. Moving the second reading of his Bill, entitled 'An Act to restrain local authorities from promoting homosexuality', he said:

> I did not think . . . that lesbians were a problem. They do not molest little girls. They do not indulge in disgusting and unnatural practices like buggery. They are not wildly promiscuous and do not spread venereal disease. It is part of the softening up propaganda that lesbians and gays are nearly always referred to in that order. The relatively harmless lesbian leads on the vicious gay. That was what I thought . . . and what I still in part continue to think, but I have been warned that the loony Left is hardening up the lesbian camp and that they are becoming increasingly aggressive.[4]

Presumably it was basic male chauvinism which prevented the noble Earl from suspecting that the opposite was true: the policies of the so-called 'loony Left', so far from politicising lesbians had, instead, begun to develop following many years' hard work and agitation by lesbian activists. Yet his observation does reveal a crucial point about the attitudes towards lesbians current among today's authoritarian Right: what they find unforgivable is that we are becoming visibly involved in the political process, and are demanding a larger share of social resources. This, of course, is classic patriarchal misogyny in operation. Halsbury's use of the words 'hardening' and 'aggressive' betray a horror and fear of women who refuse to fit into traditionally accepted patterns, who are outspoken and visibly different, and who make demands. At the same time, he clearly cannot believe that women might initiate their own actions: without the 'loony Left' to stir us up, he appears to think we would not be, in his terms, a 'problem'.

The insecurity becomes even more evident as Halsbury continues:

> One of the characteristics of our time is that we have for several decades past been emancipating minorities who claimed that they were disadvantaged. Are they grateful? Not a bit. We emancipated races and got inverted racism. We emancipate homosexuals and they condemn hetero-sexism as chauvinist sexism, male oppression and so on. They will push us off the pavement if we give them a chance.[5]

Underlying this speech is an awareness that demands are being made which, if met, will change society as we know it and lead to the erosion of the existing bases of power. The projection here is unmistakable; it is after all, the members of the ruling class who hitherto have successfully colluded to keep Blacks, lesbians and gays (among so many others) 'off the pavement'. Hence the fear that, given half a chance, we would do the same to them. It is particularly noteworthy that, not being an elected representative, and therefore answerable to nothing and no one but his own interests, Halsbury can afford to make explicit his anxieties about Black people, and to link them with his fear of lesbians and gays. Throughout this whole debate, racism has rumbled on, mainly below the surface, occasionally coming into the open, revealing a crucial clue to the real attitudes and hidden agenda of our opponents.

Already noticeable at this stage in the debate, and something which remained fairly constant in the speeches of the 'moral Right', is the deliberate invocation of hostile stereotypes of gay people, particularly gay men, which is almost invariably coupled with the disingenuous denial of any intent to stir up anti-gay hostility. Repeated encounter with this kind of whingeing hypocrisy is one of the most sickening aspects of studying the parliamentary record.

The purpose of the Halsbury Bill was outlined for the assembled peers by Lord Campbell of Alloway, who had drafted it. At this point, he was anxious to insist that the Bill would in no way prevent local authorities from funding special provisions for lesbians and gays, nor 'prohibit', as he puts it, 'the appointment of a homosexual teacher'. The aim was to prevent 'the promotion of lesbian and gay rights . . . as it is implemented in our schools', and 'the provision of explicit books of certain types . . . which', he says, 'are made available to these children'. As example, he cites the picture book *Jenny Lives With Eric and Martin*, which he confidently assumes that his audience will have read about in the press.[6] This was another feature of the whole debate: stories taken up by the right-wing press, and particularly by the less responsible tabloids, were repeated uncritically in parliament and used as evidence for the need for legislation. This point was well taken by Ken Livingstone, one of Clause 28's more forceful opponents in the Labour Party, when he commented: 'Some people have the misfortune to believe what they read in the *Daily Express*, the *Daily Mail* and The *Sun*.'[7] We would add, coming fresh from reading the parliamentary record, that we found it terrifyingly noticeable that anything which had been published in a newspaper was given total credence and weight by both peers and MPs. Even when an item of so-called news had been clearly shown to be a fabrication, the story continued to be repeated as 'evidence' by supporters of the legislation.[8] For its part, the Tory press was keen to lend itself to the Bill's support. Thus, on the morning of the day on which the Halsbury Bill was first debated, *The Times* carried a leader welcoming the proposed legislation and giving a very biased and misleading account of the situation in Haringey, where the local authority's embryo policies on lesbian and gay rights in education were coming under heavy attack.[9]

'The plain and simple intendment of the Bill', according to Lord Campbell, was 'to curb an abuse of rates': and this introduces another theme which was heard continually on the lips of the supporters of this legislation. To hear all the tender concern expressed on behalf of the ratepayer, one would think that lesbians and gay men were classes exempt from local taxation and that the sums being spent on projects related to our concerns had gone soaring through the roof.

The truth was carefully left unspoken: that even in the case of those local authorities who had begun to explore ways of fulfilling their responsibilities towards the many lesbians and gays living in their areas, the amounts of money involved were puny compared to the sums being spent on other projects and other groups. This distortion yet again reflects persistent agitation in the right-wing press.

More is involved here than resentment at a modest shifting of resources in the direction of an unpopular minority. The Halsbury Bill and its successor, Clause 28, cannot be understood in isolation from the repeated efforts of an entrenched Conservative administration to erode the powers and scope of local government. The Local Government Act 1988, of which Clause 28 is just one section, slots in alongside the poll tax legislation, the Housing Act and the so-called Great Education Reform Act as just one of numerous measures designed with this end in view. These efforts began, it would seem, as a strategy for destroying the power base of the Labour opposition, as in the case of the abolition of the GLC. More recently, and particularly since the 1987 election, the imposition of drastic restrictions on the powers and resources available to local government has found its context in increasing and very determined attempts on the part of the present administration to stamp out any kind of independent voice or action on the part of the major institutions of our society, from the broadcasting media to the Church of England.

The Halsbury Bill, and later Clause 28, were persistently presented as measures designed not to curtail the freedom of lesbians and gay men, but to curb, as their proponents repeatedly argued, 'abuses' in local government. This concern for our liberties as individuals, of course, was no bar to the lavish use of all kinds of hostile propaganda about lesbian and gay lifestyles, amounting at times almost to incitement to violence; as when Elaine Kellett-Bowman, MP for Lancaster, described the arson attack on the offices of the newspaper *Capital Gay* in December 1987 as an act which showed 'intolerance of evil'.[10] But that is in the future: let us return, briefly, to the Halsbury Bill which, interestingly enough, in view of all the battles which took place over Clause 28, passed through the Lords successfully and with little opposition. What opposition there was came, it is worth noting, mainly from representatives of the Conservative Government, Lord Skelmersdale and Baroness Hooper. The former, in a speech which returned to haunt the Conservatives during the debate on Clause 28, pointed out that while the government supported the aims of the Bill, in seeking to put an end to 'irresponsible and inappropriate teaching in this field . . . the distinction between [this] and . . . proper teaching about homosexuality cannot be drawn sufficiently clearly in legislation to avoid harmful misinterpretation. That is a risk we cannot take'.[11]

From the Labour front bench, Baroness David equivocated skilfully: she was speaking 'from a personal point of view'; on the other hand she believed that she was speaking for 'a great many people on our Front Bench' in saying that 'we are sympathetic with the aims of the Bill of the noble Earl'; however, 'perhaps this is a much more complicated matter than the Bill suggests'. She did, in fact, make some very damaging criticisms, but her tone made it quite clear that this particular issue was not one on which Labour were prepared to fight.[12] At the time the debate took place, the Labour leadership had recently embarked on a policy of publicly distancing itself from the so-called 'loony' left-wing councils, whose chief claim to insanity was their attempts to implement national conference policy on issues such as race and gay rights. These councils had recently been coming under particularly heavy attack from the Tory press; a particularly nasty feature was the singling out for specially vindictive treatment of councils with Black leaders, notably Lambeth and Haringey, and the Labour leadership's unwillingness to recognise and respond to the not very covert racism of much of the reporting.[13]

The anxieties which the issue of lesbian and gay rights was causing the Labour leaders was made very plain a few weeks later, with the leaking to the Tory press of the so-called 'Hewitt letter', written by the Labour leader's press secretary to a right-wing Labour MP, which expressed concern, in the wake of the Greenwich by-election which was won by the SDP, that the 'gays and lesbians issue' was losing Labour votes among the pensioners.[14] Not the least disturbing aspect of this incident was the fact that the author of the letter, Patricia Hewitt, had previously gained great credit on the Left as General Secretary of the National Council for Civil Liberties (NCCL), an organisation which, amongst other vital issues, has always been most assiduous in campaigning for lesbian and gay rights.

As originally worded, the Halsbury Bill would have prohibited local authorities from giving 'financial or other assistance to any person for the purpose of publishing or promoting homosexuality as an acceptable family relationship; or for the purpose of teaching such acceptability in any maintained school'. During its passage through the Lords it underwent a number of substantial changes in wording, taking on the shape in which it was subsequently, at the end of 1987, to be introduced into the Local Government Bill as Clause 14 (later 28). Noteworthy is the insertion of the word 'pretended', so that (with scant regard for sense or grammar) their Lordships now proposed to prohibit 'the teaching . . . of the acceptability of homosexuality as a pretended family relationship'. More crucial to the scope of the Bill was the inclusion of a new subclause forbidding local authorities to 'promote homosexuality', so that from being a piece of legislation aimed at affecting lesson content and the use of certain publications in state schools, and at stopping local authority grants to gay publishers, it now became a much more wholesale prohibition, potentially affecting the whole range of activities funded by local authorities.[15]

The Halsbury Bill was promoted in the Commons by Dame Jill Knight, Conservative MP for Birmingham, Edgbaston, and reached the committee stage on 8 May 1987. Dame Jill, one of the legislation's most vociferous and persistent supporters, warrants more than a passing mention. Her contributions to the debate have a flavour all their own. Every made-up story in the tabloid press seemed to have a believer in Dame Jill, and to throw her into frenzies of accusation. She introduced the Halsbury Bill in fine form:

'This Bill came into being for a very good reason . . . It is before the Committee because there is evidence in shocking abundance that children in our schools, some as young as five years, are frequently being encouraged into homosexuality and lesbianism.' By way of a bizarre excursion through the sexual abuse of drummer boys in the Indian army under the Raj, she wound up triumphantly with a peroration on AIDS:

> 'Millions outside Parliament object to little children being perverted, diverted or converted from normal family life to a lifestyle which is desperately dangerous for society and extremely dangerous for them . . . Very few hon. Members fail to appreciate the seriousness of the danger that AIDS presents to the whole of our society, yet some of that which is being taught to children in our schools would undoubtedly lead to a great spread of AIDS'.[16]

'Normal family life' was a frequent rallying cry among the supporters of the Halsbury Bill and its successor, Clause 28. More recently, addressing the General Assembly of the Church of Scotland in May 1988, a few days before Clause (now Section) 28 became effective in law, Margaret Thatcher herself invoked 'the family' as a prominent concept in a major speech evidently intended to cast a spurious cloak of moral justification around Conservative policies in general.[17] However, neither she nor Dame Jill have ever seen fit to define this 'normal family', or to defend its supposed virtues in other than the vaguest terms. Statistically, of course, the 'traditional' nuclear family, with two married parents, of whom the wife stays at home to look after their two children, is disappearing very fast. The latest figures published by the government show that the proportion of women staying at home had dropped to 37 per cent by 1985; while 14 per cent of all families with dependent children at that time were one-parent families, most of them headed by women. Moreover, there has for many years been a steady growth in the divorce rate and an increase in the popularity of cohabitation as opposed to marriage. There are many families with two parents where there has been a change of partners, with or without remarriage, and where children are being brought up by an adult who is not a biological parent.[18]

The truth is that so far as Conservative ideologists are concerned, the word 'family' means whatever serves their purposes at any given point, so that the image of the self-contained nuclear family, living in its semi-detached house, minding its own business and troubling no one slides conveniently in and out of the idea of the supportive extended family of a mythical Victorian past. What these concepts have in common is the family as a resourceful, independent unit. Clearly such families are going to be needed, for all the support services the welfare state had begun to offer – nursery provision, health care, care for the elderly, for people with disabilities and with special needs, support for the unemployed and poor – are gradually and systematically being dismantled. State education, too, has suffered a massive haemorrhage of resources in recent years, and is about to undergo a wholesale reorganisation which can only result in a huge downgrading in service for the majority of users. Soon the only available support system for the elderly, the ill, the very young, the disadvantaged, will be women, thinly disguised as 'families'. It is significant that Tory efforts to 'strengthen the family', by dumping on women an ever-increasing burden of responsibility, are plainly not striking a chord with women voters, who are turning away from the party in increasing numbers.[19]

Right-wing ideologues respond with horror to radical feminist and gay perspectives on the family, perhaps partly because they suspect that these are based on an accurate analysis. It is interesting to note that after quoting the 1971 Gay Liberation Front manifesto on the necessity for putting an end to the family, Dame Jill Knight, proposing the Halsbury Bill in the Commons, went on to say: 'We could argue for some time about how true it is that the abolition of the family would help women, but it is debatable whether it would be anything other than a disaster for the country.'[20] Similarly, the Earl of Halsbury, defending the much-derided phrase 'pretended family relationships', insisted on retaining the word 'family' in his Bill 'because', he claimed, 'it is part of homosexual propaganda that the family is a form of male chauvinism, which is not something I believe should be said.'[21] It is intriguing to see that he does not attempt to refute this claim; he simply feels it should not be expressed!

Feminists and feminist lesbians frighten people like Dame Jill and the noble Earl because we expose as a lie the myth that women and children are safer and better cared for inside the patriarchal family. The reality, of course, is that the family can be a very dangerous place: the rise in reported child abuse and the high level of domestic violence and rape are eloquent witness to this. The families of lesbians with children also challenge the idea that a woman needs a man 'to look after' her. It is interesting to note that among the various gay and lesbian books invoked in parliament to justify the need for the Clause, derision was heaped on a light-hearted American novel, *Faultline*, by Sheila Ortiz Taylor. Significantly, this book was the only fictional work about lesbians to be mentioned during the entire debate in both houses. Michael Howard, Junior Minister for the Environment, quoted the description of it in *Positive Images*, the ILEA resources guide to materials about lesbians and gays, as the 'story of a lesbian mother who lives with her lover and their children, a black gay male child minder and three hundred rabbits'. As he does not specify his objections to the book (surely not the rabbits?), the clear implication is that he is anxious about the image of lesbians and gays living with children.[22]

Despite Dame Jill Knight's eloquence, the Halsbury Bill was lost at committee stage in the Commons. It fell more or less by accident, when a couple of back-bench Labour members, who had turned up to wait for some proceedings tabled for a later point, were plainly startled and appalled by what they found going on, and forced a division. The Bill's supporters could not muster sufficient votes, on a Friday lunchtime, for the Bill to pass to its next stage. The following week the election was called; but Jill Knight still had a shot to play. In Question Time on 14 May she called the attention of the Prime Minister to the loss of the Halsbury Bill and demanded a promise that the next parliament would see government legislation to 'protect both children and the concept of the family'. Mrs Thatcher's reply is worthy of note: she commended Dame Jill for her promotion of the Bill, regretted its loss, assured her of the government's support for its objectives and most significantly, expressed the hope that she would bring it back into parliament following the election.[23] The effusive support for the Halsbury Bill which Mrs Thatcher expressed in this exchange contrasts strikingly with the official government view of previous months. What, we ask, has changed? Why is she now prepared to accept the 'risk' which only a few weeks earlier was so clearly recognised, the threat to a balanced sex education in schools? The answer can be summed up in a word: the election.

During the next few weeks the 'pavement paranoia' invoked by Halsbury was openly exploited for party political ends, with powerful help from the Tory press. At a crucial point during the election campaign, the Home Secretary, Douglas Hurd, suddenly unveiled proposals to tighten immigration controls. The measures planned (in this party of the family) included making the right of women and children to join lawfully settled husbands dependent on showing that 'proper maintenance and accommodation arrangements' had been made.[24]

Meanwhile the Labour Party continued to reveal its own problems with these issues, notably when Black candidate Sharon Atkin was sacked after she described the party as racist for its continued refusal to accept Black sections. This episode also shows the Labour leadership's lack of commitment to gay rights, which Sharon Atkin, in line with conference policy, had always supported. The candidate who replaced her, Mohammed Aslam, who was imposed on the local constituency party by the Party's National Executive, was well known for his active opposition, as a county councillor, to any recognition of the rights of gays and lesbians.[25] Incidentally, he lost what had previously been regarded as a winnable seat – an interesting sidelight on the widely-touted notion that the election was lost for Labour by the so-called 'loony Left'.

The Conservative Party was plumbing new depths in its election poster campaign. One poster in particular deliberately set out to stir up fear and hostility towards lesbians and gays, while making a calculated use of disinformation as a means of discrediting Labour. Under the heading, 'IS THIS LABOUR'S IDEA OF A COMPREHENSIVE EDUCATION?' three books in red covers were pictured side by side: *Police: Out of School, Young Gay & Proud,* and *The Playbook for Kids about Sex.* 'TAKE THE POLITICS OUT OF EDUCATION. VOTE CONSERVATIVE.', the poster shrilled. Both the latter books featured in the debate about Clause 28. A consistent propaganda ploy by the Conservatives has been to imply that education has normally constituted an area outside politics, deliberately ignoring the fact that both the covert and overt curricula in schools consistently promote images of white middle-class heterosexual family life which are of evident service to consumer capitalism and the patriarchy.

Another anti-Labour advertisement, put out by a shadowy body calling itself 'Committee for a Free Britain', featured a prominent member of the so-called 'Parents Rights Group', set up in Haringey to oppose the council's embryonic policies on lesbian and gay issues in education. The advertisement, picturing Betty Sheridan, has been cited in Chapter 3. This nasty little piece of misrepresentation – apart from anything else, Haringey's policies on sex education were still at the consultative stage and had never been implemented – was condemned by the Advertising Standards Authority, along with a number of others put out by the mysterious 'Committee', as a 'blatant violation' of the existing advertiser's code.[26] The insinuation that there is something mutually exclusive about a sound academic education and constructive and honest teaching about lesbian and gay lifestyles is a familiar smear, popular with the gutter press. It is always convenient for right-wingers to ignore the enormous impact on pupils' school performances of environmental and emotional factors, whether in the case of isolated and suicidal gay or lesbian teenagers, or of children of homeless families brought up in bed and breakfast hotels.

Clearly the Labour Party was in a difficult position. It is notoriously hard to defend oneself against accusations which have only a marginal relation to reality. Outright lies can be refuted; the truth can be positively affirmed. At a national level, Labour's formal policies on lesbian and gay issues were less than two years old at the time of the election, and there was no specific mention in those policies of school-based education. At a local level, initiatives in education were sparse, and either embryonic, as in Haringey, or very much at the level of experimental special projects, such as the ILEA work on 'Relationships and Sexuality'. Every stage in the progress of those initiatives had been greeted with a storm of jeers, sneers and outright lies from the Conservative press, and had been adroitly exploited for maximum propaganda effect by Conservative politicians. Now, with an election imminent, Labour's response to attacks on its putative 'education policy' was to keep its head well below the parapet and hope the issue would go away. It was the worst possible strategy, both for maximising the party's election prospects and for defending the civil rights of lesbians and gays against erosion. Once again, as in the case of the Hewitt letter, Labour had shown that lesbian and gay rights were an area where it felt itself to be electorally vulnerable.

The Tories did not miss the point. Nor were they prepared to drop the matter when the election was over. The opportunity to continue to score political points was evidently too tempting. During her triumphant address to the Conservative Party Conference in October 1987, Margaret Thatcher made a special point of attacking 'hard-left education authorities and extremist teachers' on the grounds that 'Children who need to be taught to respect traditional moral values are being taught that they have an inalienable right to be gay'.[27] It was a chilling and sinister moment. For it logically follows from her remark that in the eyes of the woman who has led this country for nearly ten years, those of us who identify as lesbian or gay have no inalienable right to *be*.

In the light of the events just recounted, the next development should not really have come as much of a surprise. On

8 December 1987 a new clause was proposed for insertion in the Local Government Bill, then going through its committee stage in the Commons. This clause, at first numbered 14, later 27, briefly 28, 29, and finally 28 once again, was entitled 'Prohibition on promoting homosexuality by teaching or by publishing material'. The proposer was David Wilshire, Conservative MP for Spelthorne, but the text of the clause as initially put forward was, word for word, that of the Halsbury Bill. However, this time round there was one considerable difference: government support, which the Halsbury Bill had conspicuously lacked, was now freely forthcoming, subject only to a few amendments, the most significant of which was a brief additional subsection aimed at exempting AIDS prevention work from the scope of the legislation. This 'U-turn' on the part of an administration which has always vaunted its intransigence, was noted and taken up by opponents of the new clause on its next return to the Commons, on 15 December. Their questions and challenges were in every case evaded, nor was any reason ever given as to why legislation which government representatives had criticised just a year before as unnecessary and undesirable should now receive government endorsement. The answer, clearly, lies in the adoption by the Tory Party leadership during and after the election of a posture of ostentatious condemnation towards the advocates of gay and lesbian rights; and that was less a matter of policy than of political opportunism.

More disturbing and certainly more astonishing to many lesbian and gay activists than the attitude of the party in power was the response to the proposed legislation of the Labour Party leadership. Clause 28 seems to have taken the Labour front bench unawares; at all events, it found them unprepared. To be fair, it is probably true to say that many lesbians and gay men were equally taken by surprise. One reason for this was the relative lack of publicity which had been received by the Halsbury Bill; even now, there are undoubtedly many who have marched and campaigned against Clause 28 who are still unaware of any attempts to promote such legislation prior to December 1987. However, Clause 28 certainly exposed a serious gap in Labour Party understanding of lesbian and gay issues, as well as a disturbing lack of commitment on the part of some of its leading spokesmen to the principle, first established as policy at the 1985 Party Conference, of combating discrimination towards lesbians and gay men. The resolution which established this policy also called for Labour local authorities to take action to prevent this discrimination, both by supporting lesbian and gay organisations, including youth groups, and by reviewing their own practices;[28] the kind of action, in other words, which had been so widely misrepresented in the popular press, and which was now to be repeatedly cited by government representatives and Tory backbenchers as evidencing the necessity for the proposed legislation.

The official Labour response to the clause on its first appearance was voiced by John Cunningham, Labour environment spokesman, who took the line that a ban on the promotion of homosexuality by local authorities was entirely reasonable and to be supported. However, he expressed reservations about the second part of the clause, which banned authorities more specifically from promoting 'the teaching . . . of the acceptability of homosexuality', fearing that this would hinder teachers and school counsellors in their pastoral function, and he indicated that Labour would be likely, if the government failed to address this issue, to move an amendment to the clause at report stage. The Liberal Party also, at this point, in the person of Simon Hughes, MP for Southwark and Bermondsey, accepted the main principle of the clause, though expressing rather more cogently and forcefully a concern over the possible implications of the second subclause for teachers and school pupils.[29]

From a strictly legalistic viewpoint, perhaps, the position adopted by the opposition spokesmen may be intelligible, though scarcely edifying. The powers and duties of local authorities are laid down in law. The promotion of homosexuality has never been one of the functions of a local authority; therefore, were any authority to promote homosexuality, it would be exceeding its powers. Following this line of argument through, a legal ban on promoting homosexuality does not change anything: it merely ratifies the status quo. However, in the world of practical politics, to argue thus is at best naive; at worst, thoroughly dishonest. It glosses over the widespread existence of prejudice, and the signal which such legislation inevitably gives to those who bear ill will towards lesbians and gays; and it disregards the vagueness of the term 'promote', which might arguably be stretched to cover activities previously well within the scope of a local authority's powers.

In fact, it is clear from subsequent statements by Cunningham's office and colleagues that while the position adopted by the Labour leadership was to some extent naive, in the sense that the possible implications of the clause had certainly not been fully grasped,[30] it was also disingenuous, in that the debate around the clause was initially seized as an opportunity to distance the Labour Party from what was perceived as a vote-losing association with pro-gay policies. This was implicit in the way that Cunningham, during the debate at committee stage, made only a very half-hearted effort to defend Labour-run authorities such as ILEA and Haringey from the viciously misleading charges brought against them by David Wilshire and by Michael Howard, Minister for Local Government. It became explicit two days later, when Jeff Rooker, another Labour front bench spokesman, responding now to a gathering storm of protest from lesbian, gay and left-wing party activists, was quoted in the *Independent* as saying, 'If anyone comes to me quoting Labour conference resolutions I shall point out to them that between those resolutions and now Labour has lost a general election.'[31]

The only Labour member prepared, at committee stage, to condemn the clause out of hand, was Bernie Grant, MP for Tottenham, who as one of only four Black MPs, and as former leader of Haringey Council, was no doubt better versed than Cunningham in both minority politics and the politics of sexual identity. He was also, of course, defending his own political record. He identified the clause as an attack

97

on the rights of a minority and a signal to fascists. He went on to speak of Haringey's existing policies and the reasons why they had been developed, and quoted an official document from Her Majesty's Inspectorate, *Health Education from 5 to 16*, on the need for schools to address the topic of homosexuality. His contribution was the only one which addressed itself at all adequately to the issues involved. Perhaps for this reason, it was received with evident disrespect by Tory members, and, as a final accolade, was branded 'disgraceful' by Michael Howard.[32]

The clause reached its report stage in the Commons a week later. In the intervening time, several instructive incidents occurred. On the evening of the day the committee debate took place, Dame Jill Knight was confronted on BBC radio by Neil Fletcher, leader of ILEA, who challenged her to name any school where *Jenny Lives With Eric and Martin*, by now undoubtedly the most widely-heard-of child's picture book in the country, had been made available to pupils. She replied that she did not have her files with her.[33] Similarly evasive responses on the part of the supporters of the clause have become very familiar: the 'evidence' they have cited to justify the need for such legislation has been of the vaguest, or drawn from the more inventive sections of the popular press, or else has been of a kind to which only a closed and bigoted mind could possibly find objection, such as the ILEA bibliography and video list *Positive Images*, produced by the 'Relationships and Sexuality' project, a highly responsible publication intended to introduce educators to appropriate materials for teaching about homosexuality at secondary and further education levels.

On the following Saturday an arson attack was made on the office of the newspaper *Capital Gay*; the same weekend, tear-gas bombs were thrown into a crowded gay pub in Rochester.[34] Then, on Monday 14 December, the day before the clause was due to be debated for the second time, over 800 lesbians and gay men met at the House of Commons to lobby their MPs, a mass action organised by the very recently formed Organisation for Lesbian and Gay Action (OLGA).[35] Bomb attacks, and the mass lobby – these encapsulate what we have since seen so many times and so widely repeated since the clause first reached the headlines: on the one hand, extreme violence and malice directed against lesbian and gay individuals and the institutions of our communities – a bomb found at a disco, an increase in street attacks, besides sackings and all kinds of harassment; on the other, a greater readiness on the part of very many lesbians and gays to stand up and be counted, much more effective networking and organisation, and the forging of broader alliances between often very disparate groupings of lesbians and gay men.

On the day the debate took place, Tuesday 15 December, Chris Smith, Labour member for Islington South and the only 'out' gay MP, was quoted in the *Guardian* as saying that Labour had made a tactical error by not voting against the clause when it first appeared. The Labour front bench was reported to have been still undecided the night before as to whether to seek to delete the clause.[36] Clearly the response from party activists and from constituents had shaken their complacency. In the event, they threw their weight behind amendments designed to limit the clause's possible effects, rather than seeking to have it deleted; and although John Cunningham, speaking on behalf of the shadow cabinet, was now much more determined in his attack on the clause, Michael Howard, for the government, was able to make capital out of the opposition's failure to force a vote on the clause while it was in committee.[37] Although individual Labour backbenchers, notably Chris Smith, Ken Livingstone and Joan Ruddock, made excellent speeches bringing out the disturbing civil liberties, educational and censorship implications of the clause, their appeals to the consciences of Tory members were unavailing, and the amendments were voted down. Only one speech, by Ken Livingstone, recognised the insult and potential threat to lesbian mothers in particular, of having their families officially labelled 'pretended' under the law.[38]

The two amendments tabled by the Labour front bench sought, firstly, to limit the effect of the clause by excluding from its scope anti-discrimination work and secondly, to permit the provision of information and counselling to 'any pupil . . . as to his [*sic*] personal or social development', which presumably was intended to safeguard sex education and pastoral work. In outlining the government's objections to these and other opposition amendments, Michael Howard maintained that the clause was a purely educational measure, designed to curb notorious abuses – the borough of Haringey received its usual ritual mention – and to prevent local authorities from promoting the teaching in schools 'that homosexuality is the norm'. He blandly denied that the clause would have any wider effects: 'Nothing in clause 27 will put a homosexual at a disadvantage compared to any other person'.[39] However, one fear expressed by the opposition he did not seek to allay: in reply to a question from Joan Lestor, Labour MP for Eccles, as to whether or not a lesbian or gay teacher who is open about his or her sexuality to pupils would be held to be 'promoting sexuality', he stated, 'The answer would depend on the circumstances and the context'. In other words, as Joan Lestor was quick to note, the clause was recognised by the government as a threat to the employment rights of lesbian and gay teachers.[40]

In the course of his remarks, the minister also betrayed the government's distaste for anti-discrimination work of any kind, when he described this as 'meddling with other people's conduct of their own business'.[41] It should be remembered that the primary purpose of the Local Government Act was to undermine the equal opportunities work of local authorities, by preventing them, when awarding contracts, from taking into account a contractor's employment practices, including the provision of non-racist, non-sexist employment opportunities. Clause 28 may have been an afterthought; but it fitted very neatly into a bill with such objectives. Taken as a whole, the Local Government Act 1988 is an especially devastating attack on the employment opportunities and public services available to Black people who are lesbian or gay. The Halsbury principle is becoming legitimised – make sure you keep the pavement clear for yourself.

Campaigners against the clause now had a breathing space, as the Local Government Bill at this point left the Commons for the House of Lords, where it was not due to be debated until 11 January. On Saturday 9 January OLGA organised a march through London, the first of a series of big marches against the clause. Across the country, innumerable lesbian and gay campaigning groups were organising against the clause, and many new groups and coalitions of groups were springing up. All kinds of ordinary lesbians and gays, many of whom had previously been to some degree reticent about their sexual identity, began to speak out: to relatives, to workmates, to neighbours, on local and national television and radio, in letters to the press. The activities of local government are many and varied – they range from licensing clubs to letting out premises for cultural events, and include the giving of grants to voluntary bodies and cultural groups, not to mention providing housing, recreational facilities, social services and education (including adult education). Moreover, they are major employers. For these reasons, and because the loose wording of the clause was generally feared to make it into something of a catch-all, the overwhelming majority of lesbians and gay men, however different their individual lifestyles or political perspectives, perceived the clause as a serious threat to the quality of their lives; besides reacting with anger and resentment to the crude stereotyping and disgraceful rabble-rousing which were widely engaged in by the clause's supporters.

In terms of achieving publicity, the most effective anti-clause grouping was probably the arts lobby, which was able to call on big name stars, both gay and heterosexual, and muster several journalists, in its efforts to direct the attention of the media towards the pernicious nature of the clause, particularly its feared effects on the subsidised theatre and the provision of library books. On Monday 25 January, a week before the main debate in the Lords, the arts lobby held a press conference at which many famous names from the theatre, television, film and art worlds condemned the proposed legislation.[42] The arts lobby has been criticised by some campaigners against the clause, who feel that the disproportionate attention which was given in the media to 'elitist' concerns, such as access to plays and books, distorted public understanding of the clause and distracted attention from the fears of less powerful groups such as people with special needs, many of whom live in local authority institutions or are otherwise heavily dependent on the local authority for facilities, or lesbian mothers, concerned about their children's treatment at the hands of the education system if their family relationships were to be legally stigmatised as 'pretended'.

Against this, it must be pointed out that the arts lobby never set out to hog the limelight; it received disproportionate attention from the press and television partly because it had a clearer sense than many groups of how to attract notice – and after all, who could be better at publicising a cause than performers, who live by publicity? Moreover, it did make serious attempts to publicise other aspects of the clause than the censorship fears, such as its implications for school pupils. It is to be questioned whether, if the arts lobby had never existed, public awareness of Clause 28 would have been anything like so high. The simple truth of the matter is that the national press is not, in general, nearly so interested in the worries of ordinary lesbians and gays as in reporting statements from the stars. This was shown at a press conference organised the following Friday by the Stop the Clause Campaign Education Group, where several speakers were lesbian and gay teachers and community workers, besides a gay school-leaver and two lesbian mothers. Despite the involvement of some better known figures, such as the Vice-President of the National Association of Teachers in Further and Higher Education and the SDP peer Lord Falkland, this was sparsely attended by journalists, and went almost unreported.[43] Incidentally, the education press conference could not have taken place were it not for the advice and practical support which were given by the members of the arts lobby. The concerns of ordinary gays and lesbians campaigning against the clause probably received better coverage on television and radio than they did in the press; most talk shows and documentary series seemed to feature a session on Clause 28 at some point during the campaign, although many of these programmes went out too late to influence the course of events in parliament.

Meanwhile, the campaign against Clause 28 now extended much more widely than the lesbian and gay communities or the more liberal element in the theatrical profession. The NCCL, whose opposition to the clause was hardly surprising, commissioned legal advice which formed the basis of a briefing to peers. This set out in detail fears that the vagueness of the phrase 'promote homosexuality' risked the clause's being interpreted by the courts in ways which would have an impact far beyond the field of school-based education. It also expressed fears that the clause would lead to a witch-hunt of lesbian and gay teachers, aggravate the difficulties experienced by lesbian and gay pupils, damage the confidence of children of lesbian mothers, and detract from the right of all school pupils to receive full information. Among organisations less noted for their radical commitments, the Library Association expressed its concern about the implications for public libraries of a ban on local authorities' publishing 'material for the promotion of homosexuality', since in law the term 'publish' means to circulate, make available. The National Council for Voluntary Organisations (NCVO) feared that counselling and advice organisations run by lesbians and gays would lose local authority grants, as also might organisations which operated positive policies in respect of lesbians and gays. The Family Planning Association saw the proposed legislation as a threat to sex education. Meanwhile, for its part, the Church of England studiously declined to endorse the Bill's supporters, despite the frequent lip-service given by these people to 'Christian' moral values. Instead, the Bishop of Manchester, speaking in the Lords during the second reading of the Local Government Bill, warned the government of 'the terrible dangers of encouraging prejudice'.[44] Opposing the clause was becoming highly respectable. On 29 January, Neil Kinnock, leader of the Labour Party, finally felt it safe to condemn the clause in public.[45]

One of the organisations expressing most concern about the clause at this juncture was the Arts Council, which went so far as to commission a barrister's opinion on its likely interpretation in the context of the arts, and to draft an amendment which was proposed in the House of Lords by Lord Falkland at the committee stage of the Bill. The Falkland amendment removed from the clause the catch-all ban on promoting homosexuality, and instead would have made it illegal for councils to publish material which represented 'homosexual relationships or homosexual acts as more acceptable than heterosexual relationships or acts', or to cause such material to be used in schools. There was a provision for exempting material published in the honest belief that it served 'a literary, artistic, scientific or educational purpose'. In effect, the Falkland amendment called the government's bluff: the government was still maintaining that Clause 28's implications were confined to education – well, here was an amendment, drafted on the best legal advice, designed to prevent just the kind of teaching in schools the government claimed to find so disturbing, without curbing any of the cultural or other activities engaged in by local authorities.

The Falkland amendment was not a satisfactory compromise. In particular, it retained the phrase 'pretended family relationship', so offensive to lesbians with children and their partners. However, it was widely regarded at the time as the best opportunity of watering down a clause which, it was becoming clear, the government was determined not to see deleted. The press reported government anxiety that there would be a revolt among Tory peers. There were rumours of substantial government redrafting of the clause, designed to pre-empt the Falkland amendment. In the event, when these changes were announced, they turned out to have limited significance. The most important was the insertion of the word 'intentionally' in front of 'promote homosexuality', which government ministers affirmed should be quite enough to allay the fears of arts supporters and the voluntary organisations. Opponents, including the Arts Council and the NCVO, remained thoroughly dissatisfied.[46]

During the progress of the clause through the House of Lords the deep ambivalence of the parliamentary opposition leadership was once again clearly revealed. It is significant that it was left to Lord Falkland, a hereditary peer acting, as he made it plain, as an individual and not as a representative of his party, the SDP, to lead the attack on the clause at this stage. That the Falkland amendment failed was due at least in part to the refusal of the opposition parties to match the whip imposed by the Conservatives with a whip of their own members. The Alliance parties, though critical of the clause, nevertheless enjoyed the spectacle of Labour's discomfiture, while the Labour leadership were quite evidently scared stiff by the prospect of negative publicity.

These fears were very clearly revealed in their failure to support an attempt by a Labour peer, Lord Willis, to seek to have the clause deleted. Indeed, it was rumoured among activists in London that strenuous efforts were made by the party leadership to persuade him to abandon his stand. Not for the first time in the history of its 'support' for lesbian and gay rights, did the Labour Party succeed in obtaining the worst of all possible outcomes for itself: it failed to distance itself in the public mind from an admittedly risky issue – opposition to discrimination against lesbians and gays – at the same time as it earned the comprehensive mistrust of the lesbian and gay communities and the disgust of liberals and radicals. In the process, it betrayed the principles of its own party policies, as established by the Party Conference, and disregarded the civil rights and legitimate interests of thousands of lesbians and gay men.

The debate on Lord Willis' proposal to delete the clause altogether took place at the end of the committee stage. The vote was, of course, lost, and was immediately followed by one of the most memorable episodes in the entire proceedings, when three lesbian demonstrators, shouting protests, abseiled down ropes from the galleries into the middle of the startled peers. Hansard laconically records an '*Interruption*', but the abseilers drew widespread attention from press and broadcasters both nationally and internationally. This was the first of a series of inventive stunts carried out by small groups of lesbian protesters, culminating in the invasion of BBC television's *Six O'Clock News* on 23 May, the day before the Local Government Act became operative in law.[47]

The speeches made by the sponsors of the clause during its progress through the Lords were a reprise of themes already aired: it was intended to end an abuse of ratepayers' money; it was necessary to protect young people at an impressionable stage in their development; parents (not lesbian mothers, apparently) needed to have their anxieties addressed; the family is the basic principle on which civilisation depends. And further: the clause would not affect the civil rights of homosexuals; homosexuality was abnormal; homosexuals are promiscuous and aggressive and flaunt themselves in public; homosexuals (with the aid of certain local authorities) are seeking to corrupt the nation's children . . .

More interesting and more significant are some of the observations made by the Earl of Caithness, who spoke on behalf of the government. The Falkland amendment was one of several attempts to limit the effect of the clause strictly to education, in accordance with the government's avowed purpose in supporting the legislation. All were unavailing; the government insisted on retaining the broad prohibition on promoting homosexuality. In doing so it was forced to shift its ground somewhat, and some interesting revelations emerged.

The government had begun by arguing that the clause was a purely educational measure, with no wider implications. It continued to maintain, in parliament and outside, that its intention in supporting the legislation was to protect young people from local authorities who, it was claimed, in a startlingly mendacious phrase repeatedly used during February and March in Conservative letters to concerned constituents, 'were targetting [*sic*] some activities on young people in schools and outside, in an apparent endeavour to glamourise [*sic*] homosexuality'.[48] Notice that the stress is changing: from concern about reputed 'gay lessons' to 'activities in schools and outside'. During the debate on the

Falkland amendment, Caithness had actually admitted that a prohibition directed against local authorities would have very little effect on what happened in schools. The reason is that the 1986 Education (No. 2) Act, as a result of a previous 'moral panic' about sex education, including teaching about homosexuality, had removed from local authorities all control over this part of the curriculum and placed it in the hands of school governing bodies.[49] The role of local authorities in this area was now purely advisory. This significant revelation, repeated more than once in the course of the Lords debates at committee and report stages, was not at the time reported or otherwise picked up. The situation in law is slightly less straightforward than Caithness indicated, a matter we shall return to later. Incidentally, Caithness, like Howard in the Commons, refused to give any assurances that 'out' lesbian and gay teachers and other local authority employees would not be at risk, under the clause, of dismissal; or that the clause could not be invoked against individual volumes in libraries.[50]

In order to 'justify' the clause in the light of his acknowledgment that its direct effects on school-based education could only be, to say the least of it, slight, Caithness and other government supporters began to lay less emphasis on 'gay lessons' and more on other supposed 'abuses' such as lesbian and gay youth groups, Pride weeks, and publications such as *Changing the World*, the charter for lesbian and gay rights published by the Greater London Council before the government abolished that authority. The emphasis, however, continued to be on the necessity of protecting supposedly impressionable young people against corruption.[51] Here as everywhere in the debate, the stereotype of gay people as child molesters, and the 'seduction' theory of homosexual development, were never very far from the surface. Meanwhile, some of the peers who voted for the clause seem not to have taken in any of the debate which was raging around them. At the report stage in the Lords the Earl of Longford recorded a conversation with a Tory peer to whom he had explained that the aim of an amendment which he himself was proposing was to restrict the operation of the clause to schools. The other replied that he had thought that that was the situation already.[52]

Reading through the debates on Clause 28 and its predecessor, the Halsbury Bill, in the pages of Hansard is often a disturbing experience. Both the present authors, who have identified as lesbians all their adult lives and who believed that they were entirely confident and proud in that identity, found it virtually impossible to plough through column after column of vicious misrepresentation, disinformation and extreme animosity without confronting feelings of self-doubt and personal anxiety which they had long thought dead. But there were a few heart-warming moments. One was the sane and moving speech by Lord Rea, who, in seeking to have the phrase 'pretended family relationship' deleted from the clause, revealed that he himself had been brought up by two women in a lesbian relationship, adding that he considered himself to have 'had as rich and as happy a childhood as most children who are reared by heterosexual couples, and far better than many I see in my daily practice as a doctor'.[53] This was one of the very few times in the debate that the implications of the clause for lesbian mothers and their children was given any consideration. The debate around Lord Rea's amendment won an admission from the Earl of Caithness that the second part of the clause, regarding teaching, which contains the offensive phrase, is in fact redundant, being already covered by the much wider ban on promoting homosexuality.[54] He nevertheless argued that it was important to retain it to emphasise the particularly undesirable nature of any move to represent 'homosexual relationships which have the appearance of being family relationships, in most senses of that phrase, as being on those grounds a welcome development'.[55] The government's determination to single out for special hostility stable, nurturing relationships of the kind implied here is a pointer to an important part of its real agenda, its determination to commit any absurdity or injustice in upholding the patriarchal domination of women and family life.

The Bill's return to the Commons for a final consideration of the clauses amended in the Lords was like the final act of a pantomime. A final but plainly doomed attempt was made by Labour to limit its effects by exempting work carried out 'for the purpose of discouraging discrimination against or protecting the civil rights of any person'. John Cunningham's arguments had sharpened up somewhat in the weeks since the clause had last been debated in the Commons; it is evident that he had been reading some of the briefing material put out by the NCCL and other groups who had taken part in the campaign. Nicholas Fairbairn, MP for Perth and Kinross, made a bid for the title of most offensive contributor to the entire debate when he described homosexuality as a 'morbid squint' and a 'psychopathological perversion'. He later claimed to have 'many close friends who happen to be homosexuals'.[56] We trust that if this were true at the time, it is true no longer. Dame Jill Knight was on her usual dotty form, and claimed that 'children under two have had access to gay and lesbian books in Lambeth play centres': a particularly colourful press report which had, as it happens, been thoroughly exploded following a previous airing in the House of Lords.[57] Three Conservative MPs spoke out against the clause, and two of these, Robin Squires and Michael Brown, later voted with the opposition. Michael Howard, speaking on behalf of the government, was as smooth and specious as ever. And the clause passed through parliament.

Section 28 of the Local Government Act 1988 adds a new Section 2A to the Local Government Act 1986. That section now reads as follows:

'Prohibition on promoting homosexuality by teaching or by publishing material'

(1) A local authority shall not –

(a) intentionally promote homosexuality or publish material with the intention of promoting homosexuality;

(b) promote the teaching in any maintained school of the acceptability of homosexuality as a pretended family relationship.

(2) Nothing in subsection (1) above shall be taken to prohibit the doing of anything for the purpose of treating or preventing the spread of disease.

(3) In any proceedings in connection with the application of this section a court shall draw such inferences as to the intention of the local authority as may reasonably be drawn from the evidence before it.

The wording of the section is notoriously vague, and its interpretation was acknowledged to be a vexed matter even by government representatives, and before it was passed by parliament. On 18 January 1988 a journalist from the *Teacher* consulted 'a Government spokesperson' as to the implications of 'promote', and received the cheerful admission that 'We're a little unclear what that word means ourselves. But the Government is happy with the word even though there's a little uncertainty over what it means. If it comes to trial, it'll be up to the courts to decide.'[58] This remarkable statement convicts the government of irresponsibility at best, in knowingly permitting an imprecise piece of legislation to reach the statute books; many may feel that it reveals a substantial degree of bad faith. At all events, it lends colour to the widespread belief among activists that the section has been left deliberately vague in order to cause maximum confusion and anxiety.

At the time of writing (December 1988) no court case based on the section has so far been initiated, and it is not clear whether such a case is going to take place. It seems that the section's main impact may well prove to lie, firstly in legitimating the mushrooming tendency towards verbal and physical lesbian- and gay-bashing which has received such a stimulus in recent years from the tabloid treatment of the AIDS epidemic, and secondly, in creating an atmosphere of fear and intimidation among local authorities and their employees which can only encourage repression and self-censorship. Of these, we have seen several examples already. East Sussex County Council has banned from use in its schools and colleges a resources pack on voluntary organisations produced by the National Youth Bureau (a government-funded body) which includes an entry on the London Lesbian and Gay Centre, while Strathclyde Regional Council, which is Labour-controlled, has instructed further education colleges to withhold money from student unions which fund lesbian and gay societies. The London Borough Grants Committee is now including a new condition in its agreements with voluntary organisations which forbids the use of grant money for 'the intentional promotion of homosexuality'. There is a serious fear that this may lead to self-censorship by theatre companies, some of which have done valuable education work in schools and colleges presenting plays with lesbian and gay themes.[59] Legal opinion indicates that none of the actions cited above are justifiable by reference to Section 28. It is likely, however, that what we have seen is only the tip of the iceberg. The present background of continuing financial cutbacks in local government offers councillors every opportunity to axe or deny funding to lesbian and gay projects without ever acknowledging the basis of their decisions.

The uncertainties as to the legal implications of the section were partially resolved when the Department of the Environment (DoE) issued a circular on the Local Government Act in May 1988, just before the section became operative in law. The DoE circular received considerable press publicity, particularly for its statement that the section 'does not affect the activities of school governors, nor of teachers. It will not prevent the objective discussion of homosexuality in the classroom, nor the counselling of pupils concerned about their sexuality.'[60] The circular cites the Education (No. 2) Act 1986, which placed responsibility for sex education in the hands of school governors, and which states that where sex education is given, it should be given in 'such a manner as to encourage . . . pupils to have due regard to moral considerations and the value of family life',[61] and the Department of Education and Science circular on sex education, which says that 'There is no place in any school . . . for teaching which advocates homosexual behaviour, which presents it as the "norm", or which encourages

111

homosexual experimentation by pupils.' It should be noted that the status of government circulars is solely advisory; also that the DES circular makes it clear that 'Schools cannot, in general, avoid tackling controversial sexual matters . . . and . . . should be prepared to offer balanced and factual information and to acknowledge the major ethical issues involved.'[62]

The DoE circular was prominently reported in the press as meaning that Section 28 would have no impact on school-based education,[63] an impression that the DoE was subsequently at pains to counteract. It pointed out that although the final decision on the content of school sex education now rests with the governing body, the local education authority retains an advisory role, as well as responsibility for issuing reading lists and teaching materials, and arranging visits by drama groups, and suggested that local authorities who wished to avoid legal problems should tread carefully. In what appears to have been a deliberate and politically-motivated piece of shit-stirring, the DoE cited Haringey Council's recently issued draft guidelines on the treatment of homosexuality in the classroom, *Mirrors Round the Walls*, as an example of the kind of activity that might fall foul of the law.[64]

But will it? Legal advice obtained by the NCCL, the Association of London Authorities (ALA) and other bodies suggests that very few activities previously carried out by local authorities, educational and otherwise, are actually vulnerable to attack under Section 28.[65] This does not mean that the section is not extremely damaging. The examples of self-censorship which we noted earlier are evidence of its pernicious effects, and there can be no doubt that many similar instances have never reached public attention. Yet the advice does suggest that if councillors are taken to court for 'promoting homosexuality', it might well be possible to mount an effective legal challenge.

One of the two key terms in the section is 'promote', which occurs also in the section before it, Section 27. This bans local authorities from publishing material which 'promotes or opposes a point of view on a question of political controversy which is identifiable as the view of one political party and not of another'. A legal opinion commissioned from Lord Gifford, QC, by the ALA and the NCCL notes that in this section 'the word "promote" undoubtedly has the sense of pushing a point of view with the intention of persuading people to adopt it'. Previously, the concept of 'promoting' had been confined to company law, where it means to put out a prospectus with a view to persuading the public to buy shares.[66]

The other key term, of course, is 'homosexuality', which interestingly enough has no definition in law. As the parliamentary record shows, the government defended its use specifically on the grounds that it was vague in import: 'We wish to cover the sum of homosexuality – homosexual relationships and sexual orientation; in short, every aspect of the way homosexuality manifests itself'.[67] On one interpretation, then, any support given to lesbian and gay people or organisations may be held to 'promote' homosexuality in this broad sense. This fear was widely expressed by campaigners while the legislation was passing through parliament. However, Gifford draws support both from the statutes under which local authorities were set up, which lay on them a duty of equal treatment, and from the European Convention on Human Rights, which the United Kingdom has obligations to uphold, in arguing that parliament cannot have intended to disadvantage lesbians and gays relative to heterosexual people, because to do so would bring this country into conflict with the principles laid down in these places. Therefore, he argues, the term 'promote homosexuality' must have some more limited meaning; and he concludes that it must involve 'active advocacy directed by local authorities towards individuals in order to persuade them to become homosexual, or to experiment with homosexual relationships'.[68]

The section, then, certainly does not compel local authorities to discriminate against lesbian and gay people, including those in their employment, nor does it prohibit them from discouraging such discrimination. We may conclude from this that there is no reason why policy statements on equal opportunities in employment should not continue to specify 'sexual orientation' among the grounds on which individual authorities are resolved not to discriminate; nor, in areas where policy statements do not contain such a statement, why union negotiators should not press for one to be included.

Some local authorities fund lesbian and gay youth groups, which were the subject of special attacks in parliament by government representatives and the sponsors of the section. Gifford argues that such organisations are not 'promoting homosexuality', so a local authority which funded them would not be doing so either. On his argument, moreover, there are no grounds on which local authorities must censor books with gay or lesbian themes from their central library lending stocks, or ban tours of plays, or avoid offering in-service training or advice to schools on lesbian and gay issues, provided that they avoid 'promoting homosexuality' in the sense of advocating a lesbian or gay lifestyle. However, he seems to suggest that there may be individual books and plays whose circulation or sponsoring might be held to cause a local authority to fall foul of the section.[69] It is possible that the courts may be more tolerant of recognised 'classics' than of books which do not fall into this category. It has also been suggested that any special display of books with a lesbian or gay theme might be held to contravene the section.

What of the individual school or college teacher? It is important to note that no case may be brought, under Section 28, against individual employees of local authorities; it is councillors who are directly at risk, and who, if a court finds against them, may be surcharged and barred from office. However, teachers and other employees might, of course, face disciplinary proceedings at the hands of their employing authority, if it was thought that they had taken action likely to bring the authority in contravention of the section. So far as schools are concerned, it is now a matter for the governing body, under the Education (No. 2) Act 1986, as to whether information about homosexuality should

114

form part of the formal curriculum. Nevertheless, it is worth noting that under Section 18, subclause 6 (c) (i) of that Act, if the governors' policy is incompatible with any part of the syllabus for a course leading to a public examination, their view becomes of no effect; so we shall not see school governors banning the teaching at 'A' level of Plato or Virginia Woolf. However, teachers, like college lecturers, remain at present responsible as employees to the local authority, who have powers to investigate complaints against them and to take disciplinary action. This state of affairs will change when financial management, with powers of hire and fire, is delegated to governing bodies under the 1988 Education Act. At present, a governing body has the power to recommend to the LEA that a teacher's employment at the school be terminated, but the LEA has discretion over accepting their recommendation.[70] The Earl of Caithness' statements in the House of Lords that 'The teacher is answerable to the governing body and not to the local authority' and 'what the teacher does is now the responsibility of the head teacher and the governing body' are not, therefore, entirely correct.[71] Teachers who disregard instructions from their LEA are vulnerable to disciplinary action, including loss of job, and it is at least a possibility that some authorities, seeking to cover themselves, may issue advice in relation to Section 28 which is more restrictive than the law requires. It is to be hoped that any such attempt would be strongly resisted by local teaching unions.

In general, for an authority to cite Section 28 as grounds for disciplining a teacher or other employee it would have to show that they were 'promoting homosexuality', for example by urging pupils to adopt a gay or lesbian lifestyle or to experiment sexually with members of their own sex. It is generally agreed that there is nothing in Section 28 to stop teachers from discussing homosexuality with pupils in the classroom objectively and honestly, or counselling individual pupils in a pastoral context. Nor should teachers fear to intervene in cases of anti-gay name-calling or bullying since, as Gifford points out, they have a duty, which Section 28 certainly doesn't take away, to protect their pupils' welfare.[72] But this still hasn't entirely clarified the position of lesbian and gay teachers, particularly those whose sexual identity becomes known to pupils. The reality of the matter is that in the past many such teachers have been disciplined, sacked, or forced to resign, without benefit of Section 28 to lend power to the elbows of timorous or bigoted school hierarchies, governing bodies or LEAs. Gifford argues that there is nothing in Section 28 which makes it necessary for an authority to sack or otherwise discipline an openly lesbian or gay teacher.[73] Nevertheless, it is clear that in practice the position of such teachers, depending of course on the authority and school in which they teach, may well be more delicate than previously, if only because the passing of the section has given a general encouragement to anti-gay prejudice and harassment.

Notorious problems of interpretation are presented by subsection 1(b) of Section 28, which prohibits local authorities from promoting 'the teaching . . . of the acceptability of homosexuality as a pretended family relationship'. For one thing, the phrasing is illiterate; 'homosexuality' is not and cannot be a 'relationship' of any kind. Gifford suggests that it prohibits local authorities from recommending to teachers that they teach 'that a homosexual family relationship is acceptable'.[74] It does not mean that they must go out of their way to instruct teachers to teach that it is unacceptable, nor that teachers cannot discuss the issue honestly and objectively with pupils.

At the height of the campaign against Clause 28, in January and February 1988, it was widely argued that if it were passed, local authority funding and facilities, such as the use of premises, would be withdrawn from lesbian and gay groups, library books would be censored, as would plays or films put on in locally subsidised theatres or cinemas and, of course, any mention of lesbians and gays in the classroom would become absolutely impossible. The real state of affairs is somewhat less drastic, but still grave. We have attempted to explain the apparent legal implications of the section in relation to education. The effects of the section are something else altogether, and many of these will never be publicly known. Teaching is done behind the closed doors of classrooms. Following the publicity given to the clause, many teachers are undoubtedly fearful that even to mention lesbians and gays in anything but a derogatory light is likely to see them in court (a groundless fear, of course), or at least facing disciplinary proceedings. Unhappily, one must suspect that many will avoid the topic altogether, or deal with it in such a summary way as to endorse existing prejudice.

There is still little recognition among educators and the public in general, including some lesbians and gays, of why some of us have fought, and are continuing to fight, to bring a better understanding of lesbian and gay issues into the classroom. It is common for such efforts to be smeared as dragging into schools matters which, at best, belong outside. The truth is that they are there already; that they have always been there; that they are present in a thousand vicious jokes, circulating within huddled groups of pupils – and staff; that they are present in innumerable insults, hurled every day across playgrounds and corridors, or scribbled on walls and desks; that they are present in the anxiety and bewilderment of many pupils, who have heard the insults and are not fully certain what it is all about; that they are present in the isolation, fear and confusion of many more, who know, or who are beginning to know, that words like 'poof', 'lebo' or 'buttyman' mean them. Some of these young people are among the most victimised and vulnerable pupils in our schools. Some – and no small number – have attempted suicide, or will do so in the future;[75] some – how many, we have no way of knowing – will undoubtedly succeed.

The projects which have been initiated in the last few years by a small number of local authorities, and which have received such brutal misrepresentation at the hands of the 'moral Right' and their friends in the press, are only a drop in the ocean of what needs to be done to raise the awareness of educators and provide them with appropriate materials. The purpose of these projects has never been to 'indoctrinate' pupils: on that, the most sensible comment is that made by a Conservative opponent of the clause in the final debate in the Commons. Noting that his wife was a former teacher, he observed: 'In her experience, the suggestion that one can address an average or even below average group of teenagers seeking to proselytise and expect to be heard sympathetically is unrealistic'.[76] We would say, utterly fantastic; and it is an unwarranted slur, too, on the professionalism of this country's teachers, that such a charge should be levelled. Rather, the objective is to open up a topic which has hitherto largely been taboo, to give pupils a chance to think about their own and other people's sexual feelings, and to discuss the diverse forms of sexuality and love within an honest and tolerant framework. Crucial to this enterprise is offering space to lesbians and gay men, whether in person or through their writing, to speak for themselves: to break through the silence, and provide alternative images to the vicious stereotypes of the tabloid press, or the condescending stereotypes of heterosexual social science or psychology. It is this work which is now under threat from Section 28: not because the section makes it illegal, but because the signals have gone out, both to local authorities and to individual educators, that now more than ever, such work is liable to prove expensive, either in votes, or in the personal stress which comes from constant harassment.

Lesbian and gay teachers are particularly vulnerable to this harassment; yet their personal experience of what it means to be homosexual in our society, coupled with their professional experience of classroom techniques, makes their involvement absolutely essential. A relatively small number of teachers are known by their pupils to be lesbian or gay. Some have deliberately chosen to 'come out' to their classes, some have been in a sense forced out by inquisitive and dogged questioning, or have been seen in gay pubs or on marches. Their presence in schools is extremely important, contradicting received notions of lesbians and gays as social casualties or parasites. For many of the young people they teach they are undoubtedly the only link with the reality that gives the lie to the negative stereotypes: they are, in effect, walking, talking visual aids – a difficult role, and one that deserves every respect.

To teach children to understand themselves and others better is not to teach them to be lesbian or gay. It is to start to put an end to fear: the intense fear of gay people which plainly torments so many heterosexuals; the fear of insult and attack which is the reality of life for many lesbians and gays, particularly, perhaps, those who are school pupils, and the fear of social sanctions, which affects all of us to some degree; and worse than this, the internalised fear of one's own desires. To show children that this is unnecessary, that lesbians and gays are neither threatening nor pathetic, is not to indoctrinate them, but to tell them no more than the truth.

The first British government to be headed by a woman has identified itself firmly with the interests of the patriarchy. This is entirely of a piece with its policies in general. 'Protecting the family unit', to take up a phrase of Jill Knight's,[77] is code for continuing the coercion of women into 'caring' (servicing) roles which relieve pressure on the public purse and so facilitate tax cuts for the rich – the one clear principle of Thatcherite Toryism. A feature of the Clause 28 debate is the way in which knee-jerk hostility to gays has been invoked to cover an attack on feminist ideas about the family. This is very evident in the insistence on stigmatising unconventional family relationships as 'pretended'. As Baroness Blatch put it in the Lords, in the course of an unpleasant little speech about the undesirability of children being brought up by lesbian couples, ' . . . underlying much of our discussion is a strong conviction that the future of our society depends upon the relationship between man and woman and the product of man and woman – the child'.[78] The child as product – what else? It is marvellous how these people betray themselves by the language they use. Products are not nurtured or educated – they are processed and packaged for consumption. No one asks if they are happy or fulfilled. If they are 'protected', it is in order to safeguard the owner's investment – not for their own sake. This is the rhetoric of a slave-owning society.

Slaves are not generally encouraged to think for themselves. Section 28 of the Local Government Act fits in very nicely with Tory instincts to control what can be presented to the populace. The preceding section seeks to prevent local authorities from spending money on publicising any point of view which is seen as 'party political' – such as support for nuclear disarmament, presumably. The 1988 Education Act gives the Education Minister unprecedented powers to control the school curriculum. Recently, the Home Secretary's administrative powers over the broadcasting media have been invoked in a ban on the direct transmission of statements from members of Irish paramilitary groups and their political sympathisers. Like Section 28, this prohibition is somewhat vague in its wording. Already it seems to be giving rise to some remarkable examples of self-censorship on the part of nervous media bureaucrats.[79] Meanwhile, a new and draconian Official Secrets Act is on its way. Knowledge is power – the Tories know that well. The attacks on school sex education, which have been going on now for a couple of years, and which extend much wider than attacks on teaching about lesbian and gay sexuality, are very much a part of this wider pattern.

Section 28 seeks to restrict people's choices, by restricting the information available to them. This was implicit, and sometimes explicit, in many of the speeches made by its supporters, who made it plain in their attacks on teaching about lesbian and gay lifestyles that they believed that an individual's sexuality is learned from others, or is developed as a result of particular circumstances. Conversely, a major plank in the campaign against the clause was the contention that the sexuality of each individual is fixed and innate. From this it was argued, firstly, that children cannot be taught to be lesbian or gay, and secondly, that discrimination against lesbians and gays was against natural justice, since sexuality is not a matter of choice. This line of argument, however convenient in the circumstances, betrays a naive lack of awareness of the ways in which sexuality is socially constructed. From a feminist perspective, it is also politically dangerous; the same arguments can just as easily be used to defend rape, as a 'natural' manifestation of the inborn urges of the male.

It is clear to us that the formation of an individual's sexual identity is no simple matter, and also that many people, including the present writers, experience their sexual preferences as very deeply rooted. But many people in our society are only imperfectly aware of their own sexual needs, let alone how to look for fulfilment. This is particularly likely to be true of women, who are simply not encouraged to give priority to their own needs on any level. The result in many cases is a broken marriage, child custody battles, a difficult and often painful reappraisal of personal history, a drastic cultural and social reorientation.

A damaging feature of the campaign to stop the clause was the way in which certain voices were heard more loudly than others; and though we feel it inappropriate to seek to lay blame, it is important to give consideration to those whose shouts were largely drowned out, including, in general, those who spoke from a considered feminist political perspective. Others whose voices were missed belonged to groups who are consistently silenced or disregarded in our society. At the top of the list must come people with special needs, particularly the many who because of mental or physical disabilities live in institutions or attend special schools and centres funded by local authorities. Like lesbians and gays, people with special needs are widely seen as 'other', and experience the effect in their lives of distorted public perceptions; but whereas lesbians and gay men are generally presented as preoccupied with sex to the exclusion of anything else, many people in our society experience extreme discomfort at the thought that mentally or physically disabled people have sexual desires or needs. Sex education for school pupils with special needs is thus a very delicate area in itself; a very great deal of work must still be done before there is anything like adequate recognition of those pupils (and adults) with special needs who identify as lesbian or gay.

Lesbian mothers and their partners found themselves under direct attack in the clause in the phrase 'pretended family relationships'. Many lesbian mothers experience difficulty in obtaining custody of their children in the face of bias in the legal system; now, since the advent of the clause, there are indications that judges are becoming even more hostile in their attitudes. Many lesbian mothers conceal their sexuality and their relationships, because they fear that not to do so will risk their losing their children; others worry that their children will be victimised by their peer group, or that teachers will dismiss any difficulties the children have at school as simply a result of their home background. Many, nevertheless, spoke up against the clause, on television or in letters to the press. Yet their fears were seldom brought clearly into focus in media commentaries in the way, say, that anxieties about censorship were explored: chiefly, perhaps, because of the absence of any organisation, whether lesbian-run or otherwise, to channel their protests. Bringing up children, particularly as a single parent, in most cases leaves only limited time for attending meetings and generally defending political interests.

A third group whose needs were not clearly heard in the course of the campaign were lesbian and gay young people. This is perhaps odd, because the clause was initially presented by its sponsors as an education matter. At the first appearance of the clause in the Commons, it was the educational implications that worried the Labour front bench spokesman most: by its second appearance, Labour were attempting to amend it to protect pastoral work in schools. But the main thrust of the attack in the Lords was to seek to confine the clause's effects to education in order to protect the arts, and by the final return to the Commons, Labour had abandoned its earlier amendment. This is not altogether strange; conventional political thinking identifies the welfare of young people strictly with what is generally perceived to be the wishes of their parents; self-determination is not encouraged, nor is political self-expression. However, it is disturbing that the major educational institutions – such as the Advisory Centre for Education, the teaching unions, and others – either failed to take part in the campaign, or mounted only a muted or late attack. To some extent, this was because their energies were tied up in fighting other government initiatives, specifically the 1988 Education Act which, through the imposition of a national curriculum, and the delegation to governors of powers to hire and fire staff, may yet prove far more detrimental to the welfare of lesbian and gay pupils and teachers than Section 28.

However, if the educational issues were not carried to the public at large, Clause 28 has nevertheless made ripples in the teaching profession. At the Easter Conference of the National Union of Teachers, the largest teaching union, delegates voted near-unanimously for a resolution on lesbian and gay rights, which not only commits the union to full support for its lesbian and gay members and deplores Clause 28, but makes harassment of and discrimination against lesbians and gays an offence under the union's rule book. The NUT is the first schoolteachers' union to adopt a policy of support for lesbian and gay rights. It is clear that the campaign against Clause 28 was a key factor influencing delegates' attitudes, as also was the courage of a lesbian delegate, Lena Milosevic, who 'came out' publicly on the rostrum, and received a standing ovation.[80]

One of the more positive outcomes of the campaign against Clause 28 was that discrimination against lesbians and gays became much more clearly focused as an issue in the public mind. Though many people undoubtedly found confirmation for their own prejudice in the strident bigotry of Jill Knight and David Wilshire, others were stirred to deeper reflection and a recognition of the justice of our struggles. Another positive aspect is the way the campaign has united so many disparate groups among lesbians and gays, and the way so many ordinary people have discovered in themselves in the course of campaigning gifts of expression and organisation which they hadn't realised they possessed. But there is still a fundamental problem of unequal power and access to resources which is not going to go away.

The fight against Section 28 is not over. It continues in a lot of actions by individuals and groups across the country, which are often laborious and tedious, but which are nevertheless of key importance: such as monitoring and publicising the behaviour of local authorities and other organisations, and putting out information to correct some of the widespread misunderstanding of the section's legal implications. It continues, too, in a great deal of patient work to keep the issues alive within trade unions and the opposition parties, and in constantly challenging local decisons which use the section, covertly or openly, as an excuse for withdrawing funding from lesbian and gay projects or organisations. And it continues in individual schools and colleges, in staffrooms, in classrooms, and on governing bodies, in the fight to ensure that pupils are appropriately and truthfully educated about lesbian and gay lifestyles, and that staff are not only aware of the needs of lesbian and gay pupils, and of children from lesbian families, but are prepared to take practical steps to improve their educational welfare.

Notes

1. See Nigel Warner, 'Parliament and the law', in *Prejudice and Pride. Discrimination Against Gay People in Modern Britain*, ed. Bruce Galloway, Routledge & Kegan Paul, London, 1983, pp. 83-8.
2. See Lorraine Trenchard and Hugh Warren, *Something to Tell You . . . The Experiences and Needs of Young Lesbians and Gay Men in London*, Hugh Warren, *Talking about School*, and Lorraine Trenchard, *Talking about Young Lesbians*, all published by the London Gay Teenage Group, London, 1984; also Lorraine Trenchard and Hugh Warren, *Talking about Youth Work*, London Gay Teenage Group, London, 1985.
3. They were finally made available in June 1988, after counsel's advice persuaded ILEA that none of their work, including the videos, was in contravention of Section 28. The present authors recommend them highly.
4. Hansard, House of Lords, 18 December 1986, col. 310.
5. Ibid.
6. Ibid., col. 312.
7. Hansard, House of Commons, 15 December 1987, col. 1010; cf. 9 March 1988, col. 418.
8. See n. 57.
9. 'A Grass-Roots Rebellion', *The Times*, 18 December 1986; cf. comments by Baroness Cox, Hansard, House of Lords,

18 December 1986, col. 320. See Chapter 3, 'Positive Images in Haringey'.

10. Hansard, House of Commons, 15 December 1987, col. 1009.

11. Hansard, House of Lords, 18 December 1985, cols. 335-6; cf. 11 February 1987, col. 709.

12. Hansard, House of Lords, 18 December 1986, cols. 330-1.

13. 'Kinnock blast at "zealots" for helping enemy', *The Times*, 20 November 1986; 'Cunningham strikes back at Tories', *The Times*, 16 December 1986; 'New Kinnock flare-up over left town halls', *The Times*, 18 December 1986; and cf. the remarks of Baroness Cox, Hansard, House of Lords, 18 December 1986, col. 322.

14. 'It is more anguish than panic', the *Guardian*, 7 March 1987.

15. House of Lords Sessional Papers 1986-87, Vol. V, under Local Government (Amendment) Bill.

16. Hansard, House of Commons, 8 May 1987, cols. 997-8.

17. 'Gospel according to Thatcher', *The Observer*, 22 May 1988; cf. also 'Thatcher claims Wesley as ally' and 'PM enforces responsibility line', the *Guardian*, 26 May 1988.

18. 'Household survey shows sharp increase in the number of women cohabiting', the *Guardian*, 16 December 1987; 'Britons swing to love – without marriage' and 'More women work as men take it easy', the *Guardian*, 14 January 1988.

19. 'Lady beware', the *Guardian*, 3 August 1988.

20. Hansard, House of Commons, 8 May 1987, col. 998.

21. Hansard, House of Lords, 3 February 1987, col. 181.

22. Hansard, House of Commons, 8 December 1987, col. 1209; cf. *Positive Images. A resources guide to materials about homosexuality, including lesbian and gay literature for use by teachers and librarians in secondary schools and further education colleges*, ILEA Learning Resources Branch, London, September 1986, p. 5.

23. Hansard, House of Commons, 14 May 1987, col. 413.

24. 'Hurd plans to tighten immigration controls', *The Times*, 1 June 1987.

25. 'Labour row as Kinnock sacks black activist', *The Times*, 30 April 1987; and see letter to the *Guardian* by Mick Wallis, 4 May 1987.

26. 'Mystery scare ads rapped', *The Observer*, 14 June 1987.

27. 'Dramatic steps that will carry Britain forward', *The Times Educational Supplement*, 16 October 1987.

28. Letter from Larry Whitty, General Secretary of the Labour Party, to National Executive members and others, 20 March 1986; see also Hansard, House of Commons, 9 March 1988, cols. 385-6.

29. Hansard, House of Commons, 8 December 1987, cols. 1211-14; 1216-18.

30. 'Gays angered by Labour betrayal over grants', the *Guardian*, 10 December 1987.

31. 'Gay rights outcry highlights new Labour line', the *Independent*, 10 December 1987; see also Jeff Rooker's remarks reported in 'Labour row over Clause 28 response', the *Independent*, 9 March 1988.

32. Hansard, House of Commons, 8 December 1987, cols. 1220-6, 1230.

33. As reported in 'Bigotry fear if gay sex teaching banned', the *Guardian*, 9 December 1987; see also Hansard, House of Commons, 15 December 1987, col. 1007; 9 March 1988, col. 408.

34. Hansard, House of Commons, 15 December 1987, cols. 1008-9.

35. OLGA press release, 15 December 1987; see also n. 37.

36. 'Labour in two minds over ban on teaching about homosexuality', the *Guardian*, 15 December 1987.

37. Hansard, House of Commons, 15 December 1987, col. 1016.

38. Ibid., col. 1012.

39. Ibid., col. 1017.

40. Ibid., col. 1023.

41. Ibid., col. 1020.

42. 'Clause 28 "witch-hunt"', the *Guardian*, 26 January 1988.

43. But see 'Scratched by the clause', *The Times Educational Supplement*, 26 February 1988.

44. Hansard, House of Lords, 11 January 1988, col. 965; 'Bishop warns of "terrible danger" of prejudice', the *Guardian*, 12 January 1988; cf. 'Clause 28 a threat to civil liberties, archbishop says', the *Independent*, 3 February 1988 and see Hansard, House of Lords, 11 January 1988, col. 965; cf. the remarks of the Archbishop of York, Hansard, House of

Lords, 2 February 1988, cols. 998-9.

45. '"Family-smashing" poll tax will be dismembered in Lords, says Kinnock', the *Guardian*, 30 January 1988; 'Clause 28 amended to avoid Tory rebellion', the *Independent*, 30 January 1988.

46. Ibid.; 'Lords bid to alter gays curb', the *Guardian*, 27 January 1988.

47. Hansard, House of Lords, 2 February 1988, col. 1022; 'Rope trick ladies drop in on the Lords', the *Guardian*, 3 February 1988; 'Abseil demo by women as Lords confirm gay ban', the *Guardian*, 3 February 1988; 'Gay rights protesters disrupt Lords debate', the *Independent*, 3 February 1988; 'News team repels invaders', the *Guardian* 24 May 1988; 'Gay demonstrators disrupt television news', the *Independent*, 24 May 1988; see also 'Labour row over Clause 28 response', the *Independent*, 9 March 1988; 'The gender trap', the *Guardian*, 30 May 1988.

48. Letter from 10 Downing Street signed by Margaret Thatcher, 3 March 1988. The same phrase occurs again in various letters from the Department of the Environment who, however, unlike Mrs Thatcher's office, can spell 'glamorise' correctly; though not 'targeting', it seems.

49. Hansard, House of Lords, 1 February 1988, cols. 892, 968; 2 February 1988, col. 1018; 16 February 1988, cols. 597, 607-8, 611, 613, 614, 622.

50. Hansard, House of Lords, 1 February 1988, cols. 891-2.

51. See for example Hansard, House of Lords, 2 February 1988, col. 1018; 16 February 1988, cols. 598, 605, 610, 621.

52. Hansard, House of Lords, 16 February 1988, col. 587.

53. Ibid., cols. 617-19; quotation from col. 617.

54. Ibid., col. 620.

55. Ibid., col. 627; see also col. 621.

56. Hansard, House of Commons, 9 March 1988, cols. 383, 399.

57. Ibid., col. 377; see also cols. 378, 400; and Hansard, House of Lords, 11 January 1988, cols. 1012-13; 1 February 1988, col. 871.

58. 'Letter of the law that spells fear', the *Teacher*, 18 January 1988.

59. 'Anti-gay law "is a legal non-starter"', *The Observer*, 22 April 1988; 'Lawyers support council funding of gay

groups', the *Guardian*, 16 May 1988; 'Sexuality: a new minefield in schools', the *Independent*, 26 May 1988.

60. Department of the Environment Circular 12/88 §20.

61. Education (No. 2) Act 1986 §46.

62. Department of Education and Science Circular 11/87 §21, 22.

63. 'Schools escape clause 28 in "gay ban" fiasco', *The Sunday Times*, 29 May 1988; 'Clause 28 note irks MPs', the *Guardian*, 30 May 1988.

64. 'Escape from Section 28 oversold', *The Times Educational Supplement*, 3 June 1988.

65. 'Anti-gay law "is a legal non-starter"', the *Observer*, 22 April 1988; 'Lawyers support council funding of gay groups', the *Guardian*, 16 May 1988; 'Section 28 "no bar to gay issues"', the *Guardian*, 26 July 1988.

66. *In the matter of Section 28 Local Government Act 1988. Opinion*, Lord Gifford, QC and Terry Munyard, §14, 15. We are grateful to the National Council for Civil Liberties and the Association of London Authorities for permitting us to quote from this document.

67. Hansard, House of Lords, 16 February 1988, col. 616.

68. Gifford Opinion, §2-9, 13, 16.

69. Ibid., §32, 34.

70. Ibid., §25, 26, 27.

71. Hansard, House of Lords, 16 February 1988, cols. 613, 614.

72. Gifford Opinion, §20, 28.

73. Ibid., §29.

74. Ibid., §19.

75. See *Something to Tell You. The Experiences and Needs of Young Lesbians and Gay Men in London*, by Lorraine Trenchard and Hugh Warren, London Gay Teenage Group, London, 1984, p. 145.

76. Hansard, House of Commons, 9 March 1988, col. 378.

77. Hansard, House of Commons, 9 March 1988, col. 387.

78. Hansard, House of Lords, 16 February 1988, cols. 609-10.

79. 'Broadcast ban leads terror fight', the *Guardian*, 20 October 1988; 'Terrorist ban hits pop song', *The Observer*, 20 November 1988.

80. *Spare Rib*, 190 (May 1988), p. 38; *Lesbian and Gay Socialist*, 14 (Spring/Summer 1988), pp. 13-15.

Part 2
Denying Realities, Endangering Lives, Working for Change

5 Our Issues, Our Analysis: Two Decades of Work on Sexual Violence

Liz Kelly

This chapter provides an overview of second wave feminist theory and practice in Britain in relation to sexual violence, forming a complement to Margaret Jackson's discussion in Chapter 1, which illustrates men's violence as a major issue for first wave feminists. A recent international conference in Cardiff, organised to celebrate ten years of Welsh Women's Aid, brought together women from every continent, from rich and poor countries, who are actively engaged in supporting abused women and children and challenging men's systematic physical and sexual abuse of women and children. Documenting, analysing and campaigning against men's use and abuse of women and children has become a central concern of women across the globe.

A single chapter cannot do justice to the breadth and complexity of our work on sexual violence, even where the scope is limited to Britain in the 1970s and 1980s. As with all feminist issues our history is testament to the creative interplay between our theory and practice, with as starting point our own experience. Within this broad framework the connections between the written word and national, regional and local activism are seldom straightforward. A failure of second wave feminism to date has been to neglect 'writing our own history'. How support groups and campaigns have emerged, developed and changed is not well documented, and too much history remains in individual women's heads and collections of papers and mementoes that some of us can bear neither to throw away nor to order systematically as a resource for others. With these important provisos in mind, I want to give a broad overview of how our thoughts and actions around sexual violence have developed during the last two decades.

Our understanding of, and responses to, sexual violence began from the honest discussions of our lives in consciousness-raising (CR) groups in the early 1970s. It was further influenced by groundbreaking books, long forgotten short, incisive 'think pieces' photocopied and passed on through networks, and the issues women brought to newly established women's groups and centres. What grew out of these often angry explorations were innovative ways of supporting women and children who had been victimised: refuges for women and children abused by men in their household, crisis lines and self-help groups. Our discoveries and our practical work also produced analysis: it was necessary to understand and place men's violence in the context of women's oppression. At the same time, sometimes in the same groups, feminists were engaged in critical analysis of the family and sexuality. By the late 1970s we were increasingly able to connect these critiques. It was at this point that concerted challenges from within the movement demanded that differences between women be recognised and integrated into our theory and practice.

Throughout the two decades feminists have also had to respond to events in the public sphere. We sometimes built effective campaigns and actions which highlighted the hypocrisy of the legal system, and the failure of statutory agencies to protect women and girls from assault. Some of the most successful involved making direct links within the individual women and/or their families and friends – for example, Noreen Winchester, the Maw sisters (all of whom killed their fathers who had sexually abused them) the mother of Jacqueline Hill (the last woman to be murdered by Peter Sutcliffe) and Balwant Kaur (who was murdered by her husband in a refuge for Asian women). We occasionally succeeded in getting legislative changes, such as the Domestic Violence Act 1976, on to the political agenda; the Rape in Marriage Bill 1981 did not become law. Increasingly we find ourselves fighting a rearguard action against victim blaming, sensationalist reporting and denial of the extent of sexual violence: for example, the formation of the Feminist Coalition Against Child Sexual Abuse in response to the recent Cleveland Enquiry.

These achievements may seem slight when compared to the extensive networks of support and legislative reform evident in other industrialised countries over the same period. But British activists have never had nor, in some ways, have they ever wanted, the levels of government funding available to women in other countries. The possibilities of imposed hierarchical structures, of becoming 'experts', of being 'bought off' produced a healthy scepticism, and exploration of the implications, of state funding. *How* we did our work was always as important as *what* we did. What has been achieved, therefore, is a tribute to the commitment, creativity and vision that activist feminists have brought to this work.

This combination of activist commitment and political marginalisation has led to a haphazard network of services, and occasional outbursts of outraged action. Only the refuge movement has managed to build anything approaching a relatively secure network of provision, and even that is currently under threat through changes in social security and housing legislation. The only formal political organisations to fund local projects and appoint officers whose brief was sexual violence were the ill-fated Greater London Council (GLC), and a few Labour controlled local authorities. Whilst Britain cannot boast the range of services available in some other countries, there has not yet been a 'professional take over' of the work (Kelly, 1989)!

Establishing the Framework

The first book devoted to feminist activism on, and analysis of, sexual violence was published in 1974. *Rape: The First Sourcebook for Women* by Noreen Connell and Cassandra Wilson both records and extends work begun in 1971 by New York radical feminists. Whilst the title focuses on rape, it is

131

in this book that Florence Rush first published work on child sexual abuse, and several pieces discuss sexual harassment (although it was another four years before the term itself was coined). Furthermore, many of the articles and discussions demonstrate an awareness of differences between women, particularly those of race and class. A twenty-first century historian could, from the contents list alone, construct some sense of how second wave western feminists began to explore the issue of sexual violence. The five sections of the book are: Consciousness Raising; Speaking Out; Feminist Analysis; Legal Aspects; and Feminist Action. The women's liberation movement (WLM) in the West grew out of women speaking to one another, talking about and naming their personal experiences of oppression. From shared experience emerged both the political analysis and the political commitment which is called feminism. Feminist theory develops out of women's experience; action in the world can be either a reflection of political analysis, or an enraged response to injustice which necessitates further reflection and shifts within theory.

It is this creative interplay and dynamic movement between theory and practice which characterises second wave feminism and accounts for the explosion of new ideas, new forms of organising, and new visions of radical change. The fact that the WLM has never modelled itself on a political party, that activism and theory are produced by different women in different places who may have no knowledge of one another, means that development and change is seldom logical or coherent. So although in the *First Sourcebook*, and some other early radical feminist writings (see, for example Koedt et al., 1973), explicit connections between forms of sexual violence were made and classism and racism were recognised as crucial factors affecting groups of women's experiences, these insights were not reflected in much of the subsequent research, theory and activism. Instead a unified view of women's experience predominated, perhaps because sexual violence is one form of experience that affects women across the divisions of class and race. Until recently support work, research and analysis has tended to focus on one form of sexual violence, and many groups and authors have been reluctant to explore differences between women. Had some of the early writings of activist feminists informed our work more directly we might not find ourselves 15 years later having to reinvent the wheel! The journey back to where some of us began has both resulted in important new insights and been a painful process of struggle and fragmentation.

The chronological chart which follows includes some of the most important events in Britain, the shifts in our thinking and the most influential publications over the past twenty years. It is a selective chronology reflecting my own involvement in both activism and radical feminist politics.

Whilst the chronology is selective, it none the less illustrates the complex mosaic of feminist activism which it is virtually impossible to represent or describe in linear sequence. Yet some important threads can be traced through – threads which at some points were closely woven together, at others were part of more random patchwork.

Discovering, Naming, Defining

The prerequisite to any discussion about, or action around, sexual violence was that women should recognise its existence. Women really were 'breaking silence' when they began to speak to each other and in public about the abuse they had experienced from men. Whilst in the US the first form of sexual violence which women organised around was rape, in Britain it was domestic violence. This variability in the sequence in which forms of sexual violence become public issues is reflected in many other countries, and is further complicated by the fact that certain forms of sexual violence are specific to particular cultures, or take slightly different forms because of cultural differences.

It is easy to forget that before this wave of feminism not only was sexual violence not researched, but many of the names now commonly used simply did not exist – for example 'sexual harassment', 'domestic violence', 'survivor'. Both the reality of sexual violence and the fact that it was an experience shared by many women were invisible in public

Table 5.1: SELECTED CHRONOLOGY

Date	Events/Campaigns	Theory	Publications
1969	First CR groups.	Beginning from our own experience. 'Women only' meetings.	
1970			*Sexual Politics* (Millett)
1973	Chiswick Women's Aid – the first women's refuge.		
1974	National Women's Aid Federation – split with Erin Pizzey.	Stated that battering was the result of 'women's position in society'. Refuges to include residents in all decision making.	*Scream Quietly or the Neighbours Will Hear* (Pizzey)
	International Tribunal of Crimes Against Women.	First links between male violence and compulsory heterosexuality.	
1975			*Against Our Will* (Brownmiller) *Battered Women Need Refuges* (NWAF)

1976	London Rape Crisis.	Support work to focus on enabling women to take control over their life and choices.	
	Domestic Violence Act.		
1978	7th demand of Women's Liberation Movement.	Debate about the place of men's violence in women's oppression. Recognition that sexual violence not confined to particular groups.	
	First Reclaim the Night march.	That fear of attack limits women's freedom in public space.	
1979	Occupation of a church by sex workers protesting about Prosecution of Prostitutes Bill.	Failure to develop links with sex industry workers in practice.	*Violence Against Wives* (Dobash and Dobash)
	Women's Media Action Group.	Links between male violence and the sex industry in theory.	*Female Sexual Slavery* (Barry)
		Shift from victimisation to survival.	*The Best Kept Secret* (Rush)
	'Yorkshire Ripper'.		

1980	WAVAW* campaigns against pornography.	Explicit connection of male violence with construction of sexuality.
	Angry Women.		'Compulsory heterosexuality and lesbian existence' (Rich) *Pornography: Men Possessing Women* (Dworkin)
	Sexual Violence Conference.	Emergence of debate around pornography.
1981	Rape in Marriage Campaign.		*Leaving Violent Men* (Binney et al.)
	First Incest Survivors Group.	
	WAVAW Conference.	Increasing demands by Black women that anti-racism be an integral part of theory and practice.
1982	Male Power and the Sexual Abuse of Girls Conference.		*Incest: Fact and Myth* (Nelson)
1983/4	Refuges for incest survivors.		*Well-Founded Fear* (Hanmer and Saunders)

1985	Women Against Sexual Harassment (WASH). Sexual Offences Bill.		*Ask Any Woman* (Hall) *Women Against Violence Against Women* (McNeill and rhodes)
1986	National March against Male Violence organised by Network of Women (NOW).		*The Pornography of Representation* (Kappeler)
	Glasgow Women's Support Project. Clare Short's 'Page 3' Bill.	Return to linking forms of sexual violence in theory and practice.	
1987			*The Lust to Kill* (Cameron and Fraser)
1988	Campaign Against Pornography (CAP).	Attempts to link, develop coalitions and mass campaigns.	
	Feminist Coalition Against Child Sexual Abuse. Rape and Policing Conference.		*Surviving Sexual Violence* (Kelly)

---

* WAVAW – Women Against Violence Against Women.

knowledge. Naming provided women with both words and a form of analysis – names contain within them a definition of experience as social and shared, thus challenging the previous construction of sexual violence as private and personal. This process has also facilitated research, which has increasingly revealed the prevalence of a range of forms of sexual violence. It is both feminist research and the courage of individual survivors to speak out which have undermined, hopefully forever, the myth that sexual violence is rare, and committed only by a few aberrant men. The notion that women had the most to fear in the public sphere from strangers was replaced by a recognition that women and children were most at risk at home, from male relatives and partners.

In the process of naming and documenting women's experience feminists quickly became aware of how the definitions of sexual violence which informed the law, research and 'common sense' ideas did not reflect women's experience, but rather what men defined as a violation of women. In many countries campaigns were launched to change the letter and practice of the law in relation to rape and domestic violence, and several successful campaigns have resulted in legislation which defines sexual harassment at work as a form of sexual discrimination.

The issue of definitions is, however, much more complex than this. Whilst feminists have challenged limited definitions and stereotypes, these ideas die hard. Many girls and women are still influenced by them, and do not find it easy to name what has happened, or is happening, to them as abuse or violence. For example, many more women will say they have been forced to have heterosexual sex than will say they have been raped; many more girls and women will say they have been 'touched up' than will say they have been sexually harassed or assaulted. The factors which affect the ease or difficulty women have in naming their experiences are complex and varied (Kelly, 1988), further complicated for Black women by the conjunction of heterosexism, racism and sexism. These issues have recently been recognised by feminist researchers, who are increasingly aware that *how* they ask questions affects their findings. If we don't presume shared definitions, if we do provide spaces for women to tell us what they experience as abusive, our 'results' show far higher prevalence rates (see, for example, Hanmer and Saunders, 1984; Kelly, 1988).

Here the threads from naming and defining led to understanding, analysis and campaigning. Both limited definitions and the silencing of women's voices were supported by a prevailing ideology surrounding sexual violence which either questioned the truthfulness of women's accounts or, where some validity was accorded to women's words, we were held responsible for our violation. Feminist analysis revealed the many ways in which women's experience was denied – from Freud's redefining his patients' experiences of child sexual abuse as fantasy (Rush, 1984), to the legal fiction that 'women and young children are prone to lying' (Blackstone, 1787). We also unpicked the many overt and covert methods which are used to deflect responsibility from men on to women. Understanding this helped us explain why women often blame themselves for being victimised.

'Victim blame' usually contains a variable combination of essentialist ideas about male sexuality – that men have uncontrollable urges – and the assigning to women of responsibility for setting limits on men's behaviour. Women are aware of the many ways in which they can be deemed to be 'asking for it'. Furthermore, this ideology also functions to divide women from one another, since some women choose femininity as a form of protection – behaving in ways that please men, or which at least do not challenge them. Women who opt for this survival strategy may see women who choose to resist and challenge the constraints of femininity as the ones who 'ask for it'. In fact neither route protects women from male violence, nor from being held responsible for men's behaviour.

All of these issues were evident in court cases, judges' rulings and media reporting. All became matters around which campaigns and challenges were organised.

Supporting, Acting, Campaigning

The earliest forms of activism on sexual violence were 'speak outs' and protests at legal decisions or media representations. As feminists became aware of the extent of sexual violence, the ways in which women's experience was denied and the failure of the police, the courts, social workers, doctors and therapists to provide support and protection, they recognised the urgent need for alternatives for women and children. It is in the area of providing support and advocacy for women and children who have been victimised that the most innovative and enduring alternative institutions have been created by feminists. It is one of the areas of feminist practice that unites women across the globe: crisis lines, refuges and support groups exist in many countries, and are not limited to the first world.

Chiswick Women's Aid, the first refuge for 'battered women', emerged out of the inability of a local women's centre to respond to the most pressing need of local women – a way of escaping violent partners. Since this was established in 1973, such safe houses now exist in many many countries. The first network of refuges emerged in Britain, and in 1974 the National Women's Aid Federation (NWAF) was formed, linking 27 groups; at the 1975 conference 111 groups were represented. Erin Pizzey – the founder of the Chiswick refuge – never joined the federation. The split at the 1974 conference, between a few groups supporting Erin and the majority which founded NWAF, was a combination of personal and political disputes, but Erin clearly felt uncomfortable with the growing feminism of many other groups. This was expressed through the aims of the NWAF, which included the statement that 'battering was the result of women's position in society', and in a commitment to feminist practice in the running of refuges (see Sutton, 1984). Refuges were not modelled on hostels, with live-in wardens and a hierarchical structure separating workers and residents. Instead women's ability to organise their own lives and to support one another were acknowledged and a model of self-help encouraged. The shift from 'management committees' to 'support groups' reflects this form of organisation. Unfortunately the demands of funders have recently required that some groups move backwards, adopting more traditional structures. During the 1970s NWAF devolved into national federations in England, Ireland, Scotland and Wales. They represent the only example of recent British feminism that combines local autonomy with a national organisation. There is much to be learnt from the, as yet unwritten, history of the successes and failures of this brave attempt to combine feminist politics with organisational structure.

The organic connection between theory and practice was also evident in the policies of rape crisis groups, the London line, started in 1976, being the first in Britain. Rape was understood as an assault on women's bodily integrity. So supporting a woman who had been raped should be based on enabling her to take back control over her life and choices. This basic philosophy, combined with an awareness of how police investigation and court appearances were often experienced by women as a 'second assault', led all rape crisis groups to refuse to press women to make official reports. Groups were, however, always willing to support any woman who chose to report (see Bowen and Manning, 1987).

As activism on the issues of rape and domestic violence grew, many women felt this should be reflected within the demands of the WLM. The seventh demand, which referred to all forms of male violence, was in fact the last demand to be adopted by the British WLM. The Birmingham conference, at which it was accepted after a long and acrimonious debate, was the last. Political differences between groups of women had become such that debate and consensus seemed impossible. Some socialist feminists have argued that it was the very raising of the issues of sexuality and sexual violence which 'split' the women's movement (see, for example, Segal, 1987). The fragmentation was much more complex than this, one of the major factors being our failure to build an inclusive movement – a movement in which women who were not white, middle class, heterosexual, British, able-bodied and articulate were not marginalised. It is none the less interesting that when Scottish women held a WLM conference in 1987 the theme which brought activists together was violence against women.

Towards the end of the 1970s a form of protest first seen in the US was organised in cities and towns throughout Britain – Reclaim the Night marches. These actions, in which large numbers of women claimed space at night in the public sphere, were intended to demonstrate the impact of fear of attack on women's freedom. The choice of routes for the marches, and in some cases the lack of outreach work with local communities before the march, led to conflicts, particularly in London, between activists and sex workers and Black communities. The marches which took place in Leeds and Bradford, however, in the early 1980s were supported by the local communities, particularly the community of women. Women took to the streets to protest about the murders of women by the 'Yorkshire Ripper' and about the responses of the police and media, who suggested that women should not go out at night alone, and that the murders were not 'serious' until an 'innocent woman', i.e. not a woman who worked as a prostitute, was murdered.

The early 1980s were a period of consolidation of feminist support services, and the emergence of localised actions against pornography – sex shops had windows broken and/or spray painted, locks glued up, and products covered in ink, and a couple of shops were set on fire.

Three national conferences on sexual violence were organised in the early 1980s (McNeill and rhodes, 1985) and direct action groups calling themselves 'Angry Women' formed in many cities and towns. At the same time women involved in trade unionism were demanding that sexual harassment at work be taken seriously.

In late 1985 an Asian woman, Balwant Kaur, was murdered in one of the London refuges for Asian women. Amongst the many actions in response was a national march against male violence organised by a coalition of Black and white women – Network of Women. The issues on which the march focused included domestic violence, rape, pornography, prostitution, child sexual abuse and sexual harassment, state violence against women and medical violence. The specific experiences of Black and Third World women were foregrounded. This march represents the emerging reworking of the connections between all forms of sexual violence and the possibility of coalitions of women from different communities and constituencies – potentials yet to be fully realised.

Understanding, Analysing, Theorising

Individual feminist theorists had written about the place of violence in maintaining women's oppression before the issues became priorities for feminist organising. Two of the earliest, and in some ways most influential, were Kate Millett and Susan Griffin. In *Sexual Politics* (1970) Kate Millett uses the concept of patriarchy to name the systematic subordination of women by men, which she argues has been a feature of the majority, if not all, of human societies. Patriarchy is reproduced within the family, by the state, through ideology and culture and, like all political systems, patriarchal power ultimately rests on force. Jalna Hanmer developed this argument (Hanmer, 1978), arguing that all systems of oppression employ violence or the threat of violence as an institutionalized way of ensuring compliance. Power relations are always underpinned by the threat, and if necessary overt use, of force.

In 'Rape – the all American crime' Susan Griffin begins from her own experience of coping with the threat of rape. From this experiential base she builds an analysis of how the threat and reality of rape circumscribes all women's lives. She argues that rape is not a sexual crime, but a violent political act. The reality of rape, the fact that some men rape, has the effect of controlling all women. In this short but incisive article Griffin raised a number of issues which have been developed by other women.

What this early work established was that men's power over women was political and structured. A crucial part of this structuring of power was actual or threatened violence which reproduced and reinforced male dominance. All women were potential victims, regardless of age, class or race.

Not all the theorising that went on in the 1970s is recorded. Much of it occurred in consciousness-raising groups, in working groups and during conference workshops. As we explored our own sexual histories in more depth and heard other women's accounts it became clear that for many women heterosexual romance and 'sexual pleasure' were myths rather than reality. Not only was most heterosexual sex engaged in for men's sexual pleasure, but much of it was experienced by women as pressurised, coerced or forced. When linked to men's use of prostitutes and pornography, a picture emerged of heterosexual masculinity based on the use and abuse of women. These discoveries were linked to a rejection of biologistic drive models of sexuality. Feminist theorists and activists alike conceptualised sexuality as a social construct, social interactions and understandings which take place in historical and cultural contexts. It was the combination of these revelations and the joy many women experienced in women-only work and social situations that led many activists to choose to have sexual relationships with women, to choose to be lesbians.

For much of the 1970s, most published theoretical discussions of male violence focused on rape. Rape symbolised our vulnerability, represented the ease with which women's physical and sexual integrity could be violated. A central marker in this was Susan Brownmiller's *Against Our Will*, one of the most read and discussed feminist books of the 1970s. It has been criticised recently for its grand sweep through human history, and for not dealing adequately with the issue of racism, especially in relation to the lynching of black men accused of raping white women in the US.

Another critical issue raised in *Against Our Will* has major implications for how feminists theorise about sexual violence. Brownmiller insisted that rape was not a sexual crime, but a crime of violence, and she sought to make a clear distinction between rape and heterosexual intercourse. Her argument was enormously influential, leading feminists in a number of countries to campaign for rape to be defined legally as an 'assault' rather than a 'sex crime'. This distinction between violence and sexuality is still evident in literature from rape crisis groups and has informed discussions of sexual harassment, pornography and child sexual abuse.

Catharine MacKinnon is one of a number of feminists who in different places and in different ways have challenged us to rethink this analysis. She argues, rightly in my view, that by separating rape from 'normal' heterosexuality – violence and 'abuse of power' from sex – we have disconnected our work on violence from our critique of sexuality. She reminds us that women, like all oppressed groups, are systematically disadvantaged within the economy and are denied equal, or all, access to a range of other opportunities. But what feminists discovered, and what is specific to women's oppression, is the use of sexuality in the social control of women:

> Feminism fundamentally identifies sexuality as the primary social sphere of male power. The centrality of sexuality emerges not from Freudian conceptions but from feminist practice on diverse issues including abortion, birth control, sterilization abuse, domestic battery, rape, incest, lesbianism, sexual harassment, prostitution, female sexual slavery and pornography . . . producing a feminist political theory centering on sexuality; its social determination, daily construction, birth to death expression and ultimately male control. (MacKinnon, 1982a, p.526)

She restates what many feminists know, but have sometimes chosen to understate, that it is male definitions which make clear and 'objective' distinctions between violence and sex:

> What women experience does not so clearly distinguish the normal, everyday things from those abuses . . . we have a deeper critique of what has been done to women's sexuality and who controls access to it. What we are saying is that sexuality in exactly those normal forms often *does* violate us. So long as we say that those things are abuses of violence, not sex, we fail to criticize what has been made of *sex*, what has been done to us *through* sex, because we leave the line between rape and intercourse,

145

sexual harassment and sex roles, pornography and eroti-
cism, right where it is. (MacKinnon, 1982b, p.52)

Catharine MacKinnon's work is complex and challenging.
She insists that we do not forget that women's oppression is a
sexual oppression, and that we recognise the extent to which
women's subordination is increasingly eroticised. Men use
sexuality to express and affirm their dominance; for them
coercion and force are parts of 'normal' sexuality. Dissociat-
ing sexuality from violence is also problematic because one
of the most common impacts of an experience of sexual
violence on women is that subsequent sexual relationships
become fraught with contradictions. Furthermore, by retaining the distinction we end up supporting the arguments
which men have been making for decades – that what we
experience as rape is 'sex'; that what we experience as
harassment is 'fun'. By making a theoretical separation
between violence and sexuality we undermine both our
experience of so-called non-violent sex and our analysis and
critique of the construction of (hetero)sexuality.

Adrienne Rich, in a slightly different way, has made explicit connections between sexual violence and the construction
of sexuality. In 'Compulsory heterosexuality and lesbian
existence' she examines heterosexuality not as a 'sexual
preference' but as a social/political institution. She asks how
something which has been rigidly enforced can be seen as
either 'natural' or a 'choice'. Using historical, culturally
variable and contemporary examples of the ways in which
men's dominance and women's subordination is reproduced,
Rich demonstrates that all are also ways of enforcing heterosexuality. Many forms of sexual violence are integrated into
an analysis of the reproduction of oppression and the
enforcement of heterosexuality. She shows how in recent
times the conjunction of heterosexuality and violence is
affirmed in both sexology and pornography:

[that] women are natural sexual prey to men and love it;
that sexuality and violence are congruent; and that for
women sex is essentially masochistic, humiliation pleasur-
able, physical abuse erotic. But along with this message

comes another, not always recognised: that enforced sub-mission and the use of cruelty, if played out in a hetero-sexual pairing, is sexually 'normal', whilst sensuality between women, including erotic mutuality and respect, is 'queer', 'sick', and either pornographic in itself or not very exciting compared with the sexuality of whips and bondage. (Rich, 1980, p.220)

In the 1980s there has been a re-emergence of analysis and research which looks at a range of forms of sexual violence and their role in reproducing women's oppression. Much of this analysis begins from an understanding that sexuality is not natural or biological but socially constructed, and that a central feature of the current construction of heterosexuality in the west is that it is the only 'normal' form of sexuality and that men should control sexual interaction. Valerie Hey observed that for British men the 'main topic of conversation in the pub is women's sexuality and how to control it' (Hey, 1986, p.66). Betsy Stanko suggests that: 'forced sexuality for women is "paradigmatic" of their existence within a social sphere of male power' (Stanko, 1985, p.75). Men define and relate to women sexually; women become objects for men's gaze, objects to be commented upon and evaluated, objects to be acted upon.

It is through sexualisation that men control, intimidate and humiliate women and girls on a regular and recurring basis. Because male control, and the coercion that it entails, is normalised, many women discount and rationalise their negative feelings about, and experiences of, male sexuality. As Betsy Stanko has pointed out, it is often difficult for women to define 'typical' male behaviour as abusive. Carol Ramazanoglu has documented the routine 'insults, leers, sneers, jokes, patronage, bullying, vocal violence and sexual harassment' which academic men use to keep 'uppity' women in their place, and the difficulties she encountered in naming such behaviour as violence (Ramazanoglu, 1987).

Alongside these developments in feminist theory, in the 1980s we have returned to an awareness of differences between women, and have gained a deeper understanding of the many and varied ways in which women's oppression can be experienced differently and/or compounded by other forms of oppression. For Black women their 'blackness' continues to define their sexuality, and assaults by white men combine sexism and racism. Being outside the control of individual men means that women who are prostitutes and/or lesbians are particular targets for all men. The denial of sexuality that accompanies ageing and/or disability means that sexual violence has a particular meaning for older and disabled women, and may have a particular impact on them.

Reworking the Connections

It is through working with countless women and girls that feminist analysis and understanding of a number of forms of sexual violence has deepened. Whilst the initial main focus was rape, activism, research and analysis now includes sexual harassment and sexual assault, flashing, obscene phone calls, domestic violence, incest and sexual abuse of girls and the use and abuse of women in the sex industry. Whilst some research and campaigns have attempted to move away from the separation of these issues (a particularly exciting example is the Glasgow Women's Support Project; see Bell and MacLeod, 1988), this is not reflected throughout feminist activism. In our support services, for example, crisis lines tend to focus on rape and sexual assault, refuges on domestic violence, survivors' groups on incest and child sexual abuse. Nor has the important theoretical work on sexuality and the family been systematically connected with our work on sexual violence. We have yet to explode the myth of home and family as a 'haven from a heartless world':

> But home is no safe place for women either. Women may have to deal with voyeurs and obscene phone calls at the least, brutal violence or rape by the men they live with at the worst (and everything in between). Fathers, husbands, lovers, uncles, sons – none are exempt . . . Experience of such violence makes women insecure even in the place that is supposed to be women's haven, the home. (McNeill and rhodes, 1985, p.6)

What has been missing in feminist analysis is a way of connecting routine forms of male violence to those which are more easily recognisable. When trying to conceptualise the range of male behaviour that women and girls experience as abusive I began to use the concept of a 'continuum' to express the connections between the 'typical' and the 'extreme'. What this concept encapsulates is the fact that most women experience variations of what Carol Ramazanoglu documents, on a regular basis and in a range of contexts. Whilst many women also experience rape, domestic violence and incest, not all women do, and these experiences are not as frequent in individual women's lives.

In this final section I want to suggest one way of reworking the connections and reintegrating our knowledge and analysis. Since this book addresses issues of sexuality mainly in relation to young people, I want to develop the idea of the continuum in relation to the sexual violence experienced by girls and young women.

In the past year or so the term 'child sexual abuse' has become almost synonymous in public discourse with incest. However, this term actually covers all forms of sexual violence which girls (and some boys) experience before they are deemed to be adults. Whilst the figures I will use later are based on an age cut-off point of 16, I am now unhappy with using this age rather than 18, since it is clearly connected to the age of consent for young women – the age at which men can have legitimate sexual access to women. The term 'sexual abuse of girls' covers a similar range of male violence to that which we have documented in adult women's experience – it includes flashing, touching, sexual assault, physical assault, sexual harassment, pressurised sex, coercive sex and rape. As with adult women these forms of violence are experienced in a range of contexts, the men and boys who perpetrate them being strangers, acquaintances, friends or relatives. The difference for girls and young women is that a considerable proportion of their experiences of abuse are committed by adult men – men who have the combined power of gender and age over those they choose to victimise.

When women take time to remember, discuss and analyse

their experience of male sexuality as girls and young women, a remarkable pattern emerges. Many women come to these discussions – whether in a woman's group or as part of a research project – thinking that they have never been abused. During the discussions, or sometimes after them, buried memories of repeated abuse or confusing encounters are rediscovered:

> *nearly all of us* could remember several incidents with relatives (male) which freaked us out in one way or another . . . We see this as the subtle sexual abuse of girls. (McNeill and rhodes, 1985, p.194)

Table 5.2 presents figures for the experiences of child sexual abuse recalled by 60 women I interviewed in a research project on sexual violence (Kelly, 1988). Of the 60 women, 89 per cent recalled at least one experience, which is recorded in this table.

Table 5.2: INCIDENCE OF SEXUAL ABUSE OF GIRLS

	Before age 12		Age 12–16		Total*	
	no.	%	no.	%	no.	%
Flashing	15	25	21	35	25	42
Pressure to have sex	–	–	23	38	23	38
Assault	12	20	14	23	21	35
Fondling/touching	13	22	7	12	16	27
Rape[1]	7	12	9	15	16	27

* Total figures are not the sum of the previous two columns, as some women recalled more than one incident.
[1] Includes incestuous rape.

What these figures reveal is that most girls and young women have some experience of sexual violence before they are 16. Childhood and adolescence are periods during which we are learning about ourselves and the culture of which we are a part. One of the things that girls and young women learn is that male sexuality is predatory and abusive.

The concept of a continuum enables us to reflect the range recorded in Table 5.2 and at the same time to explore experiences which are not recorded there, which women felt unsure how to define.

A number of women recalled, as I did too, how often play between boys and girls involves games which relate to sexuality. These are usually understood as innocent experimentation. For example, in our local street game of cowboys and Indians, girls were always the Indians. Our role was to be tied to the lamp-posts whilst the boys raced around us and eventually announced their victory by lifting up our skirts. This game was not 'innocent'; it reflected in microcosm two sets of power relations – we were the losers both as girls and as stand-ins for the indigenous peoples of North America. That victory was announced via our sexual humiliation was yet another lesson about male power and female vulnerability. In the first chapter of *Ice and Fire*, Andrea Dworkin recounts a similar story and explores some of the consequences of these initiations into patriarchal culture (Dworkin, 1987a). There is some interesting research to be done on how much 'play' between boys and girls is in fact a form of sexual harassment.

As girls move into womanhood, the harassment they experience becomes more explicit, although still difficult to name and challenge. It is particularly apparent during, and just following, puberty. A number of the women I interviewed recalled the pleasure adult males – relatives, acquaintances and strangers – took in commenting on their bodies and watching their subsequent embarrassment.

'I got to feel that I just couldn't go out without someone coming up to me and making a comment or something.'

'I remember at family things when my breasts had developed, uncles would make these comments about it, look you up and down – it was horrible, really embarrassing.'

These forms of ridicule and focusing upon young women's bodies are also common in relationships with peers, as the chapters in this book which address sexual harassment in schools demonstrate (see Chapters 6, 7, 8 and 10). Forms of sexual abuse are present in many of the routine encounters girls and young women have with men and boys, including their fathers.

Not all fathers sexually abuse their daughters, but many of the women I interviewed (who did not define their experiences as incest) felt that there were tensions in the father/daughter relationship which hinged on the issues of sexuality and control:

> 'It wasn't incest, but I felt sexual undertones from him.'

> 'I don't say he had incestuous feelings . . . I think some of it was *overstrong* paternal feelings, but I do think there's a sexual undercurrent to that with a girl.'

> 'When I began to want to go out with friends, he became really controlling, wanting to know everything, questioning me all the time about who I was meeting, what we did . . . and he'd never be honest and say it was boys and sex that was the issue – but it was.'

Father/daughter incest is one end of a continuum of father/daughter relationships and, as Sarah Nelson points out,

> Incest is related to a general pattern of male sexual assaults like rape . . . Incest is also a product of the family structure: but the clue lies in normal family values, not deviant ones . . . Like wife beating, incest is likely to happen when traditional beliefs about the roles of husband, wife and daughter are taken to extremes: when family members are seen as the husband's property, and sex is among the services they are expected to provide. (Nelson, 1987, p. 6)

When we apply the concept of the continuum to sexual intercourse, it is immediately apparent that for young (and adult) women there is no clear-cut distinction between sex and rape, but a range of pressure, coercion and force. In a paper given at the Sexual Violence Against Women conference in 1980 three women explored the connections between sexual initiation and rape, drawing on Simone de Beauvoir's contention that the sexual initiation of young women 'always constitutes a kind of violation': virginity is 'taken':

> As far as sexual initiation goes I'd describe it as semi-rape. He was twice my weight, on top of me, forcing my legs apart. I was too shy/embarrassed to scream to the others downstairs.

> I finally gave in to him . . . after weeks of heavy pressure.

> The subject of Sexual Intercourse constantly arose. He wanted it. I didn't . . . The pressure got progressively heavier. I was threatened with termination of the friendship . . . So I gave in. (McNeill and rhodes, 1985, p.194)

So What Is 'Normal'?

These women's experiences and those of the majority of the women I interviewed challenge the liberal view that sexuality (read heterosexuality) is a negotiation and exchange between two equal individuals. This representation fails to take account of the structured inequality that exists between men and women; it abstracts individual relationships from the cultural context in which they take place. A central feature of gender inequality is the way male sexuality is currently constructed in many cultures, embodying notions of conquest and dominance. It is this context, and women's experiences of heterosexuality, that have led some feminists to ask whether heterosexual sex can be currently seen as a 'choice' for women (Dworkin, 1987b; Rich, 1980). The fact that in private and in public, at work, at home, in the street, girls and women encounter harassment, abuse and violence means that our daily lives are structured around managing our environment and relationships with men.

> Women, in fact, are specialists in devising ways to minimise their exposure to the possibility of male violence . . . Specialists in survival through avoidance strategies women *know* what it means to be vulnerable to sexual and/or physical male intimidation or violence. (Stanko, 1985, p.1)

153

One of the shifts in feminist theory and practice in the 1980s has been a move from focusing only on victimisation to a recognition of women's strength in survival. Survival in feminist analysis is not understood in relation to concepts like 'return to normal', since sexual violence is itself part of patriarchal normality. Instead, survival involves women finding a meaning and explanation for their experience, being able to take control of their lives and make choices which are not determined by the impact of sexual violence (Kelly, 1988).

Twenty years of activism and reflection have produced a complex analysis of the extent and breadth of violence and abuse in the lives of girls and women. The documentation of our experience has revealed that 'normal' heterosexuality is frequently and repeatedly abusive, and that the abuse is systematically directed by men and boys at women and girls. The 'naturalness' of the heterosexual family has been called into question, not least because it is within so-called intimate relationships that girls and women are most at risk of experiencing sexual violence. Yet in both Britain and the US this knowledge is being suppressed and denied as respective governments seek to promote 'traditional family values', refusing to acknowledge that in doing so they are promoting child sexual abuse, domestic violence and rape.

References

Barry, Kathleen, *Female Sexual Slavery*, Prentice Hall, New Jersey, 1979.

Bell, Patricia, and Macleod, Jan, 'Bridging the gap: Glasgow Women's Support Project', *Feminist Review* 28: *Family Secrets: Child Sexual Abuse*, 136-43, Spring 1988.

Binney, Val, Harkell, Gina and Nixon, Judy, *Leaving Violent Men*, WAFE, London, 1981.

Blackstone, William, *Commentaries on the Laws of England*, London, 1789.

Bowen, Romi and Manning, Bernadette, Interview on ten years of London Rape Crisis, *Trouble and Strife* 10, 49-56, 1987.

Brownmiller, Susan, *Against Our Will: Men, Women and Rape*,

Secker & Warburg, London, 1975.

Cameron, Deborah and Fraser, Liz, *The Lust to Kill*, Polity Press, Cambridge, 1987.

Connell, Noreen and Wilson, Cassandra, *Rape: the First Sourcebook for Women*, Plume Books, New York, 1974.

Dobash, Rebecca and Russell, *Violence Against Wives: A Case Against the Patriarchy*, Free Press, New York, 1979.

Dworkin, Andrea, *Pornography: Men Possessing Women*, The Women's Press, London, 1981.

Ice and Fire, Secker & Warburg, London, 1987(a).

Intercourse, Arrow Books, London, 1987(b).

Griffin, Susan, 'Rape – the all American crime', *Ramparts* 10(3), 26-35, 1971.

Hall, Ruth, *Ask Any Woman*, Falling Wall Press, Bristol, 1985.

Hanmer, Jalna, 'Male violence and the social control of women', in *Power and the State*, G. Littlejohn et al. (eds), Croom Helm, London, 1978.

Hanmer, Jalna and Saunders, Sheila, *Well-Founded Fear*, Hutchinson, London, 1984.

Hey, Valerie, *Patriarchy and Pub Culture*, Tavistock, London, 1986.

Kappeler, Susanne, *The Pornography of Representation*, Polity Press, Cambridge, 1986.

Kelly, Liz, *Surviving Sexual Violence*, Polity Press, Cambridge, 1988.

'The professionalization of rape', *ROW Bulletin* Spring 1989.

Koedt, Anne, Levine, Ellen and Rapone, Anita (eds), *Radical Feminism*, Quadrangle Books, New York, 1973.

MacKinnon, Catharine, 'Feminism, Marxism, method and the state: an agenda for theory', *Signs* 7(3), 515-44, 1982(a).

'Violence against women – a perspective', *Aegis* 33, 51-7, 1982(b).

Feminism Unmodified: Discourses on Life and Law, Harvard University Press, Cambridge, Mass., 1987.

McNeill, Sandra and rhodes, dusty, *Women Against Violence Against Women*, Onlywomen Press, London, 1985.

Millett, Kate, *Sexual Politics*, Doubleday, New York, 1970.

Nelson, Sarah (revised edn) *Incest: Fact and Myth*, Stramullion Press, Edinburgh, 1987.

NWAF (National Women's Aid Federation), *Battered Women*

Need Refuges, NWAF, London, 1975.

Pizzey, Erin, *Scream Quietly or the Neighbours Will Hear*, Penguin, London, 1974.

Ramazanoglu, Carol, 'Sex and violence in academic life or you can keep a good woman down', in *Women, Violence and Social Control*, Jalna Hanmer and Mary Maynard (eds), Macmillan, London, 1987.

Rich, Adrienne, 'Compulsory heterosexuality and lesbian existence', *Signs* 5(4), 631-60, 1980.

Segal, Lynne, *Is the Future Female? Troubled Thoughts on Contemporary Feminism*, Virago, London, 1987.

Rush, Florence, 'The great Freudian cover-up', *Trouble and Strife* 4, 29-37, 1984.

The Best Kept Secret: Sexual Abuse of Children, McGraw-Hill, New York, 1980.

Stanko, Elizabeth, *Intimate Intrusions: Women's Experiences of Male Violence*, Routledge & Kegan Paul, London, 1985.

Sutton, Jo, Interview on early years of refuge movement in Britain, *Trouble and Strife* 4, 55-60, 1984.

6 Sexual Violence and Mixed Schools

Pat Mahony

A woman according to one group of fourth year boys is: 'scum that paints her face', 'something to kick when you are drunk', 'a thing to beat about the house', 'an ugly thing that increases population', 'a moaner', 'a slave', 'an object of ridicule', and 'a thing to use in clearing away the empty beer cans'. A man, on the other hand, is 'magnificent', 'brilliant', 'the master of women and the world', 'superior', 'stylish', 'a person who makes the world run', 'mature', 'inventive' and 'a maker of children'.

These aggressive statements stem from a poetry exercise organized by English teacher Mr Martyn Copus, of the Mons Hill School [coeducational], Dudley . . . Mr Copus was surprised and shaken by the violence of the responses. (TES, 1985)

In this chapter I shall focus on the 'sharper' end of the realities of mixed schooling. Chapter 1 has shown that a major way in which the backlash against first wave feminism was mounted was through the 'science' of sexology and Chapter 2 illustrates how the 'naturalness' of a form of heterosexuality in which males are dominant and females subordinate was carried through into the education system by campaigns which promoted a version of girls' schools as perverted, dangerous, unhealthy and unnatural. The use of sexuality in these campaigns was central. I shall try to show that in present, mostly coeducational times, sexuality is still very much an issue albeit one that is almost invisible. It is invisible perhaps because the 'progressive' ideal of coeducation has largely been achieved. It is invisible because what is happening in mixed schools is so 'normal' and 'natural' that it is barely remarkable. It is invisible because heterosexuality is rampant and that, in these gross political times, is good enough – no matter that the form of it celebrates a version of masculinity in which aggression, violence and contempt for women are central.

Previous research has shown that mixed secondary schools (ages 11-18) constitute one site amongst many where male sexual violence is learned and practised (see Jones, 1985; Mahony, 1985). It functions in school as it does elsewhere – in the social control of girls and women. What follows then is an attempt to describe and analyse some of the common forms of coercive male behaviour in schools using my more recent research material to tease out in more detail its effects, and to appraise some of the strategies which have been developed to tackle it.

In order to understand the way male sexual violence functions in school we first need to understand its connection with masculinity. Julian Wood (1982) establishes the connection very clearly:

> it was clear that learning to inhabit their form of masculinity invariably entailed, to a greater or lesser extent, learning to be sexist: being a bit of a lad and being contemptuous of women just went 'naturally' together. The boys saw all women as existing primarily in and through their physical bodies (face, legs, tits, etc.). There are precedents for this dissecting attitude just about everywhere.

> Boys . . . are encouraged to measure their masculinity via a woman-hating rapacious sexuality. This pressure to be a sort of Tarzan-cum-Ripper is sedimented into the history of how to be male. Learnt as a style it may harden into a cramped emotional range which cannot be softened. (Wood, 1982)

Here Wood is arguing that contempt for women is not the

pathological prerogative of the few but 'sedimented into the history of how to be male'. How does this happen? According to Leonard Schein (1977) the process is intrinsic to the socialisation of the human male:

> For men to become fully human, to liberate ourselves from forced sex roles and to really understand ourselves, one of the first things we must deal with is our hatred of women. We have to understand the origin of our misogyny and the full significance of the fact that we live in a patriarchal society. Patriarchy's foundation is the oppression of women. The cement of this foundation is the socialization of men to hate women. Looking at our development as males, it is easy to see how misogyny originates. As young children, our first attraction is to our mother, a woman. As we grow older, we learn to transfer our love from our mother to an identification with our father . . .
>
> As the male child develops, he knows his mother's love for him and her powerlessness. The father has the real power and is the avenue to success, excitement and the world . . . The boy must choose between continuing his identification and love for his mother . . . or transferring his identification to his father and becoming male identified . . .
>
> First we have to justify this betrayal of our mother (women). We also have to deal with our anger, resentment, frustration and ambivalence . . . The safest place to express this anger is toward our powerless mother. We rationalize her position of powerlessness, think she is in fact, inferior . . . As our consciousness develops its picture of women as inferior, we then objectify our dominant position and their subordination. Psychologically, we objectify the people we hate and consider our inferiors . . . A second situation which feeds on, deepens and solidifies our hatred of women develops a little later in time. We begin to realise our privileged position in society as males . . . Subconsciously we intuit that our privilege can only be maintained if women are 'kept in their place'

159

. . . A third factor contributing to our hatred of women is our jealousy of their powers of creation . . . Another result of the transference . . . is the double, ambivalent (good/bad) image of women. We have to find some way of continuing our loving feelings for our mother without losing our access to power. We perform this balancing act by putting our mother (and a select few other women) . . . on a pedestal . . . For the rest of the class/caste of women we create the whore/seductress myth. This degradation is expressed best in the often-heard male saying, 'Put a paper bag over her head and fuck her'.

As a psychological theory this may be inadequate: clearly there are questions to be raised about Schein's assumptions concerning the nature, universality or even necessity of the nuclear family in relation to the construction of misogyny. Questions could be asked too about what it means to say that boys 'choose' between mother and father (consider what would happen to a boy who 'chose' to identify with his mother). None the less, whatever the process, the piece does give a rather chilling account in some depth about what it means to become 'a real man'.

With this in mind let us now turn to the school to see how male control is exercised through violence or the threat of it and how girls and some schools deal with it.

Sexual Assault

It would be misleading to give the impression that sexual assault is a common feature of mixed secondary schools – it is not. None the less it does happen.

> *Female teacher*: 'I was asked to go and speak on male violence to a group of women teachers at —— school. One of the first year girls had been sexually assaulted by six first year boys. The senior management and the LEA were dragging their feet over dealing with it and some of the staff were really angry and upset that nothing was being done.'

A common way of 'dealing with it' seems to be to suspend

the boys for a limited period. Many teachers feel that this is an inadequate response.

> *Female teacher*: 'Three third year boys sexually assaulted a second year girl. She was in a terrible state, poor kid. They were suspended for a week and now they're back in school. They're regarded as heroes. I come down really hard on it if ever I hear it, but it's not good enough, the boys should have been removed permanently from the school – that kid has to live with that every day. I'd move her if I were the parents.'

Some parents do adopt this strategy and transfer their daughters to girls' schools, where these are available:

> *Female head of year*: 'A girl arrived in the second year here. She was in quite a bad way. Her mother was also upset and said she'd had a bad experience in her mixed school. It wasn't until the sixth form that the girl told me what had happened – that she'd been sexually assaulted by four third year boys. It took her a long time to get her confidence back and to this day she told me she avoids places where she might meet her old classmates.'

Beyond the traumatic effect on the victims of assault there is of course a wider message being transmitted to all pupils. This is that the sexual assault of girls by boys does not constitute a serious matter: in this respect the school does not merely reflect social values, but actively teaches them.

Values are also taught by the general visual impact of the school which can function as a legitimating backcloth to male power, constructed and maintained as it is (partly) through sexual violence.

Carol Jones (1985) has clearly described the violent sexual imagery in one school: the painting of a woman's dismembered body which passed for art, the graffiti with its woman-hating messages and the pornographic magazines passed between the boys – 'Propaganda by which men learn that it is acceptable to abuse women and girls'. The gutter press, itself a large contributor in the production of degrading and humiliating images of women, is everywhere in school. It is a

161

problem for girls:

> *Fourth year girl*: 'I remember being in the infants and me and a friend used to always go and lay out the newspaper when we had painting. The teacher thought we were being girly girls. What we were really doing was putting Page Three face down so the boys couldn't snigger over it'.
>
> *PM*: 'What do you think of it now?'
>
> *Girl*: 'I don't approve of it but the girls who do it choose to so it's up to them. It's probably money for them.'

Quite what level of choice can be imputed to young women living in a world which bombards them with objectified images of their sex is a matter for debate. Still, it is heartening to note that some years on she still disapproves.

Sexual Harassment

> *Female teacher*: 'The heavy teasing that goes on in corridors can make the whole mood of the day really wretched for girls. Seeing, when you turn into the corridor that you've got to get past that gang of boys and you know that you're not going to get through without teasing of a quite threatening kind.'
>
> *PM*: 'What kinds of things?'
>
> *Teacher*: 'Grabbing breasts and pinching bums though that would be dealt with very severely here but more generally taking things from girls and hiding them so that in the end, by the time she's got all her stuff back she's late for her lesson.'
>
> *PM*: 'Could she say why she's late?'
>
> *Teacher*: 'Well she could probably say why but she doesn't want to, she just wants to go to her lesson, she doesn't want all this all the time. The girls say this doesn't just happen once but very often it becomes a sort of pattern. With some girls it just really gets them down.'
>
> *PM*: 'Does this happen to boys?'
>
> *Teacher*: 'There is the boy who gets pushed around but it's much more the girls.'

When a boy gets 'pushed around' it is not, I would suggest,

in virtue of being a boy but because he is not the right sort of boy. Perhaps he is perceived as possessing qualities which run counter to dominant notions of masculinity. In this case he may also be subject to verbal abuse, 'poof', 'queer' and 'you've got AIDS'.

Far from finding support for his gentleness and sensitivity he may well be regarded by teachers as 'a wimp', 'a drip' and 'a born victim'. For him the lesson to be learnt is how to become a *real* man, dominant and not subordinate. For girls the message is different. It is true that they must learn their proper place but this is one of subordination, the 'done to' not 'the doers'.

The fetishisation and dissection of women's bodies into sexualised parts is a common feature of our lives as purveyed by the media. 'Heavy teasing of a quite threatening kind' (sexual harassment) functions as a reminder to girls and women of the intimate connection for men between sex and power. As part of a system of male violence which structures and maintains the subordination of women, it destroys girls' self-confidence by making them conscious of living an objectified physical existence.

Sexual harassment by way of verbal abuse similarly reminds girls of the difficulty of living life on their own terms based on their own definitions. It reminds them that primarily they are defined in sexual terms. But verbal harassment is not just a reflection of the power relation between men and women; it reconstitutes it by pressuring girls into 'going steady' with one boy, as a way of seeking protection from the abuse of the rest.

> *14-year-old girl*: 'There are a whole load of names that boys call girls – really hurtful names that are rude and embarrassing and could ruin your reputation.'
> *PM*: 'What sort of names?'
> *Girl*: 'I wouldn't like to repeat them – they're so disgusting – "slag" is the usual one and "dog" and "easy".'
> *PM*: 'What are those names saying?'
> *Girl*: 'That you sleep around – you know – lots of boys.'
> *PM*: 'So do girls get called "slag" if they sleep around?'

> *Girl*: 'Oh no. Well, yes, they do but you can get called slag if you won't go out with someone, or just if they don't like you.'
> *PM*: 'Who wouldn't get called a slag then?'
> *Girl*: 'Someone with a steady boyfriend where it's serious.'

Verbal abuse or the threat of it also affects some girls' participation in lessons:

> *16-year-old girl*: 'You get used to not saying much – just short answers where you're right or wrong – but I don't think girls really say what they think or say anything a bit risky.'
> *PM*: 'Why?'
> *Girl*: 'The boys start sniggering about you as a person – well, not as a person actually – not as a person at all, with feelings and that. They make personal comments, that's what I mean.'

This pattern of mixed sex talk is of course neither confined to nor created by schools. Nor is it necessary for male comments to contain explicit sexually abusive words for it to be effective in sabotaging women's contributions. Sometimes even so-called 'compliments' can function as sexual harassment:

> *Woman MP*: 'I was developing quite a complicated argument and suddenly one of my own male colleagues said "We could make music together". It just completely threw me: it was so embarrassing!'

When women take on servicing roles in mixed-sex conversation (supporting a man, making suggestions which help him state his view and confirming his position) then harmony prevails. When we challenge men then it is another story, as the 'debate' in parliament in March 1986 (when Clare Short tried to challenge the sex objectification of women in the press) demonstrates.[1] Boys in mixed schools both learn the techniques of domination and in practising them construct space in which *their* view of the world, *their* definitions, *their* needs and *their* interests become defined as *the* norm. Further, they learn the techniques of male domination despite their own differential access to power and privilege in a society rotten with class and race oppression. While some girls resist harassment by deliberately not entering the public space in which they become vulnerable or by entering it on male terms, there are others who refuse either of these options:

> *15-year-old girl*: 'I prefer just to get on with my work. There's a girl in our class who never shuts up. She says what she thinks. I think the boys quite admire her, but she gets a lot of teasing. I think she's right, really, even though I get irritated when she won't back down, but I couldn't do it.'

What is unusual about this view is that the girl thinks her classmate is 'right really'. Often girls seem to internalise the unacceptability of 'being outspoken', which is the phrase mostly used to describe girls who are as assertive as boys (whom one rarely hears mentioned in these terms). A girl who refuses to be silenced is then deemed to have 'asked for it' when she is harassed. A teacher recently described a first year girl in her class who was both strong and assertive as 'being full of herself', 'one of life's natural victims' who sought and enjoyed 'negative attention'. It may be no coincidence that the girl was Black. The comment by the next speaker suggests that for Black girls not only is there a struggle to retain dignity in the face of boys' behaviour, but also their assertiveness is perceived by teachers as aggression. For them the combination of sexual and racial oppression creates an even narrower tightrope.

> *16-year-old girl*: 'I won't take it from the boys. I'll always argue back, but I do have problems with the teachers always having a go about being loud, aggressive and unladylike.'
> *PM*: 'Why do you think that is?'
> *Girl*: 'I think it goes back to when my Mum and Dad were struggling. They taught us to look out for ourselves that

bit more and I just followed my older sisters. There's a tight bond between us all – me, my sisters and my Mum.'

PM: 'I meant why do the teachers have a go? Why . . . ?'

Girl: 'Racism. Right? The teachers in this school they're confused. In this lesson, right, they're saying women have got to be strong, but some of the Black girls in this class are strong so we're a nuisance to their work. Some teachers don't want girls to be strong and we're even more trouble to them.'

The extent of the racism and sexism inherent in this girl's educational experience is monumental. Whichever way one looks at it she cannot win. She receives continual sexist and racist messages about what a woman should be, based on a quasi-Victorian notion of the ideal white middle-class lady, and even in the lesson that challenges that version as sexist there is a failure to recognise that for her such a challenge is inappropriate: the result is racist.

This combination of racism and sexism in the education of Black girls makes it imperative that 'gender' issues are not treated from the perspective of white women alone (nor should 'race' issues be seen only from the viewpoint of Black men). So far only some of the effects of male violence on girls have been made explicit. There are others.

Girls service boys. They provide an endless supply of equipment (pens, rubbers, rulers), sort out arguments, shop, give food and do homework. Sometimes they are clear about why: 'everybody wants to have a good name, image and reputation'. It is hardly suprising that it should matter to girls what boys think of them. In a world where men have the power to name and to define, then girls individually and as a group are subject to these definitions. As individuals we have already seen how they tread a fine line to avoid the label 'slag'.

As a group women's role has been defined by men in terms of servicing them, and this message is deeply embedded in the curriculum: 'girls, irrespective of their class background, are more likely to learn that a woman's place and primary responsibilities lie in the home and family, not in the labour

166

market' (Deem, 1978).

It is a system which is backed by law: 'The judge said it was my natural duty to provide for the children and hers to look after them on a day to day basis' (male divorcee).

It is enshrined in family patterns: 'I was eight when my wee brother was born so I had to run the house and get up at six o'clock in the morning to get my dad's breakfast' (Dobash and Dobash, 1980); and violently enforced by some individual men:

> 'I did his breakfast in a hurry, and he complained about the grease on the plate and I probably told him I hadnae time this morning . . . I think he said he wasnae a pig, he couldnae eat that and he threw the plate at me. I think I picked up mine and threw mine at him . . . He couldn't bear it and he hit me . . . He grabbed my arm and pulled my hair . . . I didn't believe, I didn't know, that men could bloody well hit women like that, you know' (ibid.).

The common idea that violence is provoked resonates uncomfortably with what girls in school sometimes feel about 'having asked for it':

> 'I actually thought if I only learned to cook better or keep a cleaner house everything would be okay . . . It took me five years to get over the shame and embarrassment of being beaten. I figured there had to be something wrong with me' (ibid.).

Through male violence, whether sexual assault, sexual harassment, verbal abuse or simply the threat of these, boys ensure their dominance of space:

> *15-year-old girl*: 'If you want to have a chat with a friend you find a corner somewhere out of the way, otherwise they'll be on at you. Our teacher talked to us about how the boys dominate space. He suggested a girls' room, but we said no.'

Boys' dominance of space has been consistently documented over the last ten years yet redressing the balance seems to be no easy task. Some teachers have said that when girls reject the idea of space for girls they do so on the grounds of not wanting to be perceived as weak and unable to cope: 'They don't want to be seen as wallies' (male teacher).

Other teachers are indignant at the very idea:

Female teacher: 'Why should they have to go somewhere special in order to get any space at all? I think we should be putting our energies into them getting equal access to the space which already exists.'

A number of women staff and girls predict that any 'girls' only' space would: 'provoke a backlash of aggression from the boys'. Similarly, teachers who have tried to shift the curriculum away from the male point of view have encountered this 'backlash of aggression'. The next quote is a case in point seen through the eyes of a 12-year-old girl:

'We had a student last term, she was really nice, she saw a lot of things that weren't fair in our class but she didn't make you feel like it was your fault. She understood our problems. She knew a lot about things women have done, things you'd never dream of. She never got a chance though, some of the boys were awful to her. I got to hate her lessons because she couldn't control us. I think she should have expelled the boys, the rest of us wanted to work, her work was interesting. But she wasn't a good teacher.'

The dilemma in this case is not only the teacher's: on the one hand the girl appreciates her knowledge, the work she sets, her ability to recognise injustice and handle it sensitively; on the other hand the teacher cannot control some of the boys. The girl understands this as not being able to 'control us'. Where to place the responsibility for the problem shifts from the boys to the teacher, back to the boys and then rests finally with the teacher. It is worth noting that the girl's recommendation that the boys be expelled would result in something of a mass exodus (no doubt accompanied by accusations of sexism!).

At this point let us briefly consider the position of teachers in all this.

First, female staff, especially the younger ones, as well as girls, are constantly reminded by boys that their identity is primarily sexual not professional:

Male Teacher: 'One constantly sees harassment in corridors, from touching under the guise of pushing to verbal abuse and that happens with staff as well, mainly from fifth year boys. There are certainly no-go areas for women staff in corridors.'

PM: 'What happens?'

Teacher: 'Physical presence mostly, blocking a corridor, a look, often cat-calls, sexual jibes, comments on clothes. A lot of women staff have put up with it for years and not said anything. As new female staff have come in they've started to state the problem – they're not prepared to run the gauntlet all the time.'

Thus many female staff are in the same situation as girls, yet the authority structure of schools, the divisions between teacher and taught make it difficult for mutual support to be generated. It is not only the boys who sexually harass female staff, as a recent report indicates:

Some women teachers in Birmingham secondary schools have reported that good references have been offered to them if they 'co-operate' with sexual overtures made by their male superiors. Others say they have been followed home, received obscene telephone calls and had their cars and homes attacked if they have rejected sexual propositions.

The most common forms of harassment were suggestive looks at parts of the body, being the butt of sexual remarks and innuendo and being touched, brushed against, patted, pinched or grabbed. Most incidents amounted to sexual assault the union said.

Only sixteen percent of complainants said they had reported incidents. In thirty-nine per cent of these complaints no action was taken . . .

In only one case were the police called in: this concerned the petrol bombing of a teacher's house after she had rejected a sexual overture. Over a third of the women whose complaints resulted in no action said they were made to feel somehow responsible by the person to whom they had reported the incident. (*TES*, 1987)

The report cites 'pupils, colleagues, caretakers, workmen or parents' as the offenders, with proportions being 'roughly equally divided between pupils, staff and outside visitors'.

In the article, the National Association of Schoolmasters and Union of Women Teachers (the union which carried out the survey) is described as being 'greatly shocked' by the findings. While one benefit of this reaction is that an approach to the local education authority will be made in order to 'establish a new code of conduct', I am less than comfortable with the way that 'shock' functions with respect to sexual violence. This is because being shocked implies (1) that the information is new and (2) that it is unexpected. Yet women teachers have over a number of years been documenting experiences just such as these (Whitbread, 1980). As we have already seen, violence in the wider society is not new (Jeffreys, 1985) and it is certainly not unexpected (as anyone who follows the daily news knows). Of course we find stories of women, young or old, being brutally raped and murdered shocking and sickening, but the longer we continue to collude with the collective 'SHOCK!', the longer will each case stand in isolation from the rest as an individualised, unique event. An important feature of sexual violence as a system of oppression of women by men is that the instances are linked. One of the ways in which we are prevented from discovering the links is the manner in which the information is presented as unique isolated events. Another is the way the (male dominated) media occasionally talks of 'domestic violence', thereby masking the fact that the vast majority of it is by men towards women: much of the recent publicity about the sexual abuse of children has been presented as something which 'people' do to 'people'. Rarely has it been stated explicitly that what the statistics demonstrate is that practically all the abusers are men and the majority of the abused, young women.

It should by now come as no surprise to learn that male teachers as a group have amongst their ranks members who sexually harass girls.

12-year-old girl: 'Mr — came into our room when we were getting changed for the play. I think he must have had something to drink because he kept looking at us really funny.'
PM: 'How do you mean – funny?'
Girl: 'Staring at us – well, at our tops.'
PM: 'Did he say anything?'
Girl: 'Yes. I can't remember exactly – it was something about being well developed or developing – something about that.'

and

15-year-old girl: 'He's out of order that teacher, he gives me the shivers. He's always coming closer than necessary – well actually I don't mind that with other teachers. Mr H. is quite a physical person but it's different with him. That other pervert he makes me feel really weird.'

and

Female teacher: 'A girl came to me to talk about a male teacher who kept asking her out. She found it very difficult and dreaded coming to school – in fact she stayed out of school on some occasions so as to avoid him.'
PM: 'Did she tell anyone?'
Teacher: 'No not till he'd left – she was very unsure what the response would be and whether she'd get into trouble. She was still really upset about it three months later.'

In cases where girls agree to go out with male teachers perhaps the issue is a little more complicated: after all, the argument goes, they are young women and have the right to date whom they please. This female teacher does not agree:

'In one case the male teacher married the Sixth former. I think the Head had a few words with him about being a little diplomatic but it wasn't taken up, not in terms of him having a power relationship to her. You know, the girl would be under his influence because he was a teacher. You don't say no to teachers so it's going to be difficult to say no to men teachers who ask you out. It's part of the power structure of education and that male teacher abused his power – I think anyway.'

Whether or not female teachers go out with boy pupils seems to be a matter of some dispute:

Female teacher 1: 'I've never known it in twenty years of teaching.'
Female teacher 2: 'Oh I have. There was one I knew who went out with a sixth former.'
Female teacher 3: 'Yes I knew one but I think it is much rarer.'

Many feel that it is still wrong despite being different:

Female teacher 1: 'Well I still think it's wrong, teachers are in a position of authority over pupils, it's an abuse of that authority.'
Female teacher 2: 'Yes but it doesn't mean the same.'
PM: 'Why doesn't it?'
Female teacher 2: 'Well she can't force him to have sex with her or anything – but perhaps she could, you know, 'unless you do this I'll give you a low grade, I'm not sure.'
Female teacher 3: 'No but he could turn the tables – tell his mates and ruin her reputation. She'd be the slag not him. He would be viewed as having made the conquest not her so it's not the same.'

In other cases male teachers remind girls of their place as sex objects:

Female teacher: 'It's just sort of flirtatious behaviour, it's not like talking to girl students as individuals but more in terms of what they look like – treating them as sex objects which is much less tangible.'

She was clear that this affected all girls:

'Even when it hasn't got to the stage of harassment I think

there's a sort of familiarity which is sometimes upsetting (though possibly a bit flattering) to the girls who receive it. But also for the girls who don't it serves as a reminder that it doesn't matter how clever you are or how conscientious you are, if you don't happen to please the male eye, you won't get anything like as much attention as the others.'

The sexualisation of the relationship between teacher and taught is sometimes problematic for male teachers who have no desire to relate in this way to female pupils:

Male teacher: 'I'd been called to the staffroom door by a couple of Fifth year girls to sort something out. We were talking and this male member of staff came up and said "Oh God are you flirting with these girls again". I actually took him up because I was quite embarrassed by that. I said "That's out of order, first of all I'm not flirting, I'm sorting something out and your comment is flippant". He said "Well if you're not flirting with them then go away and I will". He didn't even take my point. I took it up with him later inside, I was quite livid with him because it embarrassed the girls as well – it completely changed the relationship from adult to adult sorting something out, to being something entirely different.'
PM: 'Did he take the point later?'
Teacher: 'No, he just called me a stick in the mud, you know, everyone's getting too serious, that kind of stuff.'

Male teachers sometimes make a point of reminding girls of their role as servicers:

15-year-old girl: 'It was the end of the lesson and he said to me "Pick up that rubbish!" I said "What rubbish?" I lost me contact lenses see and I can't see a thing without 'em. Then do you know what he said? He said "That rubbish, you'd better get used to looking for it, it's good training for later."'
PM: 'What did you do?'
Girl: 'I said you're sexist and I walked out. Well it was the end of the lesson but in my head I walked out.'

When female staff complain about the behaviour of male teachers they are accused of over-reacting:

Female teacher: 'A supply teacher in school was reported by a group of girls for 'teaching' them about sex in their lessons. They went to the Head to complain about him – not that they objected to the subject matter, that was what was so unusual, normally they're riveted. They felt really uncomfortable with what he was up to. The Head found the worksheets he had prepared for the girls showing details of the heterosexual act. He used these in all the lessons he covered. When the Head found out she interviewed him and dismissed him from the school. She contacted an Inspector to complain and was told that she and the school had over-reacted. The supply teacher had said that the work that he'd been given to teach was boring so he had prepared his own. The Inspector seemed to accept this for he asked the English department (in whose lesson that worksheet had been found) what work they had left . . . as though it was their fault. Incredible! The Head of English and the Head tried to get the Inspector to take some action but he refused.'

Girls often find the intervention of teachers of both sexes unsupportive:

Recent school-leaver: 'I remember being in the fifth year and this creep kept touching me up – it was very subtle, really – he kept pretending to get help but he kept putting his arm round me and just happened to keep touching my boob. I told him to stop it but he wouldn't and in the end I got so annoyed I smacked him one. The teacher had a go at *me*. I couldn't have said what was going on, not in public and not to that teacher.'

Teachers can actively disrupt the strategies girls have developed to create learning space for themselves. The following conversation took place in a science laboratory where I was supervising a young student teacher:

Karen: "'Ere Miss are you a sexist?"

PM (playing for time): 'Em . . . what do you mean?'

Karen's friend: 'No Karen you mean the other one, not sexist, feminist.'

PM: 'Yes.'

Karen: 'Well tell her Miss, she keeps saying we're sexist because we won't work with the boys.'

PM: 'Why won't you?'

Karen: 'They keep messing up the experiment and we can't get a turn on the microscope. They think they're the only ones that can do it. Will you tell her?'

What was worrying about the subsequent conversation with the girls was their total opposition to 'sexism' ever having been put on the agenda in the mixed class. Their objections were twofold. First they were heartily sick of the way boys had appropriated the term 'sexist' and were using it at every available opportunity to get their own needs met. Second, they were angry at being constantly defined as 'the problem'. They felt criticised for being insufficiently assertive and for not being interested enough in technological subjects. No one 'had a go at the boys for being mouthy' and boys' attitudes to domestic subjects was clearly not an issue in the school. For these girls, 'equal opportunities' had made life more, not less, difficult, at least in the short term.

In challenging boys' behaviour some teachers consolidate girls' low status by insisting that boys sit next to them as punishment:

16-year-old girl: 'It used to drive me mad when a teacher moved a couple of lads to sit next to us. It's like a punishment – sit with the lasses if you can't behave. He said to one of them once "Perhaps she can persuade you to do some work" and I thought "Why should I".'

This of course is heresy, for unknowingly she challenges one of the major rationales of coeducation. As long ago as the 1920s it was being argued (falsely) that: 'advocates of co-education commonly maintained that boys become more courteous and chivalrous towards women when educated alongside girls' (Dyehouse, 1981).

Today a similar claim is made: 'The boys' natural inclinations to "push and shove and barge about" are curbed by their girl co-workers' (*TES*, 1984).

Apart from the fact that such behaviour is not 'natural' (Mahony, 1985), the claim that girls civilise boys (or that they could do if the behaviour is natural) is simply false, as becomes evident from the following report. Commenting on the success of the introduction of computers in school a school inspector said:

'Children get to school before eight in the morning and don't go home until the caretaker throws them out. It's marvellous . . . The ribs of the girls are bruised by the boys because they are being pushed out of the way in the rush.' (*TES*, 1983)

What Is To Be Done?

Male sexual violence not only has horrific effects on its victims but also pressures women into seeking one man as protection from the rest. The servicing that is then socially demanded as the 'female role' in turn increases the power and status of men. Women who reject this are viewed at the very least as 'difficult', 'nagging' or 'moany old bags' and at worst as being unfit to bring up their children (Rights of Women, 1986) or deserving of physical punishment.[2] Until the politics of male sexual violence are clearly understood we shall be in no position to support girls and female staff who are the main butt of it in mixed schools, or boys who fail to match up to dominant notions of masculinity.

How then shall we organise that support? What strategies can we develop to change the situation for girls in school?

In what follows I shall concentrate on mixed schools. From the picture presented so far it goes without saying that we should protest and campaign against any further closure of single-sex schools. Whether we agree with Mr Pekin, who said almost fifty years ago that the central purpose of coeducation was 'to ensure a right relationship between the sexes' (Pekin, 1939), rather depends on his definition of that 'right relationship'. What we know of the actual relationship is that it is one of male domination and female subordination. This is not to describe the entire female population in mixed schools as downtrodden, depressed doormats. Far from it. It is a testimony to their vitality, creativity and imagination that young women in school do find ways round and through their oppression: the culture of 'having a laugh' is a rich one!

This proposal does of course lay a responsibility on girls' schools to do rather more than most have done up until now in preparing girls to understand and challenge their oppression. Discussing male violence with older girls, listening carefully to their stated needs and being prepared to widen our view in the light of these would be progress for many girls' schools. It will, I think, turn out that they need different things: for some learning to 'stand their ground' may be a place to start; but for others like the Black girl quoted earlier, positive redefinition of existing strengths is urgent – this means tackling racism. In the end any extra provision of what girls might need (for example self defence classes) will be less effective if it is not accompanied by a radical rethink of what the school teaches day by day about what counts as being a (proper) woman and how it empowers them to meet their various situations, which differ according to race, class and sexuality.

But, the argument goes, if girls' schools are to be retained then so must boys' schools, and they are nothing short of 'Rambo' factories. This is not a view shared by this teacher:

Female teacher: 'I'd work in a boys' school any day rather than a mixed one. I've never seen such displays of macho behaviour in my life till I came here [a mixed school]. There's such contempt for women – even the girls have absorbed it. Women teachers have a bad time here. I really miss seeing the boys being open and sometimes even tender.'

Since there are few state single-sex schools left such preference may be hard to satisfy. What then can be done in mixed schools?

Female teacher: 'I think we mustn't lose sight of how

important it's been to share our awareness of sexual violence. Over the last few years the awareness between us that it happens in school has grown. We've had discussions at teachers' centres and conferences have been set up to discuss it, officially sponsored in the case of one LEA and women's groups have been formed in schools to talk about it. We've named the problem and it's accepted that it exists. One strategy is to continue to make a fuss about it and continue naming it.'

Awareness is perhaps not as high as she suggests, and this makes her proposal for continued discussion even more important:

Female teacher: 'You're joking, there's no awareness at all. They wouldn't know what you're on about – well they would but not as a problem. It's a joke. It happens but it's not discussed as a problem.'

Some teachers feel that one of the most successful strategies is to tackle the issue as a whole school staff:

Female teacher: 'Two of us went to a conference and we went back into school and a small group of us put it to the staff that there was a problem. Then a small group was set up to collect evidence. Everything was confidential and we put it in terms of girls' experiences. We presented our initial findings at a staff meeting and out of that a number of further initiatives were set up. You can get quite a long way by just describing in a general way, examples of bad practice.'

But a number of teachers are becoming impatient with what is, for them, retracing old ground:

Female teacher: 'I think we need another push now – there's no excuse these days for claiming ignorance, there's been plenty written about it. I think we need to really start discussing action, what we do as individuals, what demands to make of the unions and the LEAs. We've spent long enough naming the problem.'

Others do not agree: 'I don't think we have named the problem yet. What schools are concerned with is how many girls are doing science.' (Female teacher). Similarly:

> *Female teacher*: 'One of the problems is how Equal Opportunities is understood. Equal Opps in schools has basically meant achieving a balance between what girls and boys achieve in school. I don't accept that model, it's impossible, you can't do it outside of looking at the wider power structures. Once you get on to those questions of sexual harassment, sexual abuse, rape, pornography and all the rest of it you're talking about a much smaller group of women in schools taking up these questions and often facing a lot of flak within the school for dealing with that.'
> *PM*: 'What sort of flak?'
> *Teacher*: 'Oh you know, these are the feminists, the women's libbers mockery and joking over them as women. The male identity is called into question at that stage and they can't cope with it so they retaliate.'
> *PM*: 'Are there *no* supportive men?'
> *Teacher*: 'There might be but I've never worked with them. I've taught in mixed schools for twenty years and I can't honestly say I can think of one. Sorry to be so depressing!'

The implication so far seems to be that the work already carried out on sexual violence has been productive up to a point and clearly needs to be continued, but with heterosexism, racism and classism having a much higher profile. It is important that the politics of it becomes more openly discussed, not by a few individual women who will get 'flak' but by those in positions of power within unions and LEAs. Although the vast majority of these are men, some do claim to be committed to 'equal opportunities': we need to know what this means for them so that at least we shall be in a better position to make realistic judgments about the extent or limitations of future support.

One strategy suggested some time ago (Cornbleet and Sanders, 1982), the provision of girl-only space, is now more widely on the agenda for discussion. Whether or not girls reject it seems to depend on how it is put to them:

Female teacher: 'There was a lot of argument in the school about whether having a girls' room was sexist. In the end the suggestion was dropped. Quite a few of the girls said they wouldn't go in there though at the beginning they'd been quite keen, they'd been convinced by the "it's sexist" brigade (I'm ashamed to admit I was one of them) and others said it wasn't worth all the hassle. So we had a quiet room. There are never any girls in there, it's a really heavy male atmosphere and unbelievably noisy. Perhaps we should have another go – maybe there are other people like me who've changed their minds. Anyway if it's OK to have a boys' room (which is what it is), why not a girls' room?'

On the other hand:

Female teacher: 'Our head just went in and put a notice on the door saying "girls only". She said some of the girls had asked for it and since the rest of the recreational space in the school was dominated by boys she assumed that the staff would not object. Needless to say they didn't – not in public anyway.'
PM: 'Do the girls use it?'
Teacher: 'Oh yes – it's warm and comfortable and we've put posters up and things.'
PM: 'Have there been any objections since?'
Teacher: 'No and I don't feel entirely comfortable about that. Quite a lot of teachers have misunderstood the point – they think girls need to be quiet at the 'time of the month'. We've got the room but for the wrong reason!'

Between these two extremes is a procedure recommended by most teachers:

Female teacher: 'The request for girls' space came from the girls themselves out of the school council. We went about it very carefully – full consultation of staff and a lot of preparation in terms of talking it through in tutor groups. It's crucial that it's properly prepared for other-

180

wise the boys just harangue and some of the girls take the rise out of the girls who want to use it. The process of explanation and preparation is the key.'

Where single-sex groups have been proposed for particular subjects girls' response is also mixed and again seems to depend on how 'the problem' is defined:

Male teacher: 'Single-sex groups for science were suggested but our Head of Science (who is a man by the way) reckoned the girls didn't want it. Mind you I don't know how he put it to them.'
PM: 'Is he in favour of single-sex groups?'
Teacher: 'No I don't think so, he thinks he can tackle the problem in the normal classroom.'
PM: 'What does he think the problem is?'
Teacher: 'Girls' underachievement in science.'

But in another school:

Male teacher: 'Well the girls in this school didn't object, they are very enthusiastic. Next year we're running an all-girl electronics group.
PM: 'How did you put it to them?'
Teacher: 'The Head of Department (a man) saw the whole year group of girls and told them he was fed up with seeing their work sabotaged by the boys. He put it to them in terms of an experiment to monitor the difference in exam performance once the boys were removed.'

The difference between these two accounts would suggest that where girls are defined as needing something special in order to help them cope with or be as good as boys, they reject it (as anyone with a sense of dignity would); where the problem is defined as male behaviour, girls' response is positive.

A number of teachers were adamant about the necessity of working in single-sex groups when addressing issues of male violence:

Female teacher: 'You simply cannot deal with things like sexual harassment in mixed groups, it makes the boys even worse.'

PM: 'Can you see any answer to that?'

Teacher: 'Yes. Yes I can and that's doing it with the girls and making the girls strong. Where things have changed in this country it's because there have been strong women to actually fight sexism. They certainly haven't changed because men have got the arguments. I think we should learn that message in schools. Concentrating on their strengths is also very important – it's so easy to highlight all the problems. What we've got to do is develop that confidence in themselves to fight against these injustices.'

Another teacher also felt strongly that discussion of male violence should not be done in mixed groups:

Female teacher from girls' school: 'What came out in our discussion about how girls are treated by boys outside school was the actual level of harassment that they face daily. Every girl in the group could recount some incident that had happened fairly recently – whether walking past a gang of boys and being verbally abused sexually or whether being flashed at on a bus. I asked them if they could look at different schools in the area and spot where the boys came from – whether they could differentiate between different levels of harassment according to school. They found they could. Boys from some schools were much more male than others. What was interesting was that the boys from the schools where they certainly don't have an anti-sexist policy were much less of a threat. The girls felt much safer with them. But in schools which do have a policy they felt the boys were made worse because they were made more aware of the power they had. Far from taking it from the point of view intended, that the boys become aware of their power and try to change it, the girls felt the reverse was happening – it was consolidating their power.'

It may be timely at this point to consider explicitly issues of race and class ('explicitly' because the material already pre-sented is drawn from working-class, middle-class, Black and white girls and Black and white teachers). How many people, as you read about girls identifying the more sexist boys with particular schools, thought of predominantly working-class or Black boys? It is unlikely to be none, since this has been a constant theme in discussions about the dynamics of mixed schooling. But sexual violence is *not* the prerogative of working-class and Black men: for white middle-class people to suggest that it is (and it is always someone from this group who suggests it) reveals not only a set of deeply racist and classist attitudes but also an astounding ignorance of the facts. We may not know how many judges practise sexual violence or in what forms but we do know the extent to which they condone it and underestimate its effects. We may not be able to take a count of the number of Members of Parliament who read pornography but we do know that a large number of them object to attempts to censor it. Yet one could hardly claim that judges and MPs are predominantly working class or Black.

Perhaps it is just such prejudiced responses to discussions about sexual violence in schools that have led some (white) equal opportunities workers to the view that to raise the issue of sexual violence in the first place is classist and racist and therefore to be discouraged. In my view they are wrong. We do working-class and Black girls no favours by silence, since this invalidates their own experiences of male violence. The lie that *only* Black and working-class men are sexually violent cannot be traded off against another lie – that only white middle-class women are the victims. All women are ultimately vulnerable and all women feel the effects of sexual violence (which is why we try not to walk down unlit streets alone, late at night).[3]

On the other hand, says Anna J. Hearne, all men are implicated in sexual violence: 'Black men and white men rape Black women and white women . . . White women will not help us by condoning it albeit in the name of anti-racism' (Hearne, 1986); and:

> None of us will cure the hideous evil of rape by treating it as a racial crime out of our own misguided sense of race

and prejudice. None of us will cure or curb the evil of racism by belittling the evil of rape because of racial factors.

Neither Black, nor white males should have their male violence, inclusive of rape and violence against women, protected by white women or women of colour. (ibid.)

Once having established a girls'group, this teacher felt it important to have a wider understanding of the context of male violence:

Female teacher: 'One of the problems is that many teachers grew up in the sexual revolution and as feminists have pointed out, this rarely meant freedom for women, it was more about more freedom for men to exploit women. The girls are suffering the knock-on effects from that.'
PM: 'So what do you do with the girls?'
Teacher: 'Within the context of their rights and dignity as human beings we talk through some strategies they already use. Some of them tackle it through language because they feel that's where they have the confidence – they try to make the boys and men feel small. One strategy to develop with girls is to support their own judgements about what they don't like, help them work out why and then develop something they already feel powerful in.'
PM: 'Could you have done this in a mixed group?'
Teacher: 'Absolutely not. I wouldn't anyway – it's very important for girls to be able to tap into their strength as women rather than having their oppression reinforced which is what the boys would do. When we deal with sexual harassment we try and get the girls to be a little more confident so they can deal with it. It's very difficult actually; I can't deal with it so why expect a fifteen year old to?'

Meanwhile, a rather different approach is being tried with the boys:

Female teacher: 'What the younger boys need is other models of being men. I think it's counter-productive to confront male violence head on with them. My strategy is to go for the group of boys who are shiftable – try and get them feeling pride in being gentle, support the positive qualities. I ignore the rest and hope to isolate them as a small unacceptable group. I know I'm not changing the world but maybe the girls in the class will have a better time. I don't know if it's working though.'

She is not alone in this sentiment. The whole issue of challenging male violence is given such low priority in schools that very little work has gone into monitoring the effectiveness of what is tried.

An interesting recent development has been made in one school in south London. A teacher reports:

'We'd had an Equal Opportunities Working Party but that's preaching to the converted all the time. We felt we needed time when everybody had to be there so eventually we had a half-day conference where, in small groups we were presented with situations and asked what we would do. They were often real situations around sexism in general because we know we're all guilty of it. We were in single-sex groups and whatever the situation we had one men's group discuss it and one women's group. That was interesting because there weren't as many differences as you'd perhaps expect.

When we looked at the reports about two thirds said there should be something which we eventually called the 'Helpline' where girls and women staff could take any problems to be discussed. It's separate from the pastoral structures because some girls will not go to form tutors or heads of year, they just want to talk about something and they don't want any action taken. We decided that a small group of teachers, about eight of us, who were reasonably well known in the school with a fair representation of ages and subject areas should be introduced to them in a series of girls only year assemblies over a period of a week. Men teachers kept the boys in tutor groups and the idea was that they would explain what the Helpline was to the boys. We wanted to establish that we were not thinking that all boys are brutes and villains – maybe they could do with a Helpline – but our first responsibility was to the girls.

In the assemblies we said who we were and what we wanted to do and assured them, this is the important point, that whatever they said to us would be said in confidence. We said we would talk about whatever it was and might be able to help but we'd only take action if they agreed. We told them where they could find us and that they could come at any time. Then straight away we sat down in little groups before it froze and talked. We asked them 'Do you think this will be helpful to you?' or with the older girls 'Have there been any times in the past when you might have been glad of this?' We tried to distance it a bit and brought forward quite a few openings-up of various kinds, some quite serious. In every case we could have gone on longer. The distancing was quite important – older girls saying 'I remember when I was in the third year so and so happened' but third years talking about what had happened when they were in the first year. They tended to say 'but it's better now' which we didn't believe for a moment but it made it safe to talk about.'

PM: 'Has there been much response?'

Teacher: 'It's too early to say yet, we haven't monitored it yet as the staff group involved. We made a small poster to go in every classroom as a reminder that the Helpline was there and we need to check that they are still up.'

PM: 'How did the boys react?'

Teacher: 'Some of the more sensitive boys in my tutor group were a little bit touchy about it. They said 'This is sexist Miss'. They weren't very happy about it and they aren't the ones who are involved in the persecution of girls at all. I think they thought 'We're not the reason the girls need the Helpline and we could do with some help ourselves.'

Other teachers to whom I described the Helpline were

generally enthusiastic about the idea:

Female teacher: 'From the way you've described it I think it's a really good idea. The all girl assemblies must have helped to heighten awareness and given support to girls who have been suffering harassment for a long time.'

Within this general response some were concerned that the female staff in the school should not become dispirited:

Female teacher: 'I think it's a good idea and a credit to the women who've put all the work in. I think that maybe the response will be quite limited though. It still isn't part of the wider context of the school so the Helpline could become isolated as a one-off thing. If that happens, it isn't going to be enough to enable the girls to see their identity in a different way.'

Describing the Helpline to one teacher precipitated something of an explosion:

Female teacher: 'Oh God I'm so fed up with all this. Sorry that sounds really negative. Of course it's a good thing and the women in that school are probably slogging their guts out trying to do something. Yes of course it's good. It's just that it's always women who are seen as needing the help because we have the problems. But the problem is male behaviour and when is that going to be tackled? I don't mean by those women doing the Helpline but by society at large. I'm fed up with first aid responses. It's about time the authorities started looking at what's really involved in achieving equal opportunities. Yet again we're left dealing with the effects of the problem while its cause goes untackled. Actually I'm leaving teaching altogether over just this issue. I can't stand the hypocrisy any longer.'

To what extent her reason for leaving the profession is shared by other women teachers is not known but her question: 'The problem is male behaviour and when is that going to be tackled?' is one being asked by women throughout the education service, from advisers to probationary teachers.

Sexual violence does not occur only in schools, as we have seen. Girls come to school with a wide experience of it, though they may have been discouraged from understanding it in these terms. Indeed one of the powerful ways in which its politics are masked is the benign language used to describe it. For example a boy harassing a girl on the street is redescribed as 'showing a girl you like her' (Scene, 1985), and men's brutality to women is redescribed as 'domestic violence'.

But unless the politics of male sexual violence in particular and the politics of sexuality in general are understood, we shall be in no position to understand the realities of schooling or appreciate the current debates about the role of education in shaping sexuality, and hence the quality of life for tomorrow's women.

Notes

1. The Indecent Displays Bill (Newspapers) 1986 proposed 'To make illegal the display of partially naked women in sexually provocative poses in newspapers'. Annie McKlean has summarised some of the evidence used by Ms Short: 'She has received complaints from women whose husbands buy the newspapers with these photographs who object to their children seeing such images; similar complaints have been received from school teachers. Other women have written to her alleging that these photographs lead to an increased amount of sexual harassment at work. (An article in *Woman* magazine included the following extract from a reader's letter on this subject: "A 28-year-old divorced man grabbed my breast and said: 'Give us a feel, I want to see if you're as big as Sam Fox.'" (*Woman* 30 August 1986.) She also drew attention to the contradictory messages conveyed by such pictures, which are often next to stories of rape and child abuse. She referred also to the debate concerning the link between the "rising tide of sexual crime and Page 3", and said that though as yet unproven, the "mass circulation of such pictures so that they are widely seen by children must influence sexual attitudes and the climate

towards sexuality in our society . . . These pictures portray women as objects of lust to be sniggered over and grabbed at, and do not portray sex as something that is tender and private"' (Hansard, 12 March 1986).

She continues: 'Mr Robert Adley (Conservative MP for Christchurch) speaking in opposition to the bill on 12 March 1986, described Ms Short's speech in proposing the Bill as a titillating mixture of politics, prejudice and prurience" and described the Bill as "a very sexist measure" one which " . . . deserved the booby prize." Several Conservative MPs agreed to pick out their favourite "Page 3 Lovely" and appear alongside her in the *Sun*' (McKlean, 1987).

2. A young female teacher was beaten up by a group of boys from her school while shopping at the weekend in the town centre:

'As they were attacking me they kept calling me a fucking Lezzie. No one did anything. On Monday I went to the Head and told him and his first comment was 'well you are aren't you'. I couldn't believe it, he supports the Equal Opps working party. The boys are still in school. I'm trying to get another job; the comments in school are incessant. Actually I'm not a lesbian but I refuse to say that. Where would that leave women who are? It would still be OK to beat up lesbians.'

3. The claim that all women are ultimately vulnerable does not imply that we are all vulnerable in the same ways or to the same degree. Presumably the Queen is not as preoccupied with her safety when travelling home at night in a chauffeur-driven car, accompanied by her lady-in-waiting, as the barmaid who must catch the bus.

References

Cornbleet, A. and Sanders, S., *Designing Anti-Sexist Initiatives*, ILEA/EOC, London, 1982.

Coveney, L., et al., *The Sexuality Papers, Male Sexuality and the Social Control of Women*, Hutchinson, London, 1984.

Deem, R., *Women and Schooling*, Routledge & Kegan Paul, London, 1978.

Dobash, R.E., and Dobash, R., *Violence Against Wives*, Open Books, Wells, Somerset, 1980.

Dyehouse, C., *Girls Growing Up in Late Victorian and Edwardian England*, Routledge & Kegan Paul, London, 1981.

Hearne, A.J., 'Racism, rape and riots', *Trouble and Strife* 9, 1986.

Jeffreys, S., *The Spinster and Her Enemies*, Pandora Press, London, 1985.

Jones, C., 'Sexual tyranny in mixed schools', in '*Just a Bunch of Girls*', G. Weiner (ed.), Open University Press, Milton Keynes, 1985.

London Rape Crisis Centre, *Sexual Violence: the Reality for Women*, The Women's Press, London, 1984.

Mahony, P. *Schools for the Boys?*, Hutchinson, London, 1985.

McKlean, A., 'An Evaluation of the Arguments Pertaining to the Use of Censorship in Relation to Particular Forms of Representation of Women', unpublished paper, 1987.

Pekin, L.B., *Co-education*, Hogarth Press, London, 1939.

Rights of Women, *Lesbian Mothers Legal Handbook*, The Women's Press, London, 1986.

Scene, BBC 2-Schools Education Programme, *Sexual Harassment*, 1985.

Schein, L., 'All men are mysogynists', in *For Men Against Sexism*, J. Snodgrass (ed.), Times Change Press, Albion, USA, 1977.

TES, (*The Times Educational Supplement*) 'The micro fanatics', 4 November 1983.
   'Still puzzling over the sex equation', 17 February 1984.
   'Sexism in the fourth year', 19 September 1985.
   'Union shocked at sex harassment', 6 February 1987.

Whitbread, A., 'Female teachers are women first: sexual harassment at work', in *Learning to Lose, Sexism and Education*, The Women's Press, London, 1980.

Wood, J., 'Boys will be boys', *New Socialist* 5, 1982.

7 Asking the Wrong Question: Schools' Responses to the Sexual Abuse of Children

Carol Jones

Introduction

The daily tyranny of sexual violence against children has remained a largely silent issue within education. Yet those of us who teach or work with children and adolescents work – whether knowingly or unknowingly – with survivors of child sexual abuse daily.

In this chapter, drawing upon my experiences as both a classroom teacher and as a feminist who has counselled survivors and campaigned against child sexual abuse, I intend to show that the haphazard way in which schools respond to sexual abuse actually serves to silence girls, maintains commonly held notions of male sexual behaviour as acceptable, and ultimately promotes heterosexuality – either directly or indirectly.

In recording some of my own experiences, in providing an analysis of this experience within the context of male violence against women, and by making recommendations for other teachers and local authorities, I hope to alleviate the isolation of survivors and to provide support for other feminist teachers struggling with the often conflicting feelings of fear and responsibility

Incest and Sexual Abuse of Girls[1] – the Reality

Before considering the ways in which schools respond to

sexual abuse it is worth reminding ourselves of some of the truths.

> In the current climate of concern it has been rapidly forgotten that what made child sexual abuse a public issue was the courage of adult women survivors of sexual abuse who spoke out about their experiences, along with the pioneering support work of feminist organisations such as Rape Crisis Centres; Women's Aid and Incest Survivors Groups. (Feminist Coalition, 1988)

The last time the sexual abuse of girls aroused public concern was during the wave of feminism in Britain at the end of the nineteenth century, when women campaigned around many of the issues we are still debating today (for example, women doctors carrying out medical examinations, the importance of women police officers carrying out investigations and the need for refuges and 'safe houses' for girls; also see Chapter 1, 'Sexuality and Struggle').

As far back as the end of the nineteenth century, pioneers against the sexual abuse of girls recognised that this was an abuse of male power and that 'men of all classes are among the offenders, those of good education and of bad; those whose character has never been called into question, as well as those of no reputation' (NSPCC Occasional Paper VVIII, in Jeffreys, 1985).

The NSPCC also recommended that sexual assault might be remedied by teaching about incest and sexual abuse in schools (ibid., 1985). Second wave feminists have continued to campaign against the sexual violence directed at girls and women.

Between the 1960s and 1980s we set up Women's Aid refuges, rape crisis centres and, later, refuges for incest survivors. Second wave feminist theory has developed out of making sense of our own lives, beginning with the real lived experience of women and girls. We have come to realise that the sexual assault of girls includes any intrusive sexual act which makes a girl feel uncomfortable, ranging from exhibitionism and genital manipulation to rape, and that it is a gender-specific crime almost overwhelmingly committed by men and boys usually when in a position of trust and authority (Hamblin and Bowen, 1987; Nelson, 1987; London Rape Crisis Centre, 1984; *Feminist Review*, 1988).

Abusers may be fathers, stepfathers, uncles, grandfathers, lodgers, babysitters, teachers, family friends or house fathers of children in care, to list but a few. Sexual abuse also includes peer group and sibling abuse committed by any male. We also know that the sexual abuse of boys is a crime committed by men who are almost overwhelmingly heterosexual (MacLeod and Saraga, 1988).

The sexual abuse of children is part of a whole 'continuum' of violence against women and children perpetrated by men and boys (Kelly, 1987; see Chapter 5 'Our Issues, Our Analysis'). As with all forms of male violence, sexual assault remains a largely unreported crime, for many reasons. Girls may fear recriminations; they may not be believed; they may feel stigmatised if reporting sexual abuse and may well face the same harrowing 'guilty until proven innocent' treatment that women in general experience at the hands of men's legislature. Girls from Black and ethnic minority families as well as working-class families often experience specific difficulties in disclosure of sexual assault because of the racism and class structure of British society which often affects the way statutory agencies and the police respond to disclosure of abuse. Nevertheless, the state is coming to terms with the fact that the sexual abuse of children is rampant.

Feminists have used the figure – based on both American and British research – of '1 in 4' for some time:

> The few prevalence studies which have been conducted in the U.K. have produced varying findings, mainly due to differences in methodology. But what they have shown is that child sexual abuse is vastly more prevalent than was previously acknowledged and occurs right across the social spectrum – to children, predominately girls, regardless of class, race and regional differences. (Feminist Coalition, 1988)

Most sexual abuse goes undetected: men are usually rigorous about not physically scarring girls, who may also be threatened with death should they disclose the abuse.

Much of the reality of sexual violence against girls is only now beginning to be acknowledged by the state. But this has been relatively recent. Since the mid-1980s certain events have made 'child sexual abuse' a public issue. It is, I believe, thanks to the pioneering work of feminists, along with the apparent, sudden 'epidemic' of child sexual abuse that the issue is being discussed and disputed on the public stage.

A few years ago the mass media became awash with the issue, reporting the death of children whom, it was claimed, Social Services departments had failed to protect (the scape-goating of professionals has become popular). 'Child abuse' became a vague term which described what 'adults' did to 'children'. The issue became sensationalised; dubious 'statistics' were bandied around and 'Childline' was set up. By 1986 headlines such as 'Childline swamped by numbers of callers' (the *Guardian*, 12 December 1986) highlighted what survivors and feminists had known all along – that sexual abuse was at epidemic proportions and that there are simply insufficient resources to meet the demand.

Although many women and survivors had campaigned to bring the suffering of children into the open, we were fearful of how the state would actually respond. In some ways, we were right to feel fearful. It was almost as if the sexual abuse of children was a new phenomenon – accounts were reinter-preted in the media; 'experts' in the field (usually men) appeared on television discussing the (uncontrollable) sexual behaviour of certain 'adults' and describing 'symptoms' of 'victims'. It was never made clear that abuse is gender speci-fic or inclusive of peer group and sibling abuse.

A whole cottage industry developed, making anatomical dolls to be used by family therapists who subscribe to the 'dysfunctional family' orthodoxy. This orthodoxy, developed by certain influential family therapists, focuses on the family unit rather than particular individuals who may be abusers or have been abused.

In this approach, much is made of the notion that each

member of a family system influences and is influenced by everyone else . . . Thus incest is caused by, or is a consequence of, the family's dysfunction, not the abuser's abusive behaviour. (MacLeod and Saraga, 1988)

Family therapy, in working with all family members aims to maintain the family unit, each member being encouraged to take responsibility for the abuse. Many feminists have remained critical of this approach, which hides the abusing male behind the family; the standard misunderstanding that mothers 'collude' comes into play,[2] and it fails to accept that because men as a group inflict sexual abuse upon girls the issue must be about male power.

The most recent public dispute on sexual abuse has centred around the Cleveland crisis. It is beyond the scope of this chapter to document this crisis, which has been recorded and analysed elsewhere (see *New Statesman & Society*, 1 July 1988; *Feminist Review*, Spring 1988; *New Statesman & Society*, 31 July 1988; *Marxism Today*, August 1987) but it is worth noting that the state – appearing to be in crisis on this issue – has, through the mass media, generally come down on the side of 'parental rights' and the scapegoating of professionals (particularly women) in order to ignore the fact that the British (men) may well be 'a nation of child abusers'. Moreover, it has been inconceivable to some individuals (for example, Stuart Bell MP) that so many children could be being sexually abused.

So there have been enormous changes in the public awareness of child sexual abuse since I first became a teacher ten years ago. Each change has affected my experience and the experience of girls I have worked with; and at each point new issues for feminist teachers have been raised.

Incest and the Sexual Abuse of Girls – Dilemmas and Experiences as a Feminist Teacher
The 1970s

As a new teacher in the 1970s I knew little about the nature or scale of men's sexual violence against women and girls, which just goes to show how many of us must forget and invalidate our own experiences of such violence.

One of the myths that I had absorbed before becoming a teacher was that incest was 'a taboo in every society' and that as such it did not happen. Many women/survivors must have sat through innumerable 'sociology of the family' lectures in the 1970s in which 'incest as a taboo' was displayed at the front of the lecture hall and students made copious notes.

It is hardly surprising, then, that I was totally unprepared for the reality of working with survivors of sexual abuse in the classroom, for I was like 'The mother (grandmother, aunt, sister, friend) who does not see because she cannot see what she has been told does not happen' (Ward, 1984, p.5).

As a probationary teacher, school case conferences taught me that incest and sexual abuse does happen, but there are inconsistent and haphazard ways of dealing with the offence and, at best, patronising ways of working with survivors. I learnt that as a form teacher I could be called upon to attend case conferences; to be encouraged to perceive a young woman who had been sexually assaulted as 'a problem' (either her behaviour was 'too aggressive' or she was 'too withdrawn'; she was 'too precocious' or 'too immature'). When and if sexual assault was discussed it was only when the most extreme and always illegal abuse had come to light – incest in the family (father-daughter rape) rather than peer group/sibling abuse.

The fate of the survivor was always in the lap of the authorities and individual social services departments who, in 1979, appeared to have few clear guidelines on the issue: would the survivor be taken into care or would the father be removed?; what effect would the procedures have on the girls/women in the family? and so on. The girls themselves were rarely consulted about what they themselves might have wanted, despite the fact that they were of secondary school age.

Within the mixed school in which I worked there was no whole school discussion on the issue. Once I had completed my probationary year (and therefore felt more secure in my job) I started a young women's group after school. The group developed quite spontaneously out of discussions in subject lessons in which girls accused the boys of monopolising most of the space at school. Women's posters around my classroom enabled girls to start discussing 'women's issues'. The after-school group met regularly and became instrumental in future discussions amongst staff and pupils about sexual politics and power in the school.

At the same time I decided to research the sexual harassment of women and girls in schools by interviewing staff and students at the school. I was now in the process of reading, consciousness raising and researching around male violence against women. For the first time the male violence that I had experienced and which I saw all around me made sense: Women are not 'mad', 'to blame', 'victims' – but we were silenced. I began, with other women and girls, to make sense of the world as we experience it and to understand that any man or boy may be guilty of sexual violence. Furthermore, my research on sexual harassment in schools highlighted that mixed sex schools are, indeed, dangerous places for girls and women; that they serve to promote male domination and women's subordination and that when we 'fight back' we are severely punished (Jones, 1985). Pat Mahony has researched the effects of mixed sex schools on girls and has concluded that they are indeed 'Schools For The Boys' (Mahony, 1985 and Chapter 6, 'Sexual Violence and Mixed Schools'). Nevertheless, 'knowing' all this did not stop me from feeling immobilised with helplessness when some of the girls at the school confided in me that they were not only being sexually abused at school by boys or male teachers, but were also being sexually abused at home. I experienced then what I now know many teachers experience – the dilemma over confidentiality and disclosure.

Confidentiality and Disclosure

Women counselling survivors of male sexual violence have come to appreciate the importance of confidentiality for survivors. Counsellors have discovered that many girls and women have had their often painful experiences negated when disclosing and pressing for a conviction from the state

(London Rape Crisis Centre, 1984). Furthermore, the feelings of isolation, fear, anger, possibly self-disgust and mistrust need to be acknowledged sensitively and in a way that enables women and girls to regain the feeling of control, as male violence is actually about taking control away from women.

Confidentiality is not to be confused with failing 'to do' anything about the abuse itself. Were the state to respond to women by believing us, were it to be supportive and positive to women, confidentiality might not be such an important issue.

There is for women teachers however, a moral, professional dilemma if girls confide in us – as there was for me when I was a teacher. We want the abuse to stop; we want to best support the survivor; but the very state which demands that we disclose to those in authority fails to protect survivors once they disclose, indeed disclosure may well harm survivors if the girl is not believed/the perpetrator not removed.

At that time in my teaching career I could find no professional guidance. Senior teachers and head teachers appeared to be unclear as to what to do themselves. More experienced teachers had decided from bitter experience to support girls by referring them to confidential feminist counselling agencies which provided then – as now – the only reliable service available to women who needed to talk to someone who would always believe them.

My response to disclosure then was to believe the girl, disclose if she wanted me to and maintain confidentiality (yet advise her to contact a counselling service) should she ask me to. A small group of girls and myself then worked through the official procedure for reporting sexual abuse, and ways of supporting each other, all in order to help them make decisions about what they wanted to do. Some of them contacted the Incest Survivors campaign or the local rape crisis centre. They became a self-help group for each other, staying with each other when afraid.

Young women were also disclosing to other women teachers. Some girls were being sexually assaulted by their brothers or brothers' friends, many of whom we taught. This fact was openly displayed when boys wandered into classrooms to tease their friends' sisters because the brothers had been bragging to their friends that they'd had sex with their sisters.

Some girls resisted by shouting back. Others remained silent.

Three years later I left and started working with unemployed school leavers, all of whom were young women. Again, incest and sexual abuse was everywhere. As I visited young women who'd recently left school I found that not only were many of them rapidly absorbed back into the domestic exploitation of the home – doing all the housework, looking after younger sisters and brothers or having babies themselves – they were also lumbered with unemployed fathers and brothers who now had access to them during the day.

My aim, which was to set up a group made up of the young women I met, was sabotaged by fathers who wouldn't let their daughters out, who punished them when they developed their own self-confidence and who watched me constantly when I visited the young women. From all of this I learnt several things: firstly, that male violence against girls affected, in some way, every girl I came into contact with. Secondly, that schools were reluctant to intervene in peer and sibling abuse (indeed, aggressive, socially ascribed 'macho' behaviour was actually encouraged as 'normal') and that the very institutions which insisted on disclosure often failed to provide an adequate response to that disclosure.

There was far more abuse than the institutions themselves were prepared to recognise. Girls generally remained totally silent, fearing for their lives should they disclose. Above all, I learnt that men/boys will do anything to stop women/girls having access to each other through separatist provision; for example, fathers, and boys in mixed schools and youth clubs can become extremely hostile – indeed, violent – if separate 'girls' nights' are set up (ILEA Youth

Service, 1984).

The 1980s

My return to teaching from youth work in the mid-1980s coincided with the increase in public discussion of sexual abuse in the mass media referred to earlier in this chapter.

Given that child sexual abuse was now being discussed and children were being encouraged to disclose, indeed reassured that they would be listened to, more girls at the school I then worked in appeared to be coming forward to disclose to teachers. Yet the procedures for dealing with disclosure had hardly changed. Legislation surrounding sexual violence remained the same, making disclosure, prosecution and conviction a nightmare of hurdles for some young women and girls.

One education authority, anticipating the 'epidemic' of disclosure following initial media coverage of child sexual abuse in the mid-1980s, issued a circular to schools advising teachers to report immediately to head teachers any disclosure of 'child abuse'. It demanded that teachers record all incidents, which would then be sent to the authority's newly created 'EWS Designated Officer for Child Abuse'. That was in 1984; those posts have yet to be created. An increase in disclosures, yet very little change in the state's response, created further new difficulties for teachers, myself included. I think the following case study highlights some of these difficulties.

A Case Study

Some years ago now in a school in Outer London a young woman of 14 (who shall be called Sharon to preserve anonymity) and whom I taught, confided in me at the end of a lesson that her father had 'been sexually abusing' her. The consequences of her previous disclosure to her head of year and educational social worker who had reported to social services was that she was being held responsible for her mother's subsequent illness. A social worker who had visited Sharon's home found (not surprisingly) that the father – a

200

middle-class professional – denied all allegations. A friend of the family's – also a professional man – was, quite unwittingly, informed by one of the professionals involved. Pressure was put on Sharon by the two men (father and friend) to retract the allegations.

Sharon became terrified. Not only was she now mistreated by her parents who also argued with each other about the 'truth' of the allegations; not only was her mother ill as a result of the stress, but also Sharon was unable to trust anyone in authority to actually 'do' anything to help her. She wanted me to help her by accompanying her to her head of year, and appealing again for help. The year head was extremely supportive, believed Sharon (and said so), and confessed, herself, to feeling frustrated at the support agencies' failure to intervene.

Despite being allocated a social worker who was meant to counsel Sharon in confidence (but who in fact betrayed this confidence to Sharon's parents) nothing more was done. Sharon's life became more and more intolerable. Her only support was from the confidential counselling service that she had decided to telephone who gave her the opportunity to talk about her feelings and who helped her to decide what she might want to do. None of the case conferences called to hear Sharon's 'case' could agree on what needed to be done. After all, Sharon was a model student who had no 'behaviour problems', who was 'academic' and who was, apparently, coping. There was, apparently, insufficient evidence to intervene. The father was presented as a 'victim' of Sharon's allegations.

Sharon became increasingly withdrawn and afraid. As a teacher I could only support her by listening if she wanted to talk, telling her that I believed her and that she was not responsible for her mother's illness and by officially presenting her 'case'. But that could never have been enough.

Social services failed to visit for three months, ready to 'drop the case'. Sharon ran away and contacted me via the school some time later to inform me that she was safe and in the care of a different social services department. Her younger sister (who was in my form), who was clearly distressed and missing Sharon, cried to me one day that she thought her sister had run away because of what their father was doing to her. They had shared a bedroom and the younger sister had been woken up by the father's night-time visits. The young sister claimed that she herself had not been abused by the father, although I often wondered whether she would ever have trusted anyone to respond effectively even if she had been abused. After all, the state had failed her sister. Two other survivors who had similar experiences following disclosure ran away some time later.

One wonders whether girls were learning from each other's experiences that if they ran away at least they might be taken into care, which was preferable for these girls anyway (though not for all) to not being believed and being left to cope.

Yet again I had learned several things from these young women's experiences. Firstly, that any girl who discloses may not be believed, particularly if she does not display 'anti-social' behaviour and if the abuser is a respectable professional. Secondly, that there was little cohesive inter-agency cooperation or trust between the agencies concerned. Thirdly, that men bond in order to maintain a conspiracy of silence around sexual violence. Furthermore, because Sharon had not actually been raped and because there was insufficient 'evidence' it was, apparently, difficult for agencies to intervene in the family. So there is a definite problem in what constitutes serious and non-serious abuse. We can only ask what children are expected to tolerate before the state takes their experiences seriously. I myself was thrown into experiencing the ongoing feelings of conflict about confidentiality and disclosure. Apparently disclosure was not always effective, indeed quite the reverse, yet I had new thoughts about teacher–pupil confidentiality.

Being a classroom teacher in Britain in the 1980s becomes more difficult for any teacher. Fewer resources mean larger classes with less non-contact (with students) teaching time for preparation, marking, counselling and all the other tasks that teachers have to take on above their direct teaching time. In addition, an increase in administrative tasks fostered by the various new initiatives and public examination changes means that time for face to face contact is minimal.

Disclosure may take place after a lesson to any teacher – after all students seek out, as we all do, those individuals whom they trust to listen to them and take their feelings seriously. How, then, does the individual teacher create a calm and trusting atmosphere on her way to the next lesson when a girl requires at least half an hour's counselling? How may the teacher facilitate the young woman using a telephone for confidential counselling when the only telephones in a school are in the offices of senior teachers (and she has no privacy at home)? Even if the survivor tries to ring a counselling organisation it's quite likely that the line will be permanently engaged due to the general increase in calls to women's organisations on sexual assault. Moreover, it may not be entirely appropriate for girls to receive counselling by teachers, for good counselling means enabling girls to talk about painful and complicated feelings within a trusting relationship. Teachers may feel in a dilemma over their conflicting roles by acting, for example, both as a confidante and yet possibly as an enforcer of discipline (or certainly being in an overly powerful position) at the same time.

The State's Response to the 'Epidemic' of Child Sexual Abuse and its Effects on Schools

The results of the most recent public enquiry into the Cleveland dispute will undoubtedly bring about changes in family law and have repercussions for schools. The immediate response of professional organisations to the now public recognition of the existence, at least, of child sexual abuse has been the demand for more resources. Whilst accepting that this is important, I think it is also important to ask what form these resources would take, who would control them and what perspective on sexual abuse is to be adopted.

For example, it has become fashionable amongst some education authorities to focus on prevention work in which children are taught to 'say no'. Whilst accepting the advantages of teaching children to respect their own and others' bodies and to understand that they do not have to do anything that makes them feel uncomfortable, it really is not enough to focus on making children, rather than abusers, responsible for their actions. Survivors' own testimonies inform us that saying 'no' is not enough to stop men choosing to abuse their power.

The most recent DES circular (No. 4/88; 6 July 1988), entitled 'Working together for the protection of children from abuse: procedures within the Education Service', to be sent to all schools, acknowledges the increasing concern about child abuse specifically in relation to the report of the enquiry into child abuse in Cleveland. It emphasises the importance of and provides guidance on cooperation between the agencies concerned with children's protection. It acknowledges that 'it is rare for children to make false accusations of sexual abuse . . . this should be taken seriously and deemed to merit investigation' (p.2).

The DES circular makes a number of recommendations:

1. Senior teachers should be appointed in each school to coordinate the school's response to sexual abuse. (This will, I hope, prompt schools to engage in entire staff discussion and discussion with governors to develop a whole school policy; see O'Hara, 1988, for further suggestions).

2. It accepts that 'it is regrettably the case that some teachers and other members of school staff have in the past been found to have committed child abuse' (p.2; still ungendered).

3. Referring to the Education (No. 2) Act 1986, which increases school governors' responsibilities in devising school policy, it recommends that governors consider ways in which the school curriculum may include education about sexual abuse.

4. Adult students who may have been abused as children and who attend further and higher education institutions should, according to the circular, be entitled to receive guidance on local sources of help and counselling.

5. Teacher training courses should include preparation on

the awareness and recognition of child abuse; and in-service training for teachers coordination/teaching about child abuse is to be implemented.

Despite the fact that the DHSS Child Abuse Training Initiative attached to the circular lists under 'in depth treatment training' Great Ormond Street Children's Hospital, and training to be conducted by 'key figures' such as Dr Arnon Bentovim of the family therapy lobby which feminists/survivors object to, the circular is helpful in (a) recognising the existence – indeed the seriousness – of child sexual abuse and (b) recommending inter-agency cooperation. Inter-agency cooperation may prove difficult as agencies often have different approaches to sexual abuse, but in my view a whole borough/area policy which is clear to all professions and potentially more effective for survivors is preferable to the current often haphazard response from statutory agencies. This inter-agency policy on sexual abuse is already successfully under way in Islington and Haringey in London (Boushel and Noakes, 1988), being the product of discussions, initiated by the social services department, between all of the statutory agencies. Both these authorities have clearly been influenced by feminist work and theory of sexual abuse in devising policy. However, inter-agency co-operation can prove difficult, so we need to discuss across agencies our differences as well as similarities in working together. For example, it may not be appropriate to invite the police into schools to talk to children about how to 'avoid strangers' (1) when most children are sexually abused by males already known to them (London Rape Crisis Centre, 1984); (2) if that agency fails to take children's/women's allegations of sexual violence seriously or fails to provide supportive conditions for medical examinations to be carried out by women officers; (3) until that agency, indeed all agencies, adopt an anti-racist perspective in dealing with sexual assault. Hence, the state's response to the increased public awareness of child sexual abuse is varied.

We have already seen how the results of the Cleveland enquiry have led to recommendations on how education authorities should respond. It needs to be acknowledged that individual social workers and some social services departments (such as Islington and Haringey) are responding to the disturbing reality of children's lives despite diminishing resources, but there is no agreed national policy on effecting responses to disclosure. I am aware that there can be no 'right' procedure for everyone and of course there are children whose very lives are endangered by sexual assault and rape. It may be possible to help a young woman of 15 to make her own decision about what it is best for her to do, but it is not the same for a six-year-old. We must not stand on the sidelines of indecision whilst children are being routinely tortured. But this really illustrates the complexities of the discussions that we must engage in. There can be no neat, easy solutions to the sexual assault of girls of different ages and in different situations. Feminists/survivors of child sexual abuse have a role to play in helping agencies to devise policy, whether as individuals in the field, or as voluntary organisations. After all, it has been the testimony and experience of women and girls that has informed our work and forced us to set up voluntary organisations to support and campaign with other survivors of sexual abuse.

However, in my opinion, the state through its institutions (one of which is school), is merely responding to an apparent epidemic rather than asking what causes it. Were the state to ask, it would need to turn the whole issue of sexual violence on its head by asking the awkward question of why men/boys do it. Once we start asking this we are forced to consider the nature of male sexuality and power and ultimately of heterosexuality itself.

The Cause of the 'Epidemic': a Theoretical Understanding and the Place of Schooling Within It

Given that the sexual abuse of girls is a crime committed almost overwhelmingly by men and boys, we cannot fail to make connections between male violence and male sexual behaviour as it is socially constructed and reconstituted by male supremacy.[3]

The full extent of men's sexual behaviour has been documented and analysed elsewhere (Coveney et al., 1984) but it is worth noting here that men's sexual domination and women's subordination is most successfully reinforced within the political institution of heterosexuality. So vital is heterosexuality to the maintenance of men's power to regulate women's behaviour that it has, at different periods during this century, actively been promoted – from the sex reform movement in the 1920s (Jeffreys, 1983) and the rise of the science of sexology (Jackson, 1983; and see Chapter 1, 'Sexuality and Struggle') to the growth of the sex industry, including child pornography, from the 1960s onwards (Coveney et al., 1984).

This understanding is of value when considering the sexual abuse of girls. For it is in the heterosexual family that men have easy and legitimised access to women and girls. Furthermore, it is in the family that we first learn that we are expected to please men and boys. It is part of our normal training to seek male approval, to learn to be flattered by men's attention. Within the family men bond with each other, encourage boys to develop a machismo befitting those who come to view women as acquisitions to sexually service them. Every state institution defends this as proper and even 'natural'. Indeed, some have argued that 'incest is an everyday event in the normal family' (Leeds Revolutionary Feminist Group, 1982). Whilst the mass media pumps out the cute, sexy, sweet, little girl stereotype, at the same time, it is capable of blaming any girl who is assaulted as being 'sexually provocative'.

Education and Schooling

Education has a major part to play in teaching and reinforcing notions of masculinity and femininity and in promoting the idea that heterosexuality is right, indeed 'natural'.

Chapter 1 has shown the lengths to which sexologists and others went at the beginning of the century to construct a form of heterosexuality which 'institutionalises and sexualises male power and female submission, thus harnessing women's bodies to the service of men's needs and placing them under male control' (Jackson, Chapter 1). We have also discovered that those same individuals believed in 'coeducation' as a way of 'training the sexual emotions' towards heterosexuality and that advocates of coeducation in the inter-war years believed that 'mixed schools would make girls more adjusted to the demands of heterosexuality' (Faraday, Chapter 2). It has been illustrated that (mixed) education in training for male domination and female subordination has been fairly successful, always at the expense of girls' safety (see Mahony, Chapter 6).

Despite anti-sexist policies developed by certain education authorities in the 1980s, and initiated by second wave feminists since the early 1970s, very little work has focused on successfully challenging male sexual behaviour. Rather, policies tend to have emphasised equal opportunities by which girls are taught merely to become proficient in adopting male values. Were authorities to adopt an anti-sexist perspective, notions of masculinity central to the male domination of women would be critically reviewed. Indeed, heterosexuality itself might well be threatened – once masculine behaviour is exposed for what it actually does to women and girls. This should be the starting point for looking at the sexual abuse of girls as part of the whole continuum of male violence against women.

In failing to address the uncomfortable issue of why men and boys do it and how they continue to 'get away with doing it', schools – through the overt and hidden curriculum – transmit the idea that male sexual behaviour is acceptable. As such, sexual violence perpetrated by male teachers and boys against girls remains largely unchallenged. Students as well as staff may internalise those values and anyone who resists is perceived as 'deviant'. Just as education authorities have been reluctant to understand male sexual violence within schools as an issue of sexual politics, so they have experienced difficulties in making sense of sexual violence outside of the school, including that within the family.

Despite education authority regulations that child sexual abuse must be treated seriously, reported immediately, authorities appear to have a naive faith in the state's ability to safeguard girls and women's lives. Should all cases of sexual abuse be reported, mixed sex schools would have queues of girls waiting to disclose sexual behaviour from men and boys which has actively been fostered as 'natural', 'healthy' behaviour. But that is not what the authorities understand by sexual abuse. Rather it is identified as something rare, unusual, only taken seriously if sufficient evidence of a particular form of sexual violence can be provided.

Myths, about incest in particular, implying that abuse is limited to certain groups or communities, although untrue, have the effect of creating a silence about the prevalence of men's sexual violations. Survivors themselves, in internalising these myths, may feel 'abnormal' and certainly isolated. So girls are trained to seek out the 'protection' of individual men. Boys, meanwhile, are encouraged to measure their masculinity by a woman-hating 'rapacious sexuality' (Wood, 1982). And the two sexes will, apparently, 'meet' in heterosexuality.

In training both sexes to hold an idealised view of the heterosexual family as normal, indeed 'safe', in having faith in the sanctity of fathers' rights and in holding the view that male sexual behaviour is acceptable, schools continue to promote heterosexuality. This is further enforced by schools' failure to challenge the oppression experienced by anyone who 'steps out' of the heterosexual line, i.e. young lesbians and gay men (Hackney Lesbians Stop The Clause Education Group, 1988). Indeed the Conservative Government's most recent legislation – Section 28 of the Local Government Act – as well as its direct (and unprecedented) intervention in the teaching of sex education in schools, which says that it must have 'due regard for moral considerations and the value of family life' (Section 46, Education (No. 2) Act 1986) is the action of a desperate government responding to mounting evidence that the family is indeed harmful to children and women, as well as to the feminist initiated campaigns around issues of sexuality. In this way we see the state in crisis.

It is hardly surprising then that schools' response to the sexual abuse of girls is to regard it as unusual, limited to certain groups and to have haphazard ways of dealing with it.

For they are failing to ask the right question. Or perhaps they cannot ask it.

The best and most courageous prevention work educationalists could engage in would be to (seriously) challenge male sexual behaviour, review the institution of heterosexuality, and enable girls to develop their own forms of resistance; to re-educate boys in preparing them for non-violent, caring ways of engaging in relationships and by posing alternatives to heterosexuality including lesbianism, homosexuality and celibacy.

This would mean a reassessment of the harmful effects of mixed schools and the benefits of single-sex schooling for girls. Instead we find ourselves responding within a framework set by the state which accepts the desirability – the promotion – of heterosexuality and enforces this through schooling.

Unless we ask the right questions and look at the cause of child sexual abuse, and from that draw up effective school policy, we will be failing to safeguard children's lives.

Recommendations on Working Against the Sexual Abuse of Girls in Education

What follows is a list of recommendations which have two objectives: to challenge male sexual behaviour through education (and thereby address the question of why men/boys abuse) and to suggest improvements for disclosure. Both working for and within the state has been combined with a feminist approach to addressing and changing male behaviour.

1. Recognition of the fact that child sexual abuse is an abuse of male power (and is, therefore, gender specific) over girls of all social classes, races and regions.

2. That girls disclosing abuse be believed.

3. (a) That whole inter-agency discussions begin on the nature of, effective response to, and eventual elimination of sexual abuse; (b) that feminist organisations that have been working around the issue for years be invited to participate in these discussions with the view to producing guidelines for everyone in contact with children.

4. That LEAs make recommendations to school governors in advising on anti-sexist and anti-racist policies to challenge male sexual behaviour.

5. That school governors, in consultation with staff and students, devise effective whole school policies for dealing with disclosure of abuse both within the family and at school.

6. (a) In line with the 1986 Education (No. 2) Act, that there should be teaching of a balanced perspective on sexuality, including a review of male sexual behaviour and alternatives to heterosexuality; this may best be facilitated in single-sex groups; (b) that sex education which encourages pupils to have 'due regard to moral considerations and the value of family life' (Section 46, 1986 Education (No. 2) Act) should enable schools to encourage a full evaluation of both the positive and negative aspects of the heterosexual family including domestic violence, and sexual violence against women and children.

7. (a) That in-service training for staff should include an assessment of male sexual behaviour; (b) that in-service training for women teachers on counselling survivors of sexual assault be set up.

8. That children disclosing abuse should be informed of all of the options open to them, and should be given emotional and practical support in making their own decisions about what to do next.

9. That each school be encouraged to employ an outside woman counsellor from a long established feminist organisation to visit the school on a regular basis to (a) provide confidential counselling for children and (b) provide counselling for mothers and daughters who are living in families where men are sexually abusive.

10. (a) That women's groups in schools provide women with opportunities to consciousness-raise around the issue, support each other and provide a link with girls experiencing sexual violence; (b) that girls/young women's groups in schools would enable students to support and confide in each other. These would also provide a 'safe space' for girls from boys' harassment.

11. (a) That telephone numbers of counselling organisations be displayed around the school for students to use should they choose to, (b) that students as well as women teachers should have access to telephones at school which allow for confidential telephone calls.

Conclusion

I have argued in this chapter that the sexual abuse of girls is a product of men's socially constructed behaviour most legitimately expressed and sanctioned through the institution of heterosexuality.

Whether we work in voluntary or statutory organisations we need to develop effective policies of responding to disclosure of sexual abuse as well as developing an anti-sexist education which challenges commonly held notions of masculinity, male sexual behaviour and heterosexuality.

In addition to devising 'policy' we need to begin with the question of why/how men maintain their power to sexually abuse. Men who claim to want to improve conditions for women/girls have a role to play in challenging themselves and other men in this. Schools, in treating abuse as abnormal, in educating children to accept male domination, male sexual behaviour and heterosexuality, uncritically promote the very institution which endangers children's safety.

As feminists/survivors we have pushed the issue of child sexual assault into the public arena. Now we need to draw up the agenda which will challenge male sexual behaviour and ensure the safety of children.

Further information

1. The Child Abuse Unit at North London Polytechnic provides an up to date reading list on child sexual abuse, at a small cost. Contact them at Ladbroke House, 62-66 Highbury Grove, London N5 2AD. Tel. 01-607 2789 ext. 5014.
2. The London Rape Crisis Centre, which also has the telephone number of rape crisis centres outside London, provides a 24-hour confidential counselling service for

women and girls who have been raped or sexually assaulted. They may be contacted on 01-837 1600 – PO Box 69, London WC1.

Notes

1. In this chapter I usually use the term 'girl'/young woman instead of child although I recognise that both sexes are sexually assaulted when children. However, this serves to remind us that according to all research the sexual abuse of girls is far more prevalent than the abuse of boys; both sexes are assaulted almost overwhelmingly by heterosexual men.

   I have always worked with survivors who are girls and as such can only draw upon that experience.
2. This belief is a popular one amongst family therapists and the state in general. We know that the issue is far more complex than this and is to do with feelings of powerlessness to change a situation that many women have; not all mothers do know; many women experience violence from husbands themselves. For a more thorough analysis see MacLeod and Saraga (1988) and Nelson (1987).
3. It is important here to stress that the notion that men have some kind of innate sexual drive is, in my view, nonsense. This argument has been used to gain sympathy for behaviour which is often sadistic and violent and which is invariably a conscious abuse of power.

   I subscribe to the view that sexuality is a social not a biological construction; and that men/boys benefit from their abuse of power because it maintains their domination and women's subordination through force or the threat of force.

References

Boushel, Margaret and Noakes, Sara, 'Islington Social Services: developing a policy on child sexual abuse', *Feminist Review* 28: *Family Secrets: Child Sexual Abuse*, Spring 1988.

Coveney, Lal et al., *The Sexuality Papers: Male Sexuality and the Social Control of Women*, Hutchinson, London, 1984.

Feminist Coalition Against Child Sexual Abuse, Briefing Document, unpublished, June 1988.

Feminist Review: *Family Secrets: Child Sexual Abuse*, Spring 1988.

Hackney Lesbians Stop the Clause Education Group, *Sexuality and Sex Education – A Balanced Perspective*, unpublished, 1988.

Hamblin and Bowen, 'Sexual Abuse of Children in the Home' in *Women Against Violence Against Women*, Onlywomen Press, London, 1982.

ILEA Youth Service, *Working With Girls and Young Women – A Progress Report*, 11 January 1984.

Jackson, Margaret, 'Sexuality and the social construction of male sexuality', in Coveney et al. (1984).

Jeffreys, Sheila, 'Sex reform and anti-feminism in the 1920s', in *The Sexual Dynamics of History*, London Feminist History Group, Pluto Press, London, 1983.

The Spinster and Her Enemies, Pandora Press, London, 1985.

Jones, Carol, 'Sexual tyranny: male violence in a mixed secondary school', Gaby Weiner (ed.), in *Just A Bunch Of Girls*, Open University Press, Milton Keynes, 1985.

Kelly, Liz, 'The continuum of sexual violence', in *Women, Violence and Social Control*, Jalna Hanmer and Maynard May (eds), Macmillan, London, 1987.

Leeds Revolutionary Feminist Group, 'Incest as an everyday event in the normal family', in *Women Against Violence Against Women*, dusty rhodes and Sandra McNeill, Onlywomen Press, London, 1985.

London Rape Crisis Centre, *Sexual Violence: The Reality For Women*, The Women's Press, London, 1984.

MacLeod, Mary and Saraga, Esther (eds), *Child Sexual Abuse: Towards a Feminist Professional Practice*, Report of Conference, of that title, Child Abuse Studies Unit, P.N.L. Press, North London Polytechnic, London, 1987.

'Against orthodoxy', in *New Statesman & Society*, 1 July 1988.

Mahony, Pat, *Schools For The Boys – Co-Education Reassessed*, Hutchinson, London, 1985.

Nelson, Sarah, *Incest, Fact and Myth*, Stramullion Press, Edinburgh, 1987.

214

O'Hara, Maureen, 'Developing a Feminist School Policy on Child Sexual Abuse', *Feminist Review: Family Secrets: Child Sexual Abuse*, Spring 1988.

Ward, Elizabeth, *Father–Daughter Rape*, The Women's Press, London, 1984.

Wood, Julian, 'Boys will be boys', *New Socialist* 5, 1982.

8 Sex Education in Schools: Keeping to the 'Norm'

Julie Melia

Sex education in schools has long been identified as a 'controversial' issue, with regard to the form, content and delivery of this part of the curriculum. It can be seen as an important aspect in the social and sexual development of children and young people and is therefore of prime importance within the educational process.

In this chapter I shall be looking critically at the most recent Conservative Government initiatives concerning sex education and in particular will focus my attention on certain key documents relating to this. I hope to demonstrate that these documents clearly set out the attempts by the present government to impose a particular moral code on all those involved in education. Further, I will suggest that this moral framework, whilst both confused and contradictory, is also an attempt to promote a particular view of heterosexuality which patently discriminates against all of us who exist outside of the 'normal' stable married heterosexual unit.

Feminism and Education

Education has historically been a location for organised feminist activity. Nineteenth-century feminists fought long and hard for the education of girls and women, and feminists have never ceased the seemingly unending battle against the education we have been offered. In recent years feminists have put forward criticisms of such diverse areas of the educational process as the treatment of girls in the classroom by teachers, mixed schooling, classroom materials, careers advice, harassment of students and staff, and of educational theory itself. (See e.g. Deem, 1978; Spender and Sarah, 1980; Stanworth, 1983; Whyld, 1983; Mahony, 1985 and Chapter 6 in this volume, 'Sexual Violence and Mixed Schools'). It has been argued that education can play an important part in the coercion of girls and women into the acceptance of a subordinate social role.

Much less has been written about the part played by education in the socialisation of girls into a particular (hetero)sexual role, and in particular, the part played by sex education in this process. The work of the London Gay Teenage Group (LGTG) and other young lesbians and gay men has been instrumental in drawing attention to the harmful effects of an education which attempts to force young people into the acceptance of a narrowly defined sexual role.

Homosexuality is rarely mentioned in schools; in one survey only 2.6 per cent of the survey population said that homosexuality had been dealt with as part of their 'sex education': 'At school, they mentioned it in the 6th form, in sociology. It was mentioned under deviancy. You know, lumped between murders and the insane' (Trenchard, 1984).

For young people in schools where homosexuality was acknowledged, many found it worse than useless: 'School sex education said that it was perverted, that if your glands over-secrete then you're gay' (Trenchard and Warren, 1984).

These young people are quite clear about what they want from education: an acknowledgment of their existence and the right to a self-defined sexuality. Failure to deal with heterosexism in any form serves to alienate young lesbians and gay men and prevents their full and equal participation in the educational process.

The Future of Education?

Any criticism of sex education inevitably needs to be set within a wider educational context. It is essential at this time that we look particularly at proposed educational reforms which promise a radical restructuring of the education system in England and Wales, in conjunction with the recent addition of Section 28 of the Local Government Act 1988 to the statute books (see Chapter 4, 'Section 28 and Education'). Although the varied nature of school curricula, teaching styles and pupils' experiences preclude generalisation, it is important that we look closely at the pressure being exerted by the present government on all those involved in education to make us promote their particular view of the world.

The Education Reform Act passed into legislation at the end of July 1988 and can perhaps be seen as 'The most far-reaching reform of the education system since 1944' (Hirst, 1988).

This piece of legislation shifts the balance of power and control in education from local education authorities and teachers to central government and school governing bodies. Financial management of schools is to be given to governing bodies and headteachers, and schools will be allowed to 'opt out' of local education authority control and become grant maintained by central government. The Act introduces compulsory bench mark testing at the ages of 7, 11, 14 and 16 against which individual pupils and whole schools will be tested. The Act establishes a 'National Curriculum', the basis for which will be the 'core' subjects of English, mathematics and science.

These reforms seem set radically to transform education in this country. Whilst some of the implications are still unclear, and will remain so until the implementation of the Act, some of the proposals are of direct relevance to sex education.

The proposed National Curriculum clearly defines the syllabi to be taught and completely eliminates the teaching of social studies from the curriculum. It further proposes that 'health education' be taught as a 'theme' in biology. Under the new proposals, it seems likely that sex education will be slotted into 'appropriate' subject areas such as science, which may well have space to explore the dimensions of sexuality and relationships only within a limited framework (DES, 1987a).

The Department of Education and Science (DES), responsible for the administration of the education system in England and Wales, points out that

> Whilst the physical aspects of sexual behaviour may well be encompassed within the teaching of biology, opportunities for considering the broader emotional and ethical dimensions of sexual attitudes and mores may arise in other subject areas. (DES, 1987b, para. 16)

We can only speculate on precisely how much space 'other subject areas' will have for such matters under the rigours of a national curriculum subject to sustained assessment and testing.

Sex Education and the Law

Sex education in England and Wales is currently delivered according to the directives of the Education (No. 2) Act 1986. Section 18(2) of this Act gives responsibility for the organisation of sex education in schools to governing bodies:

> The articles of government for every such school shall provide for it to be the duty of the governing body –
> (a) to consider separately (whilst having regard to the local education authority's statement under Section 17 of this Act) the question of whether sex education should form part of the secular curriculum of the school: and
> (b) to make and keep up to date, a separate written statement –
>> (i) of their policy with regard to the content and organisation of the relevant parts of the curriculum; or
>> (ii) where they conclude that sex education should not form part of the secular curriculum, of that conclusion. (HMSO, 1986)

It is the responsibility of school governors to determine exactly how and whether sex education should be provided, and governors are given an apparently free rein if they decide that pupils should be presented with a range of information with which to make informed decisions about their sexual lives.

The Act appears to make no demands on the form and content of the sex education that governors decide upon, although Section 46 does exhort governors to:

> Take such steps as are *reasonably practicable* to secure that where sex education is given to any registered pupils in the school it is given in such a manner as to encourage those pupils to have due regard to moral considerations and the value of family life. (HMSO, 1986; my emphasis)

This gentle reminder to governors of their moral obligations when defining the form and content of sex education need by no means be interpreted in a restrictive or narrow way and clearly recognises the practical considerations of teaching itself.

In this context, the 'value of family life' need not be prescriptively defined; pupils could be encouraged to look at the value of a variety of family arrangements, including lesbian families, single-parent families and extended families.[1] It is precisely this apparent ambiguity which is firmly and irrevocably qualified by the DES circular, *Sex Education at School*, in its moral framework for sex education.

Sex Education in Schools: a Moral Framework for Education

The reader of *Sex Education at School* (Circular 11/87) is directed by paragraph 3 to place it 'Within the general context of new statutory provisions relating to the school curriculum contained in the Education (No. 2) Act' (DES, 1987b). It clearly states the intention of the DES that this document be used to put the flesh on the bones of the framework for teaching about sexual matters contained in the 1986 Act. It seems that:

> The Secretary of State for Education believes that local education authorities and governing bodies will welcome guidance for the provision of sex education established by the 1986 Act and on other aspects of treatment of sexual matters within the school context. (Ibid., para. 3)

It is my assertion, however, that this 'guidance' is by no means as welcome as the Secretary of State might wish, since it sets up a blatantly discriminatory and hence anti-educational framework.

The circular opens with a brief explanation of precisely why sex education is so important, as 'An important element in the work of schools in preparing pupils for adult life' (para. 1). It is considered that schools should take on this responsibility, since parents may often be unable or unwilling to take on this aspect of their children's education. However, the circular emphasises that 'The teaching offered by schools should be complementary and supportive to the role of parents' (para. 2).

At this point in our reading of the circular, we have no reason to suspect that the parents whose role teachers are to complement in their teaching belong to one particular group, and we could be forgiven for assuming that lesbian and gay parents could offer sensitive and caring advice to their children. However, the moral framework that the circular sets out would seem to deny many parents the right to expect complementary teaching in schools where keeping to the 'norm' takes utmost importance.

The ideology of the family embodied in this government document would seem to suggest that all of us do, or should, live within a particular set of family relationships. It is in direct conflict with the argument put forward in favour of a National Curriculum, to 'Enable schools to be more accountable (to parents) for the education they offer to their pupils' (DES, 1987a). The only parents to whom the sex education proposed by the DES might be acceptable and hence accountable might be those living within the 'normal' family prescribed by the DES.

Although schools are bound by the 1986 Act, teachers can perhaps take some small comfort from Section 18(2) of this Act, reiterated by circular 11/87. The sex education policy drawn up by governing bodies in accordance with the regulations need not be strictly adhered to 'Where that policy is incompatible with any part of the syllabus for a course which forms part of the curriculum and leads to a public examin-

221

ation' (DES, 1987b, para. 4).

Paragraph 12 again takes up this point, quoting biology syllabi as an example where teaching may well extend beyond the letter of a sex education policy agreed by a governing body. Teachers within arts and humanities departments may well, particularly in the context of GCSE subjects, make reference to the social construction of gender, sexuality and relationships. However, as already stated, the proposed National Curriculum will clearly define the subject parameters in such a way as to limit teaching to a more traditional approach.

The circular makes explicit the role of governors in curricular development, a role that the proposed National Curriculum will extend far beyond sex education, to ensuring the implementation of this curriculum in schools. It is, however, quite clear that governors will be allowed no discretion, since 'It will not be possible for them to modify the national curriculum' (DES, 1987a).

Some discretion is however, expected in the context of sex education. Governors have to take account of 'Any representations made to them by any persons connected with the community served by the school' (DES, 1987b, para. 6). Such representation could, of course, come from lesbian and gay groups, such as lesbian mothers' groups and lesbian and gay youth groups, and could allow space for radical discretion in the form and content of any teaching about sexual matters. Governors could, in theory, have the authority to take into account the work of such groups in challenging heterosexism when drawing up the specifics of their sex education policy.

However, it seems clear from paragraph 9 that the only 'discretion' the DES can envisage as required is not toward those individuals and groups concerned to combat discrimination, but toward those parents who have 'Strong objections on religious grounds to their children receiving sex education' (ibid., para. 9). The (then) Secretary of State for Education, Kenneth Baker, himself stated, at the 1986 Conservative Party conference that the new regulations concerning sex education were partially intended to alleviate the 'concern' felt by parents 'When sex education uses *unsuitable* books and methods' (Smith, 1988).

Paragraph 8 of the circular further elucidates for governors their role within curricula development, envisaging that 'Governors, as part of their responsibility for deciding policy on the *content* of any sex education to be offered, may determine their school's overall approach to teaching about sexual matters' (DES, 1987b, para. 8; emphasis in original). Quite how this might affect subject syllabi is unclear, although the circular takes pains to point out the possible ramifications of such extended control on teachers' practice, stressing that the role of governors should not impinge on the 'Exercise of professional skills by the headteacher and staff' (ibid., para. 8).

It seems unclear at this point exactly how much professional discretion is to be allowed to teachers, particularly in the context of exemptions for public examinations. It also remains unclear what the role of teachers will be under the proposed National Curriculum. However, as will be demonstrated later, it becomes apparent from the DES directives on AIDS education precisely what this professionalism should entail.

The DES appear to be openly intent on inhibiting any radical possibilities that might be opened by the giving of control over certain parts of the curriculum to governing bodies. The circular makes it explicit that the organisation of sex education will provide a further means of severing the bonds of local authority influence by suggesting that 'Governors will be obliged to have regard to the relevant parts of the LEA's statement [on sex education] *but will not be bound by them*' (ibid., para. 14; my emphasis).

Such a clause is obviously open to a number of interpretations, including the possibility that school governors might feel hindered by a prescriptive heterosexist policy on teaching about sexual matters. However, within the current political climate, particularly the moral panic concerning homosexuality generated since the AIDS phenomenon, it seems very likely that such a directive could be used to undermine the equal opportunities work of radical education authorities who seek to place heterosexism firmly on the educational agenda (see Chapter 3, 'Positive Images in Haringey').

'A Moral Framework for Sex Education'

Having clearly stated *how* sex education is to be provided in schools, the circular moves on to its crowning glory, its moral framework for sex education. Although the form of sex education, and therefore to a large extent also the content, has been defined in a fairly comprehensive manner by paragraphs 1–17, the DES is at pains to leave no radical stone unturned by setting out its definitive 'moral' guide to sexuality. Paragraph 18 repeats the wording of the 1986 Act with regard to 'moral considerations and the value of family life' but seems most anxious to elaborate on precisely how this should be interpreted.

The initial statements regarding the nature of this morality seem at first sight most welcome to educationalists, since 'The aims of a programme of sex education should be to present *facts* in an *objective and balanced* manner so as to enable pupils to comprehend the *range* of sexual attitudes and behaviour in present day society.' (DES, 1987b, para. 19; my emphasis.) There appears, however, to be some concern that any such 'facts' must be located within a clearly defined set of morals, based not simply on subjective definitions of right and wrong, but of normality and abnormality.

The circular recommends that 'Pupils should be *helped* to appreciate the benefits of stable married and family life' (ibid., para. 19; my emphasis).

As Margaret Jackson points out (see Chapter 1), we need to examine very critically the reasoning which suggests that young people need to be 'helped' to understand the benefits of an apparently natural process. It is clear at this point that the notion of 'family' with which we are familiar from Section 46 of the 1986 Act, has been coupled with 'stable married', and the position is irrevocably qualified.

The transformation of 'family' into 'stable married' in the course of two government documents reveals the clearly discriminatory nature of the circular. Not only are the experiences of lesbian and gay pupils and families to be invali-

224

dated by a programme of sex education which extols the virtues of the stable married family, the experiences of single parents, including those who are divorced or separated, children being cared for within extended family arrangements and children whose parents are unmarried, are rendered invisible at best, and at worst, inferior. Any sex education programme which fails to consider the value of different family arrangements must inevitably be highly subjective and unbalanced and will lead to an unsatisfactory educational programme.

To provide the desired balance and objectivity in a programme of sex education, it would of course be essential to present to pupils the facts in relation to the extent of child sexual abuse, rape and murder that takes place within the 'stable married' heterosexual family unit (see Chapters 5 and 7). The 'benefits' of this particular type of family arrangement need to be examined clearly and critically in order to help pupils make informed decisions about their own sexual choices.

After its lengthy assertions regarding morality, the circular acknowledges that 'Schools cannot, in general, avoid tackling controversial sexual matters, such as contraception and abortion, by reason of their sensitivity' (DES, 1987b, para. 21). However, just in case teachers were 'Prepared to offer balanced and factual information' as paragraph 21 recommends, the following paragraph unambiguously clarifies the moral position that should be adopted in relation to other controversial sexual matters such as homosexuality:

> There is no place in any school in any circumstance for teaching which advocates homosexual behaviour, which presents it as the 'norm' or which encourages homosexual experimentation by pupils. (Ibid., para. 22)[2]

Such an assertion has profound implications across the curriculum; the definitive 'in any circumstance' suggests that work in the arts or humanities, for example, which questions stereotyping or attempts to problematise the concept of 'normality' would be deemed unacceptable.

Teachers are grimly warned that 'Encouraging or procuring homosexual acts by pupils who are under the age of consent is a criminal offence' (ibid., para. 22). It is, however, unclear precisely what could constitute encouragement or procuration in the classroom. We can at this point only speculate on possible action that could be taken with regard to teachers who attempt to give help and guidance to pupils questioning their own sexuality, or that of others, whether such help take the form of giving pupils the telephone numbers of lesbian and gay organisations, or of being open and positive about their own sexuality. Such action may well constitute encouraging behaviour outside the 'norm' and could mightily displease governors who, under the currently proposed educational reforms, will have new powers of hiring and firing staff in schools.

The language used in the circular with regard to teaching which encourages, advocates or procures a particular form of sexual attitude and behaviour perhaps inevitably evokes a clear association with the equally spurious concept of 'intentional promotion' employed in Section 28 of the Local Government Act 1988. The DES seems, like the authors of Section 28, to be a little unclear precisely what form of teaching and learning it seeks to prohibit, yet it is apparent that the aim of objectivity and balance hitherto so desirable will not be deemed appropriate in relation to homosexuality (see Chapter 4, 'Section 28 and Education').

Advice to Pupils Under 16?

The circular moves on from its moral framework to make recommendations for teaching about AIDS and then sets out guidelines for teachers giving 'Advice to Pupils Under 16'. A distinction is drawn for teachers between

> Providing education generally about sexual matters . . . and . . . counselling and advice to individual pupils particularly if this relates to their own sexual behaviour. Good teachers have always taken a pastoral interest in the welfare and well-being of pupils. But this should *never* trespass on the proper exercise of parental rights and responsibilities. (DES, 1987b, para. 25; my emphasis.)

However, I would suggest that, in practice, such a distinction sets up artificial limits for teachers and gives no indication of how teachers are to operate in the teaching and learning situation.

Good educational practice must, of necessity, respond positively to the needs of the individual, and the pastoral role of teachers involved in the daily care of young people leaves little room for the separation of 'education' and 'advice'.

The work of young lesbians and gay men has highlighted the urgent need for teachers to respond positively to the needs and experiences of young people in schools, and the consequences of failing to do this:

> Being a lesbian at school my worst fear is that I will be found out and that it would lead to physical victimisation from other pupils – yes it does happen. Is it fair when pupils have been physically attacked because of their sexuality? Is it fair that they feel that they can't even turn to a teacher because they are not sure if they will support them because of their sexuality? (GEN, 1987, p.43)

The DES sheds very little light on its definition of a teacher's 'professional' responsibilities. Teachers are unequivocally given the role of moral custodians of the young people they come into contact with every day.

The DES and AIDS Education

There is one aspect of education in the area of sexual matters in which a consideration of homosexuality is at least not expressly forbidden. As the circular points out,

> Whatever the overall policy on sex education adopted by the governing body, particular attention should be given to the forms of sexual and other behaviour which carry the risk of infection with the AIDS virus and about ways in which risks may be avoided or lessened. (DES, 1987b, para. 23)

It should, in theory, be possible for teachers to use this part of the sex education curriculum to counteract stereotypes and prejudice by looking critically at the disjunction between the medical facts about AIDS and the moral panic that has been generated around the issue. If, as teachers, we are to be as fair, objective and balanced as the Secretary of State for Education and the DES would like us to be, then we surely owe it to pupils to discuss the fact that celibacy, lesbianism, or at the very least non-penetrative sex are by far the most physically safe sexual practices. However, lest we still be labouring under the misconception that we should aim for balance in our sex education programme, the materials produced by the DES with regard to AIDS education tell us exactly how we are to proceed.

The AIDS education package 'Your Choice for Life' was sent to all state schools in England and Wales in the spring term of 1988. This package comprises a 24-minute video and a set of notes for governors, headteachers and teachers. The video itself is by no means an ideal resource for a teacher concerned to look critically at myths and stereotypes, and opens with an unqualified reference to homosexuals (whom we presume to be male) and drug users as most at risk from infection. It does not discuss lesbian and gay lifestyles – indeed lesbians are never mentioned – but it does avoid moralism and threats. Whilst many criticisms have been levelled at the video itself (see for example Panter, 1988) as a teaching aid it could prove a valuable springboard for discussions relating to sexuality, relationships and physically safe sexual practices.

It is, however, the accompanying notes from the DES which stress that 'The video should be used *only* in conjunction with this guide' (DES, 1987c).

On a practical level it seems incomprehensible that such prescriptive instructions be given concerning the form *and* content of discussions surrounding safe sexual practices. The booklet of notes is very comprehensive and stresses that, at all times, 'Teaching should emphasise that young people can avoid AIDS by avoiding sexual experimentation' (ibid., section 3.2). Teachers are urged to focus specifically on 'The virtues of abstinence and restraint' (ibid., section 3.9). Whilst we can perhaps safely assume that responsible teaching would by no means encourage or advocate promiscuous sexual behaviour, teachers do need to be prepared to discuss with concerned pupils the practicalities of safe sex.

However, with the reiteration of a concept of the family as 'stable married' and an emphasis on the centrality of marriage in sexual relationships it seems apparent that the primary concern of the DES is to safeguard the moral, rather than the more practicable physical, safety of young people in schools. Teachers are severely warned that

> In discussing these issues with pupils . . . it should be made clear that the fact that a form of sexual behaviour may be legal and may not carry a risk of infection with the AIDS virus does *not* mean that it is morally acceptable. (Ibid., section 3.1; emphasis in original)

Quite what these particular forms of sexual behaviour *are* is at no point clarified in the DES notes on the video, although it seems morally unacceptable to question the physical safety of penetrative sex. The lesbian experience is rendered completely invisible by the DES, since even the few references clearly refer to gay men. The instruction notes simply quote the directives from paragraph 22 of the circular on teaching about the 'norm' and can find no space for discussion about the variety of human sexual feelings.

The moral framework for sex education set out by the Department of Education and Science clearly defines for us the parameters for debate regarding matters of sexuality and relationships in schools. The *legal* aspects of teaching about sexual matters laid out by Section 46 of the 1986 Education Act have been precisely interpreted by the DES in such a way as to make good practice in sex education virtually impossible.

I would suggest that a balanced programme of sex education should cover a range of issues that are of direct relevance to young people's lives today. Sex education should promote discussion of a wide range of different lifestyles and make explicit reference to the ways in which various institutions and groups seek to mould and prescribe our social and sexual roles. Such education should be used to counteract some of the racist, sexist, heterosexist and classist elements that characterise young people's education today and should be designed to equip young people with the knowledge and skills with which to take control of their own lives.

If we are to follow the directives of Circular 11 to the letter, firmly located within the context of retrogressive educational reforms and restrictive legislation concerning local authority spending, with which we are by now only too familiar, then the education given to young people in schools will simply present a series of half truths about a mythical heterosexual family. It is imperative that we remember that Section 46 of the Education (No. 2) Act 1986 may at present be open to more radical interpretation. We should endeavour, at this time, to concentrate our energies on providing this much-needed radicalism in our schools.

Acknowledgments

I would like to thank Margaret Jackson and Pat Mahony for their helpful comments and suggestions on an earlier draft of this chapter.

I would also like to express thanks and gratitude to Tracey Smith; without her constant help and support this would not have been written.

Notes

1. Section 28 of the Local Government Act 1988 is by no means as ambiguous in its reference to homosexuality as a 'pretended family relationship'.
2. As Margaret Brown asserts, the use of the word 'norm' here is problematic: 'It is not altogether clear what this assertion is supposed to mean . . . Is it saying any more than that homosexuals are a minority? Or are we being invited to read some connotation of abnormality into whatever is supposed to be the opposite of the "norm"?' (Brown, 1987).

References

Brown, Margaret, 'Keeping to the "norm"', *The Times Educational Supplement*, 2 October 1987.
Deem, Rosemary, *Women and Schooling*, Routledge & Kegan Paul, London, 1978.

DES (Department of Education and Science), *The National Curriculum 5-16: A Consultation Document*, Welsh Office, 1987(a).

Sex Education at School (Circular No. 11/87), London, 25 September 1987(b).

Your Choice for Life: AIDS Education for 14-16 Year Olds, Welsh Office, 1987(c).

GEN, *Challenging Heterosexism*, Women in Education, London, March 1987.

HMSO, Education (No. 2) Act 1986, London, 1986.

Hirst, Judy, 'Class war', *Spare Rib* 194, September 1988.

Mahony, Pat, *Schools For The Boys? Co-education Reassessed*, Hutchinson, London, 1985.

Panter, David, 'The AIDS case', *The Times Educational Supplement*, 15 January 1988.

Smith, Tracey, 'Outside the 'norm': homosexuality and lesbianism in sex education', unpublished MA dissertation, University of York, 1988.

Spender, Dale and Sarah, Elizabeth (eds), *Learning to Lose: Sexism and Education*, The Women's Press, London, 1980.

Stanworth, Michelle, *Gender and Schooling*, Hutchinson, London, 1983.

Trenchard, Lorraine (ed.), *Talking about Young Lesbians*, London Gay Teenage Group, London, 1984.

Trenchard, Lorraine and Warren, Hugh, *Something To Tell You*, London Gay Teenage Group, London, 1984.

Whyld, Janie (ed.), *Sexism in the Secondary Curriculum*, Harper & Row, London, 1983.

9 North London Young Lesbian Group: Specialist Work within the Youth Service

Jane Dixon, Gilly Salvat and Jane Skeates

Introduction

This chapter concerns work with young lesbians in the Youth Service, as this is where the good practice with young lesbians is to be found. In order to explain this work it is necessary to discuss the history of 'specialist' youth work, as far back as the setting up of the London Gay Teenage Group (1976) and the first Girls' (now Young Women's) Projects (1979) and before that the rise and fall of the 'first wave' of girls' work beginning in the later nineteenth century.

Work with Young Lesbians – Where Is the Good Practice in the Education Service?

Schools are one of the institutions in our society which uphold, reinforce and shape heterosexism, that is, the institutional view that heterosexuality is the superior sexuality and lifestyle and that lesbians and gays are second-class citizens. Young lesbians who are consciously or unconsciously resisting heterosexuality and aware or becoming aware of their lesbianism in school (70 per cent were aware of sexuality when at school)[1] are seen as a threat, at best ignored and at worst harassed and abused (38 per cent suffered abuse because they were thought to be gay).

Schools are a breeding ground for ignorance and fear about lesbianism, and practically nothing is ever done to challenge these ideas or to dispel myths.

Unofficially, that is outside the classroom/curriculum, lesbianism is used as a form of control: for example girls are threatened with the label 'lesbian' if they do not conform to heterosexual 'feminine' stereotypes. This threat can come from teachers as well as other students (only one young person with a disability and no young Black people felt able to confide in their teacher/s about his/her sexuality).[2] Yet this unofficial/playground profile is hardly mirrored officially at all (76 per cent never had homosexuality formally mentioned at school).

Due to legislative change – the DES circular on sex education, school governors' new powers, and Section 28 of the Local Government Act 1988 banning local authorities from promoting homosexuality – it has become ever more difficult for lesbianism to be positively discussed in the classroom and for lesbian teachers to 'come out' at schools and therefore act as role models for young lesbians.[3]

So if positive ways of working with young lesbians in the Education Service are to be looked at, we have to examine the Youth Service. The case study that will be discussed is that of the first Young Lesbian Group (YLG), which was set up in 1979. This group will be looked at in detail – its history, the reasons for setting up the group, how it works and what happens each week, its functions, and its political importance. The good practice laid down by this London-based group has been used as an example by other groups following on. There are now 18 other lesbian and gay youth groups in London and several outside London.

It is also important to note that it was not the Inner London Education Authority (ILEA) or other London education authority hierarchies who started to do this work, but lesbians and gays within these youth services who struggled for years to persuade them to take it on. In the case of the ILEA, for example, the fact that it had an equal opportunities policy gave youth workers something to start organising around. ILEA recognition was valuable in terms of mainstream status, money and facilities. When this recognition was won, it came out of hard political struggles which are still being fought. Youth workers had to prove the need that they knew was there and are constantly having to justify that need.

Why is the Youth Service part of the Education Service?

As it is often not understood, it is important to explain why the Youth Service is part of the Education Service (and not Leisure and Recreation Services) and why youth work comes under the category of social education.

Youth work takes place with young people outside of school time and settings, and with young people in their 'leisure' time, whether those young people are at school, work, unemployed or on one of the many government training schemes. Social education is a process which gives help and support to young people to develop relationships with their family and friends, and with society at large. It can offer support through the difficult period from childhood to adulthood, so that young people can make more informed choices about how they live their lives as adults.

There is of course a recreational aspect to this process, but it also offers skills acquisition, space and time to discuss, find out, develop ideas, try things out, and a place to sort out problems, be they practical or emotional. It takes a non-judgmental attitude to all young people. The major aim of the Youth Service is to work with *all* young people at those times when they ask for it and in a less formal structure than is offered at school or in the workplace.[4]

The History of 'Specialist' Youth Work

In describing how and why young lesbian groups were initially set up it is important to place the groups in an historical context. Youth work with young lesbians came out of youth work with young women and also with young gay men. These developments in youth work came through identification of neglected and/or oppressed groups throughout the beginnings of the formulation of equal opportunities policies. This development in turn grew out of liberation politics. The struggle for independence in India and the ideas of Gandhi, the Civil Rights movement of the 1950s and 1960s initiated in the USA by Black people and supported by many white liberals, contributed an important political impetus to twentieth-century politics. These important struggles led to the reaffirmation of equality for all peoples, and the reality of common oppression as a rallying point for political action, and for a common consciousness. This model, developed by Black people, highly influenced the development and ethos of both the women's liberation movement and the gay liberation movement.

Youth Work with Young Women – the Setting Up of the First Young Women's Projects

Youth work with young women was started in 1880 with the establishment of the first youth clubs for girls in London's East End. This was some years after clubs for boys were set up, and was a result of the concern expressed by religious groupings, socialists and others about the utter deprivation experienced by the working class in that area. Girls' clubs went from strength to strength until by the 1930s there were 325 registered girls' clubs in London alone. Established in every part of the country, they were brought together under the umbrella of the National Association of Girls' Clubs. In the 1940s, however, due to World War II, the new ideas about coeducation and the fact that women were encouraged to return to the home as the men came back from the war, the thriving and active girls' club movement went into decline. In the late 1940s and 1950s people involved in working in youth clubs were encouraged to take up training. Slowly, a largely volunteer group of workers (women) gave way to paid professionals (men). Male workers then gradually took over the National Association of Girls' Clubs, until by the early 1960s its original purpose had all but disappeared and its name was changed to the National Association of Youth Clubs – an organisation serving mixed clubs, 80 per cent of whom were boys. The National Association of Boys' Clubs, however, still maintained its autonomy and today is the wealthiest youth club association in the country.

In the 1960s workers' reports indicate that they found girls 'a problem' and without motivation.[5] With the Association's change from a girls' to a mixed organisation went resources and properties that had been gained for girls, worth several hundreds of thousands of pounds (including camp sites, residential centres and a swimming pool)[6] (National Organisation for Work with Girls & Young Women; 1983). By the mid-1970s this history had been firmly hidden from women youth workers; all women who embarked on girls' work at that time were totally ignorant of their history. The lesson to be learnt from this past is that mixed youth organisations did not serve the needs of girls and young women, whereas single-sex ones did. It had been shown that 'merger' meant 'take-over'!

The 1970s and 1980s

By the 1970s young women had all but disappeared from the clubs. After the age of 14 or 15 the needs of girls were not catered for. The Youth Service was geared towards young working-class men and was, in the main, sports and activity orientated. Workers were concerned primarily with male youth sub-cultures, male offenders and the problems they presented to society.

In the mid-1970s, because of greater awareness of the demands of the women's movement and the growing number of women taking advantage of increased opportunity in training and further education, women began to join the Youth Service as professional workers. At this time only 20 per cent of the full-time youth workers employed by the ILEA were women. A few of these women were active feminists, and it became apparent very early in their work with the Youth Service that there was a glaring absence of girls and young women in the clubs and projects.

In 1977 a few women youth workers started to meet together at the London Women's Liberation Workshop (the unofficial 'headquarters' of the women's liberation movement). This is significant, as it shows the feminist base from which these women's new ideas sprang. They met together not only to talk about their work but to plan strategies to rectify their situation. They also came together to support each other in the face of the massive amount of sexism they were all experiencing in the male-dominated Youth Service. This small group very rapidly grew and soon had to be divided into borough-based groups. In North London the workers from Camden and Islington worked together. These times were euphoric for many of them in their common struggle. They worked in complete trust and sisterhood, supported each other and went to each other's aid in times of stress and the violence many of them suffered from young men. In order to set up this work they often 'bent the rules', working secretly and voluntarily to organise young women's activities, such as single-sex work with girls. They had to do this because the opposition was sometimes so vicious, uncompromising and violent. (Single-sex work with boys was acceptable, the 'norm', and there had never been any opposition to this, of course.)

Feminism had taught them to share, and they shared resources and finances to make things happen (not a frequent occurrence in the competitive ethos of the male Youth Service). They used sport, arts and craft, music, discos, self-defence, assertion training, discussion groups, sex education and a whole bag of activities which young women had asked them to provide. They used their own personal skills and talents and taught each other new skills so that they could pass these on to young women. The network of sympathetic women grew as the friendship networks of young women in the area developed.

It became apparent that work should be concentrated on the needs of young women, and that specialist young women's provision should be established. From these informal beginnings women from Camden and Islington became involved in steering their ideas through the bureaucratic process and the shifting sands and cold feet of the Youth Service hierarchy and its committees. Pressure was brought to bear, pickets were organised and leaflets given out as the Youth Service suddenly discovered that it had consented to a dangerous new departure – single-sex youth provision for girls! Most of the men involved in the decision-making processes, along with the young men who used the clubs, were shocked by the assertion of these women. Right from the start they accused the women youth workers of being lesbians who wanted to convert wholesale all of 'their girls' to lesbianism(!), and felt that this new departure would open the flood gates not only to 'stroppy' feminists but to lesbians as well. The fact that heterosexual and lesbian feminists worked together in common cause gave the girls' work movement strength. It also meant that heterosexual feminists had to come to terms with being accused of lesbianism.

Camden Girls' Project was set up in July 1979 (the first feminist orientated young women's space since the early part of the century). Islington Girls' Project followed in October 1979. Each project had full-time paid youth work staff, a £500 setting-up grant and one room. The work was always designed to include *all* girls but very soon, as needs were identified, work began with *particular* groups of young women who were isolated or in need of special provision. For example the age range (missing from mixed clubs) of the 14-21s was targeted. Work began to concentrate on Black and minority ethnic young women, those with children, young lesbians and those who were interested in non-traditional female activities such as sport and rock music. Work was also carried out in mixed clubs to enable special provision for young women and raise their participation. Workers found that by example they had to teach young women to value each other's company and learn to function in groups, instead of just with their best friend. Young women soon began to gain strength and to analyse their oppression and value the positive aspects of being with each other.

Youth Work with Young Gays – the Setting Up of the London Gay Teenage Group

Around the same time as women youth workers were meeting to discuss girls' work in the mid-1970s, ideas of working with young gays were being discussed by young gay men and gay male youth workers.

At the Campaign for Homosexual Equality's Conference in Sheffield in 1975 a group of young men, for the first time, expressed that the issues discussed there were irrelevant to them, and as young men, they felt excluded. They got together to demand rights for themselves. The Gay Youth Movement was subsequently set up under the auspices of CHE (Campaign for Homosexual Equality), but the original members soon pulled out and set up their own organisation. A small group of young men started to meet at Oval House in London, with the assistance of two ILEA gay male youth workers.

The London Gay Teenage Group was launched in 1976 and started meeting at the Grapevine Project in Islington. This non-aligned voluntary youth group soon grew in numbers and young women began to be involved too. The voluntary involvement of youth workers was, at this time, unrecognised by the Youth Service and it was by agreement with the management committees, who managed these workers, that support for this group could take place. These workers did this work as unpaid extra to their actual youth work jobs – just as women youth workers had adopted this tactic in setting up work with girls.

In 1978 the London Union of Youth Clubs recognised this group as a bona fide youth group. This was the first youth organisation to do so. The next battle to be won was recognition by the ILEA Youth Service. It was (and still is) important for voluntary youth groups to have this recognition, because with it comes access to resources such as equipment grants, part-time youth workers to service and support the group, training opportunities and a link with youth services and opportunities throughout the country.

The registration process for the London Gay Teenage Group took two years (1977-1979). The group was considered highly controversial by the ILEA hierarchy, but the members of the group systematically set about putting their case forward to youth officers, committees and members of the ILEA. This situation was almost unique in the history of the Youth Service because it was primarily the young people (aged between 16 and 21) who, as youth group members, fought this campaign for registration. One of the main issues in the Thompson Report 1981 (a government report on the aims and objectives of the Youth Service) was that of youth participation and its importance. Usually 'normal' groups that can prove they are well run and managed and can show commitment to the young people they cater for are welcomed to the Youth Services voluntary sector; this was not the case with the Gay Teenage Group. (Senior officers and members of the ILEA were by this time being bombarded by protests from organisations such as the Festival of Light and other extremist religious and political organisations.) Reports were written on every side, by police, psychiatrists and lawyers. The legality of the group was discussed endlessly. Letters were written in support by youth workers. Members of the group undertook visits to the youth committees of many different boroughs around London asking for registration so that they could meet and be fully recognised. At last, in 1979, Islington's Area Youth Committee recognised the London Gay Teenage Group as a bona fide youth group. The London Gay Teenage Group still exists today. It is primarily managed by the young people themselves, with some support from youth workers and other sympathetic adults. It now employs two part-time youth workers who are managed by the committee.

The Young Lesbian Group (now the North London Young Lesbian Group)

The Young Lesbian Group (YLG) was set up because the need was there for young lesbians to have a separate space for themselves, away from boys and heterosexual girls, in order to gain support and friends, and to explore relevant issues. Lesbian youth workers knew from their own experience and that of other lesbians that they had, in the main, been alienated and unhappy as teenagers because they felt that they were 'the only one'. They recognised these feelings in some of the young women attending their youth clubs, and knew that they were feeling unhappy, rejected, lonely and isolated. Many of these young women had no other lesbian friends, and no heterosexual friends that they could trust. Some had a poor school record and were looked upon as 'loners' or 'withdrawn' at school. However, it was also realised that most young lesbians were not attending youth clubs at all. Fifty-two per cent of young lesbians and gays and 66 per cent of young Black lesbians and gays never attended a mainstream youth club,[7] and of those that did, not one of them felt comfortable growing up as lesbians, knowing that it was seen as, at worst, mentally sick or criminal or, at best, sad and pitiful. Their self-esteem and feelings of worth were badly affected by these negative attitudes. They received hardly any positive feedback from family, friends, school or work.[8]

Some of these young lesbians were 'found out', some chose to 'come out', some were beaten up, sexually abused, thrown out of home or locked inside their homes. Some were forced to see psychiatrists or to date boys or to marry. Some were harassed at school or at work. Some had breakdowns and attempted suicide.[9] Some ran away and lost their families for ever. Some turned to early marriage and motherhood in a desperate attempt to 'please', to eradicate their lesbianism, because other people's attitudes caused them so much pain. Some ran away to big cities, especially London, homeless and jobless, becoming involved in prostitution and with drugs and alcohol, sometimes ending up in borstal and then prison. Some took refuge in lesbian or gay clubs where everyone was, or seemed, much older and more experienced. And, of course, teenage lesbians were also, amidst the pain of rejection, isolation and physical abuse, often experiencing the real joy of self-discovery on their own and in their relationships with other women. Most of these young lesbians had nowhere to go to talk things over, no one to whom to relate their joyful experiences, or with whom to talk about their normal everyday problems.

Some of these young women had been attending the Gay Teenage Group (and some were also participating in girls' work in the area). Those that attended the Gay Teenage Group had increasingly become aware that many issues relevant to young lesbians could not be explored in a mixed setting. They felt that many such issues were not entirely of primary concern to young gay men, and wished to have separate space in order to deal with them.

The wish to be separate coincided with the setting up of the two girls' projects and workers from those projects were asked to facilitate this new group which began in the autumn of 1979. This proposition was an entirely new kind of youth work – highly controversial and with no previous examples of practice to draw upon. The two workers, one Black and one white, knew that to maintain this group, work undertaken would have to be well considered, careful, and by the letter, in terms of good youth work practice. They used lessons learned in the women's movement, gay liberation, Black liberation and girls' work practice as a framework for this new departure. In a typical youth work setting (table games, music, refreshments etc.) they concentrated on social and political education, counselling and self-help to enable young women to centre themselves and gain in confidence and strength.

The Young Lesbian Group was set up for lesbians, by lesbians. It was agreed that it was important that lesbians worked in the group and that any outside speakers who came in would be lesbians. This was to counter the complete lack of lesbian role models in society at large and to give young women in the group the feeling that it was 100 per cent OK to be a lesbian for those few hours a week, as they were in an all-lesbian environment.

Space and emphasis was also laid on the cultural identities and needs of those young lesbians from minority ethnic backgrounds. Work was carried out with regard to the position of Black people in this society, and pride and solidarity with those young lesbians was encouraged. Anti-racist work was integrated throughout the work of the project.

For example, with white group members, it was important to establish a group atmosphere which was explicitly anti-racist. For Black and minority ethnic members, it was important to show positive role models and information about Black lesbians. This was done by collection and use of resource materials and through contacts with Black and minority ethnic lesbians. Since the early 1980s lesbian groups for Black, Chinese, Cypriot, South Asian, South Armenian and other lesbians have been set up. Young lesbian group members have regularly gone on to join these groups – some initiated them. Issues of cultural identity often developed for group members at a point when the issues of sexual identity and confidence within lesbian identity had been established.

Within the group's meeting space was quiet space for discussions, an office for counselling and the telephone, and a 'noisy' space for music, pool, darts and informal chat. The underlying ethos was self-help and self-improvement. Young women were encouraged to socialise together and form support and friendship networks which in turn operated for new young women coming into the group. This has proved to be a very successful part of the work. Nine years later we find that within all the different age ranges there are good support and friendship networks which stem from this time.

Quite soon, particular ways of working emerged and good practice was built upon. Aims and functions were drawn up and an informal programme of work was developed and improved over the first few years. The functions of the group, which have remained the same over the nine years of its existence, are listed below:

1. To enable young lesbians to work out their sexual/emotional identity in a supportive environment which does not condemn them.

2. To provide space where young lesbians can talk about relevant issues together, to learn how to survive in a hostile world and to improve the quality of their lives.

3. To help young lesbians involved in crisis situations.

4. To enable young lesbians to participate in the running of the group.

5. To go on trips and visits, both social and cultural, to engender a sense of identity and pride as lesbians and in lesbianism.

Over the years these functions developed into a programme of work, and have been carried out through a combination of group discussion, individual counselling, and practical help and guidance. The group has had discussion on: coming out, lesbians and feminism, lesbian history, sex education, class, incest, disability, motherhood, race, the police, housing, violence, and other issues.

There have been guest speakers from Lesbian Line, Lesbians and Policing Project, and Sappho, and courses run by the Group include self-defence, and silk screening. Youth participation has been encouraged by joint organisation of activities and fund-raising events, such as jumble sales and discos. Also, by having young women members to answer the telephone (possibly to distressed callers), and by encouraging members to reply to pen friend requests (young lesbians ring from all over Britain) members are also involved in group management. A high proportion of members (compared with youth in general) have gone on to do part- and full-time youth work and youth work training. Members have been invited to other 'mixed' youth clubs to talk about the YLG. The group has been on seaside trips, organised and attended the first National Young Lesbians' Summer Camp in Yorkshire, been to Amsterdam for 2-4-day holidays, stayed for long weekends at Oaklands (Wales) and Horton (Yorkshire) Women's Holiday Centres. It has attended the theatre, cinema and social events, been on Lesbian and Gay Pride Marches, and appeared on Esther Rantzen's TV show and on lesbian and gay youth videos.

Group workers have counselled young women who are in distress: for example the lover of a 16-year-old was killed in a car crash and the young woman was unable to confide in anyone until a year later, when she rang the group. Workers will also refer on to specialist agencies, such as Rape Crisis. Other young women arrive in a crisis where more than counselling is called for, i.e. practical help. Some of them have literally run away from home that day and alternative accommodation must be found. They may need to be taken to casualty if they have been beaten up. One young woman had been raped in the hostel where she lived and another had run from years of physical abuse by her father which had changed to sexual abuse when her lesbianism was found out.

In these situations different options have to be discussed – whether or not to involve the police, support around possible pregnancy, pregnancy testing and so on. Others want to leave home and need help and advice about whether this is the best alternative. Sometimes we have ended up meeting and counselling parents as well as their daughters! Young women's older brothers and/or fathers have followed them to the group (this has happened on more than one occasion) and have been very threatening to their sisters/daughters as well as to group workers and members. This has meant getting local support from other youth workers, housing workers or social workers.

Local support and personal contact between group workers and other caring professionals in the members' area has not always been forthcoming. For the first few years, before there were other YLGs in London, young women came from all over London and the Home Counties, from Hemel Hempstead to Croydon, from Dagenham to Hounslow! Therefore workers had to deal with other professional workers over a very wide catchment area, usually having to 'educate' other professionals as to the needs of young lesbians.

On a typical evening in the group, when there would be two or three workers there, while one worker is talking to a very disorientated new member in the office, another might be listening to an older member's story about splitting up with her girlfriend. A group member may be talking on the telephone to a young woman from Devon who rings up sometimes for a supportive 'chat', and the rest of the group may be having a discussion/argument with or without a worker, or playing pool or darts, planning a fund-raising benefit, or just sitting and feeling 'at home'.[10]

Young women hear about the group from Lesbian and Gay Switchboard, Lesbian Line, from teachers, social workers and other youth workers, from stickers and handbills and from the group's 'plug' in 'Out in the City' in *City Limits*. On one evening at the group, in December 1987, members were asked why they attend and why the group should exist. These are some of the answers that they gave:

'To meet other young lesbians – to do things and go places I wouldn't do alone.'

'People don't want to feel they're the only one . . . they need confidence to meet people.'

'If the Group didn't exist I'd be alone and have no confidence.'

'I come to talk about what it's like to be a lesbian . . . to get strength and courage to "come out" to my mum.'

'To find out what's going on in the area and get more courage to go places.'

'We meet and go out socially.'

'To make lesbians think it's not wrong – for support and someone to talk to.'

'For people who think they might be . . . it makes you feel – if there are so many of us – it can't be wrong.'

'Because you know everyone else that comes is a lesbian.'

'You are isolated – because there is no other way – if other young lesbians were "out" at school it would be different.'

'I have to lead two lives – make excuses and cover up.'

'The "scene" is full of older women – I would have been a bit lost.'

'To experience political things – work things out – bounce ideas off each other.'

The above young women could have been making the same statements nine years ago. It is true that homosexuality and lesbianism are talked about more now, but change is very slow and sometimes moves backwards as well as forwards (as in the case of Section 28).

Section 28 of the Local Government Act 1988 has shaken up a few assumptions, made many people less complacent, shown lesbians and gays who their friends and enemies are, and brought some lesbians and gays 'out of the closet' but it

246

has not as yet brought about the demise of YLGs. However, it is possible that in the case of the ILEA and its abolition, YLGs and gay youth groups may be cut as part of general cuts packages, along with other 'fringe' or 'specialist' groups.

Young lesbians today still feel acutely isolated and rejected, they are still beaten up, raped, made homeless and spurned by their families. Groups like the Young Lesbian Group are vital to them. They are sometimes the only places, if only for a few hours once a week, where young lesbians can relax, just sit and be themselves knowing that they do not have to hide, act differently, protect themselves or lie. These are places where boyfriends, husbands, marriages, engagement rings, and heterosexual sex are *not* topics of conversation; here they can find out who they are, free from pressure and in an open and accepting way. They are places – again, often the only places – where heterosexuality (or the pretence of it) is *not* compulsory or taught or assumed.

There are 18 lesbian and/or gay youth groups in London as well as a number outside London now. These groups are all vital and necessary, not just as a 'social service' to improve the lives of young lesbians maybe sometimes keeping them *alive*, but also to make society more aware of heterosexism and as part of a political resistance to it.

Notes

1. The figures cited in these pages are from research by Camden Council into the lives of lesbians and gays, Association of London Authorities.
2. Ibid.
3. Section 28 banned local authorities (1) from 'intentionally promoting homosexuality' and (2) from teaching the acceptability of 'pretended family relationships' – it is part of the Local Government Act 1988 which became law in May 1988. No local authority has in fact been taken to court since then and the government circular on the section accepts that, as governors are responsible for the teaching of sex education, a local authority cannot be taken to court over (2). For further discussion see Chapter 4, 'Section 28

and Education' and Chapter 8, 'Sex Education in Schools'.

4. See the Thompson Report 'Experience and Participation – Report of the Review Group on the Youth Service in England' – DES, Session 1981-82, October 1982.

5. See, for example, the *Annual Report* (1960) of the London Union of Youth Clubs, formerly the London Association of Girls' Clubs.

6. National Organisation for work with Girls and Young Women; *Youth in Society*, London, June 1983.

7. Figures from Camden research, op.cit.

8. There is evidence of this throughout *Something to Tell You*, London Gay Teenage Group, London, 1984.

9. Ibid.

10. Workers' report for Islington Girls' Project *Annual Report*, 1983.

10 Challenging Heterosexism in the Curriculum: Roles for Teachers, Governors and Parents

Pip Scott

The lengths to which the state has gone to enforce heterosexuality and the role that coeducation plays in promoting this are clear (see Chapters 1 and 2). This same state has failed utterly to address the problems of male violence and sexual abuse against young women and girls (see Chapters 6 and 7) whilst at the same time trying to enshrine the sanctity of the heterosexual family through the current legislation on Sex Education: the Education (No. 2) Act 1986 and the Local Government Act 1988. However, if laws are needed to enforce the teaching of (hetero)sex education it is implicit that sexuality can be socially constructed and therefore taught. If it can be taught it can also be un-taught and a range of options and alternatives presented.

If we are to challenge heterosexism in education, it is important to understand how schools operate, both overtly and in the 'hidden' curriculum. We need to look at what information is being given to parents and students and what messages the schools are sending out, not only in terms of what materials teachers use; what information is available; how it is presented and by whom; but also at the whole ethos of the school and its effect on the day to day reality of lesbian and gay students, lesbian mothers with children in school, lesbian and gay teachers and support staff, and indeed anyone who chooses to live outside the Tory model of the heterosexual family unit (white, middle-class, Mummy, Daddy, and 2.4 children).

In this chapter, using my experience as a teacher and media resources officer in secondary and further education, and by quoting the experience of lesbian mothers and their children and those of lesbian and gay students, I will illustrate this day to day reality, look at how these overwhelmingly negative experiences can be challenged and not repeated, and consider how it is possible to challenge heterosexism in a variety of ways. This means not only looking at 'sex education' but at the whole range of subjects taught and all the interactions of the whole school community with regard to sexuality.

The Reality

It would be easy to fill several volumes with the horror stories told by lesbians and gay men, lesbian mothers, their children and lesbian and gay pupils about the reality of school life: the violence, fear, lack of validation, abuse, prejudice and ignorance.

> They survived through crises few older people would without the support of society. Rejected by parents, or coping with being institutionalised. Dealing with alienation, harassment, break-ups, and not least, death – without a shoulder to cry on, without people to talk to, to share the hurt, without the support of family, the understanding of teachers. (Trenchard, 1984)

> 'I really did think I was the only gay. That's what made me take the tablets, attempt suicide.' (Male, aged 16, in Warren, 1984)

> 'I told my teacher who sent me to a psychiatrist.' (Female, aged 19; ibid.)

After a year of researching the lives of young lesbians and gay men living in London and from a diverse range of cultures, classes and ethnic groups, the London Gay Teenage Project published their findings in the book *Something to Tell You* (Trenchard and Warren, 1984). Subsequent pamphlets, *School* (Warren,) and *Talking About Young Lesbians* (Trenchard, 1984) catalogue further damage done by heterosexism and document the experiences of these young people at school.

> 416 young lesbians and gay men filled in an extensive questionnaire [with] a series of questions about their schools and personal experience there. The majority of these young people (60 per cent) said that at their schools the topic of homosexuality had *never* been mentioned in any lesson at all. Furthermore, 80 per cent of the people who said the topic had been mentioned said it was in a way that was not helpful to them. Thus less than one in ten said that homosexuality had been talked about at their school in a way they found personally helpful. (Warren, 1984)

Many young people complained that being lesbian/gay at school had created problems for them which were not recognised by any of the staff in the school. It is also important to remember that many lesbian and gay young people have additional struggles in their lives: many are Black or from other minority ethnic or cultural groups and suffering already from living in a racist society.

> 'As a Black lesbian I fight alongside those same brothers and sisters (Black lesbians and Black gays) for recognition of our sexuality within our own minority ethnic communities. The battle that I wage with my family for acceptance is the same battle that all lesbians and gays fight with their families, and the assumption that it is different is racist. For Black lesbians and Black gays the battle is a tougher one to take on because it means fighting with the same family and community that cushions and tries to protect you from the racism within the wider community, but it is the same battle.' (Femi, 1987)

> 'People, especially the boys, kept saying "Poof, gay black bastard". The usual uneducated names.' (Male, aged 19, in Warren, 1984)

'Being a muslim doesn't mean I'm not a lesbian, though I can't talk to my mum. I can't talk to anyone at school either.' (Female, aged 17, in Scott, unpubl.)

'It's hard to think that you're normal, especially when everything in the media, television, adverts etc. portray the happy man and woman image. It's the media and the way you're taught to think that makes you feel abnormal.' (Female, aged 19, in Warren, 1984)

'Abuse, both verbal, mental and physical. School sent me to a psychiatrist after I had attempted suicide as a result of said abuse.' (Male, aged 20; ibid.)

'The only book it was mentioned in was the bible.' (Female, aged 19; ibid.)

'Feelings of insecurity and paranoia that people knew.' (Male, aged 20; ibid.)

'Having to lie, leading 2 lives.' (Female, aged 17; ibid.)

'I was unable to cope with the fact that I felt/saw things differently from everyone else.' (Male, aged 20; ibid.)

'I could never be myself.' (Female, aged 20; ibid.)

Others have physical disabilities or learning difficulties and are rarely consulted about their needs or experience. These problems are often exacerbated by a complete neglect of lesbianism/homosexuality in all areas of the curriculum; a willingness by the school community to condone anti-lesbian and gay attitudes; and the inability or refusal to provide any positive support or counselling to young lesbians and gays with problems at school.

It is a sad indictment of education that so many young people have experienced such pain and distress, in schools, even to the extent of seeing suicide as their only perceived solution.[1] It is important to be clear how many young people we are talking about:

There are lesbian and gay students in *every* school in this country. Research has indicated that between 1 in 5 and 1 in 20 of the population define themselves as bisexual or homosexual. A frequency of 1 in 10 is the most commonly quoted and widely accepted figure. This means that if, for example, a school has 1,000 pupils, it is likely that 100 of them will be homosexual, or will come to that realisation. (Warren, 1984)

Included in this chapter is some of the testimony of the young people interviewed in *School* by Hugh Warren, which is essential reading for everyone involved in schools. None of us who are concerned with the welfare and education of *all* our students can fail to be deeply affected and moved by the accounts of these young people's lives:

'I had difficulty concentrating on school matters because I didn't understand myself. There needs to be an acknowledgement that teenagers can make decisions about their sexuality at an early age.' (Female, aged 20, in Warren 1984)

'They called me "queer" because I never played football and hung around with girls. I got beaten up and had my face slashed. The teachers didn't know how to deal with it. I had to leave school because of the threats.' (Male, aged 19; ibid.)

This insistence, often unconscious, on presenting heterosexuality as the only acceptable way of being, affects not only young lesbians and gay men but also the children of lesbian mothers and the lesbian mothers themselves.[2] Using the case studies of two such lesbian mothers and one of their daughters, it becomes clear how heterosexism damages and invalidates, and how difficult it seems to challenge it, but at the same time how important it is that we take up this challenge if we care about choice and safety and life.

CA: A Case Study

I talked to CA, a lesbian mother with two young boys, K and J who are at primary school.

PS: 'Are you "out" as a lesbian at your children's school?

I've talked to a lot of lesbian mothers who feel that it is very difficult to put their children at risk by being open.'

CA: 'Yes, I am. I know a lot of women who choose not to be "out" for the reasons you say, and I totally respect their right not to say that they are lesbians, but I don't agree with not being out. It *is* hard on our children but there is no easy way round it. I am not willing to go along with someone else dictating where and when I'm out. If it creates difficulties, it's not us creating them, it's them. It's our right to be out when and where *we* decide.'

PS: 'Do you think having sons rather than daughters makes a difference in terms of how they are treated at school?'

CA: 'Yes, it is much easier having boys than girls. It is easier for boy children than girls – the gender difference gives boys an easier time, they cannot be accused of being a *lesbian* by association: girls can. They also often get pity, "Poor lad, his mum's a lesbian". For me, I think a lot is said in terms of children's rights – school is *their* environment, their place of work – which is obviously true, but I want my children to take on the struggle against heterosexism just as much as I expect them as boys to take on the struggle against sexism. They are privileged because they are boys and white, I don't want them to be protected from that struggle.'

PS: 'How do they handle it?'

CA: 'J will acknowledge that he has two mothers, but doesn't dwell on it. K on the other hand is much more open. A lot of the children who we know as open, cheerful and friendly amongst friends are regarded as loners, difficult, withdrawn or sullen at school because they refuse to discuss their home lives and choose to keep themselves separate. Children with lesbian mothers receive no validation about their own realities. The words lesbian and gay are not heard at school except as abuse; children are repeatedly told that they "can't have" two mothers. Lots of them end up making up stories about their home lives in order to fit in with the concepts of the family they see presented at school. I know a child who drew a series of pictures of his "father" and then one of him dying in a car crash. The effects of all these things means that kids have a split sense of reality about home and school. It must be the same for kids from different cultures.'

PS: 'How did you go about choosing what school to send them to? How much did the issue of you being a lesbian affect what you did?'

CA: 'Well, before deciding on schools, we knew we wanted a small school, local and positive about having a child with disabilities. (K has cerebral palsy.) We both talked to the head teacher (C and her partner). We told her about our relationship and the children and she was very straight-forward about it and said she didn't see that it was a problem. I felt however that it is because she sees the whole school as being full of "problem families" and we were just part of that. One example of what I mean is one time we were trying to get a helper for K (because of his disability he is supposed to have specific help). The school had the inter-views without letting me know until afterwards. So I asked the Head whether she had told the helper about us being lesbians because K talks completely openly about us and I wanted him to be validated in his experiences, and she said that she had, but, "don't worry it was in complete confi-dence". Well of course, that just showed how she had missed the point. I want K to be validated about talking about us, but she just couldn't hear it, she just went on about confidentiality.'

PS: 'But what about confidentiality in terms of custody and so on?'

CA: 'Of course teachers must be made aware of this and be sensitive, but they *must* listen to individual parents and not make assumptions. I want the words "lesbian mother" to be used in schools as a matter of course without any fuss.'

PS: 'Have there been any particular incidents which have been hard for either of the boys to have to deal with?'

CA: 'Not so much for J because he won't say much to anyone at school, but K is very open and less fearful about what he says. There is one thing that happened though. Someone was organising a project where parents and chil-dren were going to write little stories about themselves. One of the parents was particularly keen for me to get involved, I

think mainly because they wanted something about disability. I talked to J and K about it. J wasn't interested but K got
quite excited about doing it. So, we wrote a little adventure
story about a journey on the tube and how K got on to the
train and I didn't, and how we eventually got back together
and so on. It was a story with choices in it – like – if you want
to know about cerebral palsy turn to page so and so, and if
you want to know why K has two mums, turn to page so and
so, and on these pages were quite simple explanations. We
had fun doing it and K was excited about it. What was
supposed to happen was that everybody would bring their
stories in and they would be read out to all the children.
Now, of all the stories, guess which story was handed in and
somehow "got lost"?'
PS: 'Oh no!'
CA: 'It has never turned up.'

A – A Case Study

A is 45 and has two daughters at school, B who is 16 and C
who is 14½.

PS: 'Are you out as a lesbian at the girls' schools or to any
of their teachers?'

A: 'To some of the teachers, but only once I've sussed out
who is trustworthy. I've always felt that school is my
daughters' space and they ought to have the chance of
dealing with their own struggles in their own time and their
own way. So I've never wanted to impose anything of myself
– my sexuality included. I was also fearful that if they started
having negative experiences at school because of my sexuality they would reject me. So there was quite a lot of fear
around it.'

PS: 'How did it make *you* feel?'

A: 'I spent a lot of the time being terrified that someone
would find out – every time one of them came home from
school upset, I always thought, "Oh my God, someone has
twigged it and is giving them a hard time". It's been quite a
strain.

'To offset it I've tried to be the perfect mother – helping at school Christmas parties, being a governor – I've always done more than a lot of parents who were more confident. It's almost like having a bank balance and making sure your assets are enough to offset the day when you make a large withdrawal.'

PS: 'Do you think you would have felt differently if you'd had sons rather than daughters?'

A: 'I think it would have been easier in a lot of ways. I haven't had sons and I don't want to stereotype, but I get a sense of one's relationship to sons being no less intense but maybe less protective. Also because they are not girls they couldn't be accused of being lesbians.'

PS: 'Guilt by association?'

A: 'Yes. One painful thing that happened two years ago – when B was very upset and it turned out she was frightened of being a lesbian, very difficult to deal with. She'd absorbed a lot of negative things about lesbians, and being one myself made it very painful. It was complicated by the fact that a close friend of hers had started a relationship with a boy and B felt very rejected and upset and wondered if the feelings she was having meant that she was a lesbian. What came out as she talked was her absolute horror and disgust at the thought that she might be. She said she would rather commit suicide than be a lesbian. On the one hand it was painful and oppressive to me – but on the other, here was a kid who was beside herself and who needed my support.'

PS: 'Do you think you resolved it with her at all?'

A: 'I don't think I handled it very well at the time. We talked it through and I told her about when I first knew about myself. I tried saying, what does it matter if you are a lesbian, but that didn't help. I found myself almost reassuring her that she probably wasn't – even though actually it would be fine by me if they both were. So I got in a terrible muddle about it. The best I could come up with was that if she was that it was OK, and that she'd get a lot of support, and if she wasn't there was nothing to worry about. So she could just take her time with it . . . but it was very painful.'

PS: 'Do you think these fears are about being frightened of how the other kids would treat her? I know that when I was 11 in the fifties that it was a bad thing to be, but I knew I was one and I knew the word, but where had I learned it from? There wasn't much openness or publicity in those days.'

A: 'I think she has internalised a lot of negativity from school, especially secondary school. She has moved from saying "I don't think it is a problem but the world is very prejudiced", to "it's disgusting", and "I love you but I wish you weren't", and then to feeling ambivalent about it – I remember the words she used – "I don't agree with it, but lesbians are people you can really love". Then she thought she was, and then her Head of English, a gay bloke, asked her to put something together about a book he was compiling and she started off, "Not only is mum a warm, loving, caring person, but she's a lesbian and I'm proud of her for that". Then she went on to describe all the stages she went through – bitter, very confused, how she had a hard time. She has always made up a lot of stories to cover up.'

PS: 'Yes, I wanted to ask you about that.'

A: 'When she was first at secondary school she was quite open about D (my partner). If she was ill at school and the teacher said "Is your mum at home?' She'd say "No, but D is". Then the teacher wanted to know who D was and she'd say "She lives with us". But as she got older, friends started coming home and one day when she was obviously feeling edgy, she made up this incredible story about how D had been married to a soldier, they had been moving house, he got sent to the Falklands and got killed and she missed him so she'd stayed with us ever since. Which of course was brilliant because it all got focused on this poor, mythical bloke who had been killed in the Falklands!'

PS: 'Brilliant, what a creative solution!'

A: 'Yes. But I still don't know whether my attempt to give them space to work it out for themselves has been the best strategy. By the end of her time at school she was really wanting to tell someone, her friends, and the teachers about how oppressive they had been. A lot of the homeworks they got involved talking about the people they live with. She used to say "I can't write about that, D hasn't even got a name". She thought about telling the truth in her English GCSE oral exam. I think she would have done, but with the whole pressure of exams she decided not to. She wanted to do it but was afraid that she couldn't handle the consequences. Now, I don't know whether that's because in my attempts to enable them to build their own strengths at their own pace, I've done the wrong thing – maybe I should have been "out" and said there is nothing to be ashamed of – and maybe then they would have been stronger.'

PS: 'Don't you also feel that by letting them come to it in their own time that, in retrospect, was the right thing to do?'

A: 'Well, I don't know, but if a kid of 16 writes what she did, and says, well, I've got two mums and it is the world that is the problem, then I suppose at least some of it wasn't a mistake.'

PS: 'Yeah, sounds like a success story to me.'

A: 'But maybe if I'd done the other, she'd have got further quicker, or maybe she'd have gone under. I don't know.'

PS: 'Just listening to you talking about the stages she's gone through reminds me of all the stages I went through around coming out. It is the same sort of process – knowing you are one, feeling bad, hating yourself and then gradually wanting to tell people . . . but it is very frightening.'

A: 'Yes, that's exactly right. C has been very different. As a very little kid she said "It's no big deal. People should do what they want". But she has got quieter and quieter about it. When a friend of mine asked her about it recently she was quite indifferent . . . "it's not a problem", she said. Although I've had all the uproar about it with B, somehow it is healthier. I don't feel entirely comfortable with C's silence around it. Either she is OK about it, and indeed she doesn't seem messed up according to all the conventional indicators, she's doing well at school, has an active social life and so on. But how can it not be something of a problem for a 14 year old? She can't be that sussed out and self-contained.'

PS: 'What sort of things has she written about home for schoolwork?'

A: 'I remember when she was six she was very open. She'd say anything. I remember one time she wrote, "We went to the seaside and my mum found a dead fish on the beach and took it home and cooked it for our tea". I can remember being very worried that the teacher would really think I gave them dead fish for their tea! Around sexuality I've found it difficult to guide them, I've not wanted to undermine myself and let them think I am ashamed of being a lesbian, but I've wanted to warn them that the world is prejudiced, and they need to be a little bit careful.'

PS: 'Do you think you need to give them that warning, don't you think they know?'

A: 'I think they don't know. I actually know kids who have gone to their infant schools and written, "My mum is a lesbian . . . Miss, how do you spell lesbian?"'

PS: 'But it amazes me how time and time again really young kids know not to write the truth.'

A: 'That's also true, but sometimes they don't know when they are giving the game away. So if they have to write a story about their family, my kids would write about mum and dad and sister and cat and they might add a dog for good measure. They weren't saying, "my mum is a lesbian", but they were always saying, "mum and D took us on holiday", or "mum and D did this with us", so they don't know when they are giving the game away. There were a couple of times when anyone with a brain between their ears would have known what the circumstances were. It was that which used to frighten me, because if the kids thought they were hiding it because they weren't ready to take it on, then they were making mistakes about what they were writing. I never knew quite what to do – I didn't want to freak them but I didn't want them to drop themselves in it if they weren't ready.'

PS: 'There is the issue about how your lesbianism is going to affect your daughters, what harassment they might get, but there is the whole issue about custody for lesbian mothers.'

A: 'Well, I think I used the custody issue for longer than it was a reality. I felt guilty towards other lesbians for not being out. I felt I lacked courage and dignity too.'

PS: 'But it, custody, is an issue isn't it?'

A: 'Yes, for a lot of women it is.'

PS: 'The information schools have about kids, how they label them, confidentiality and so on.'

A: 'Yes. I want two things for my kids, not to hand it on a plate to teachers that if anything went wrong in their schooling it was because I was a lesbian. There was a time when B was playing up – not because I was a lesbian, but because the teacher kept singling her out as an example to the other girls as an excellent pupil. Predictably she got called "Boffin" so started being naughty to get the approval of her classmates. Secondly, I didn't want it to be any different for my kids than for any others – that is I wanted them to have the opportunity to develop and find their own strengths with my support, and have room to grow up without a load of hassle. It is a romantic view of childhood maybe, I know the world isn't like that – but I just wanted them to be kids. They both have very strong friendships with other girls and I've never wanted that to get destroyed by any nonsense about lesbians because it has always seemed a very healthy and lovely feature of their lives. I don't want the world crashing in and saying, "Ugh. Look you're taking after your mother . . . dirty queers" etc.'

PS: 'Were there any "out" lesbians at their schools?'

A: 'No unfortunately. There was just one gay man at B's school.'

PS: 'Would it have made a difference to you if there had been?'

A: 'Oh yes, it would have been possible to network and for them to support me as a lesbian mother, and for me to support them in my role as a governor. I remember B coming home once absolutely over the moon because one of her teachers had worn a feminist earring. She had a really good relationship with that teacher.'

PS: 'Yes, I remember one of my nieces coming home one day and saying that her new teacher had the same "style" as me. What she had realised was that she was a lesbian. She was taught by her for a year and then by a gay bloke so she thinks all teachers are lesbians or gay men.'

A: 'Lucky girl.'

PS: 'Yes, fat chance, but nice to have the experience . . .

So what do you want schools to do?'

A: 'I want them to stop assuming that the only natural, normal and good way to be is heterosexual. I want them to start telling the truth, and start saying how, as a matter of fact, people live their lives in many different ways – some are celibate, some live in groups, gay or straight etc. Start telling it like it is – as a matter of course. What I don't want them to do is a big project about lesbian mothers. Imagine it, now who's got one? B, you have haven't you? I just want them to be honest about how the world actually works, that heterosexualtiy is not all that it is cracked up to be – to stop this highly selective version of it.'

PS: 'Is there anything else you want to say?'

A: 'Yes. I've never ever had any support or recognition from any of the schools my daughters have attended, to make it easy for me to be open and honest about who I am. At the moment the Tories are really big on parents' rights. Well, I'm a parent, I'm a lesbian parent. The Tories assume that all parents are heterosexual. Well we are not.'

B's Story

B is A's 16-year-old daughter. What follows is the writing she did about her mother and school.

'To a lot of people it is only natural that their mum is special but this is even more so for me, not only because she is a wonderful, accomplished and loving person but because she is a lesbian. It is only recently that I have been able to feel proud of her for being this. For a long time I felt bitter towards her, because of the pain and uncertainty I went through, the lies I told and still tell today. Not many people know and those that do keep it to themselves, both for my mum's and my sake.

'My mum and dad divorced when my sister and I were young, but before this during the times when my dad (who is equally important to me although not in the same respect) was away working, we had a woman staying with us. At the time I thought nothing of it although, and I think this must have been very hard for my mum to do, my mum was always open about her sexuality with us, when she was sure of it.

'So it did not seem unusual to go and live in an all women household. I hated the women who lived with us, yet became extremely upset when they left. I hated them for what they were. How could I explain to my junior school friends that these women my mum had bought a house with were lesbians?

'I was never able to sort out my feelings about her sexuality, but then came D. It's uncanny the way that people think that she and I are mother and daughter, and how D and mum look like sisters. I get on extremely well with D and love her very much. I suppose one could say I have two mums.

'I do feel like I live a life of deceit, lying about my mum to my closest friends and saying D is our lodger, aunt or whatever (one day I will be caught out). I feel guilty and as if I am letting them both down, but I refuse to suffer the prejudice of the world, they would be so ignorant of the situation. I have often thought recently of telling my close friends just before I leave school, but this takes so much courage and I do not know what to expect of their attitudes. I do not want to have to cut myself off from them completely if they cannot understand.

'I wouldn't want my mum to be anything else. We get on extremely well and unlike most of my friends my mum and D are the closest friends I have. I have two wonderful mums, while everyone else has one. That is worth all the pain I went through. This in itself was released when I was able to speak to mum and D about how I feel. I don't think I could have done that if they weren't lesbians, mind you I wouldn't have had the problem then! This has made them, I feel, more warm and loving and able to talk about their feelings freely.

'The one regret that I have is that there are no books or anything for children of lesbian mothers. Although I know I am not the only one, I felt I needed some reassurance – a message for us out there.

'Because the school curriculum assumed everyone was heterosexual, homosexuality was *never* mentioned, no teacher ever mentioned it, no sex education including it was ever taught, in fact the only time it was talked about was when girls "joked" about "poofs" and "lessies". My response to this varied throughout. When I and my peers began to mature I was able to defend homosexuality in a sort of manner, but often I would laugh with them so that they would never guess. Then I would feel guilty like I was letting everyone down, me, mum, D and my friends because in a way I was lying to them.

'My friends naturally made assumptions about my mum, because of the heterosexist society we live in and partly because mum went to great lengths to "compensate" for her sexuality, in other words, appear a "good mother". I was aware of this but could never quite decide whether I would rather she kept well away just in case people found out.

'As a school they never did anything, indeed could not do anything even if they had known the situation I was in, how can you change what is assumed and has been assumed and encouraged for centuries?

'Finally I would just like to mention my open study that I did for my GCSE English Literature folder. It compared the life of young lesbians in fiction and reality. It was suggested by an English teacher who was himself gay and knew about my position. This was the only support I received at school and it was *individual*. However it certainly brought about some sticky moments: e.g. I was interviewed by a university student studying the new English exam and introduced as the author of 'an exceptional open study'. She asked me why I had chosen the study I had. HELP! What could I say? "Oh, this teacher of mine, he's gay you see and he knows my mum's a lesbian, so he suggested I do it and supported me in writing about the bloody society we live in!" Well, in the end I said I thought I'd be original, everyone else was writing about racism and sexism etc. so I read a lot of books about the subject and wrote something different.

'This open study, I feel, released a lot of anger from me, that I had with everyone; myself, mum and those who made my life the way it was. I was only able to think about writing this after my open study.

'I love my mum, or should I say my two mums, and I wouldn't want it any other way, but it has taken me a long time to come that far with my feelings in such a turmoil. After all, I couldn't have written this last year.'

The Way It Is . . .

The Education No. 2 Act 1986 states that a *balanced* perspective on sex education and relationships should be presented, including discussion of sexuality as a whole. It is overwhelmingly evident from the preceding testimony that any notion of balance in the existing curriculum is non-existent. What is presented is completely heterosexist; the only model for relationships is heterosexual; sexuality is never presented as a continuum where choice might be involved; if lesbian or gay relationships are mentioned at all, it is likely to be in the context of sexually transmitted diseases and as a problem. Educational TV is saturated with 'How To Have A Baby' programmes which are presented by men and show white mummies and daddies. They present the biological version of parenthood without any discussion about sexual attraction, passion, pain, responsibilities or the implications of having children. Indeed the problematic areas of nuclear family life, already well documented in this book, and more specifically the problems of male behaviour – sexual abuse of young women and girls, domestic violence – are rarely mentioned. Similarly issues of consent, safety and the law relating to sexuality are notably absent. If young people are to have a genuine opportunity to control and make sense of their own lives, and be able to make real choices, challenge gender stereotypes and, in particular, male power as it is constructed they must be given the opportunity within the school curriculum to discuss and understand issues of feelings, power, choice, responsibility, self-image, self-esteem, and the oppression of specific groups, Black people and other cultural minorities in this country, and people with disabilities.

In the majority of schools discussions, such as there are, about sex and sexuality are either confined to biology, which concentrates on human 'plumbing', or to either personal and social education programmes or the pastoral curriculum. The tendency has been to assume that subjects are value free, which of course they are not.

In the 'hidden curriculum', the ethos of schools, messages re-inforcing heterosexuality are everywhere. Even when schools have understood the need for some sort of equal opportunities policy of race and gender there is rarely a mention of sexuality. The messages on the walls (unofficial, in terms of graffiti), are uniformly anti-lesbian and anti-gay; officially, in terms of posters and displays, they rarely give information or validation to lesbian and gay pupils. It is universally assumed that parents, pupils, teaching and non-teaching staff, governors and visitors are heterosexual; engagements and weddings are celebrated quite uncritically. The message is that schools are one large, happy heterosexual world. Even when teachers or other workers are honest in answering children's questions about their sexuality, they are not believed. For example, when asked by a group of fifth-year girls whether I was a lesbian or not, I answered 'yes'. They found it almost impossible to believe me because the myths they had absorbed about lesbians did not match up to the fact that they liked me.

Despite the propaganda, we know that schools are made up of diverse groups of people, lesbian and gay as well as heterosexual. We know it is a myth that everyone in school is heterosexual, and we have to engage in the struggle to challenge this assumption. The next section attempts to outline how we might mount this challenge.

Taking Up the Challenge

In spite of the odds, none of us are helpless in the face of heterosexism. In spite of the way it is constructed and promoted, thousands of us have resisted and made our own choices. All education workers, parents and governors have a part to play in challenging the myths. While inevitably teachers are in the front line in presenting alternatives, schoolkeepers, technicians, cooks, media resources officers, librarians, clerical and canteen workers can all ensure that heterosexism never goes unchallenged.

The formation of attitudes and prejudice starts at home and is nurtured at nursery and primary schools. The Haringey Council Report *Equal Opportunities – The Lesbian and Gay Perspective* (1988) presents five areas where heterosexism can be challenged. These are: the way in which the concept of family and family life are portrayed, sexual stereotyping, the presentation of gender in children's learning materials, verbal abuse and, finally, answering children's questions.

It is essential that all children are encouraged to develop a positive self-image, to be proud of themselves, their families, their language and all the aspects of their culture which they value. The children of lesbian mothers receive none of this validation, as we have seen. The words lesbian and gay are never heard except as terms of abuse; children are repeatedly told that they 'can't have' two mothers and may end up fabricating stories about their home lives in order to fit in with the concepts of family they see presented at school – if they do not, of course, they risk having their stories 'lost'. Other children respond by refusing to discuss their home lives, and cheerful friendly children find themselves labelled as sullen or withdrawn. Few children of any age tell their friends that their mother is a lesbian: they have learned what a negative reaction that brings. In essence they are being forced to deny the reality of their lives: to lie. This means that other children and parents, along with their teachers, are never made aware of the alternatives.

To overcome this, children should be presented with the whole range of alternatives and lifestyles, not just that of the nuclear family, in all their books and learning materials. By all means use their experiences and celebrate them – but do not lose their lives like young K's. Creative play should not be an occasion to reinforce traditional sex roles, rather use it as an opportunity to explore and develop self-expression in a variety of roles.

Just as many schools now have policies which make it unacceptable to use abusive terms which are racist and sexist, so it is important that this is extended to include derogatory terms against lesbians and gays. When it comes to answering children's questions it is important to bear in mind the age and ability of the child to understand what is being said, but there is no reason why they should not be given honest and factual answers to their questions in an objective and appropriate way.

In secondary schools too, it is important that existing equal opportunities practices and policies are surveyed and evaluated – there are, increasingly, plenty of examples of good practice where lesbians and gay men are being given more equal treatment in different areas of the curriculum, if only through the use of more thoughtful language (e.g. 'partner' rather than 'husband' or 'wife'), or by refusing to make the assumption that all people are (hetero)sexually active. Teachers and other workers have a part to play here. They can make themselves aware of the variety of ways in which they may, if they are heterosexual, be reaffirming heterosexual lifestyles: for example, by wearing wedding rings, talking about their heterosexual partner, showing family photos and so on. They must realise that they do these things without thinking, while lesbians and gay men are always aware that by talking about our lives in this way we are putting ourselves at risk. In realising this, they may become more sensitive to our oppression.

As pupils with disabilities will be increasingly integrated into mainstream secondary schools, it is important to bear in mind that sexuality is an issue for them too. This must involve the school and governors in careful discussions as to how these young people's needs and interests will best be served, particularly if they are lesbian or gay. Adolescence is the time when many young people start to develop or question their sexuality. This can be a confusing period for all young people but for young lesbians and gay men this confusion can lead, as you have read, to feelings of extreme isolation and despair. It is a terrible indictment of our education system that the same fears I had as a young lesbian over thirty years ago are still echoed with devastating similarity by young lesbians and gays today. If these young people are Black and/or disabled, girls or working class, the problems are compounded by sexism, racism, class and lack of awareness.

Successful education depends on good home–school liaison and on children not being made to feel ashamed or undervalued because of their home backgrounds. It is inaccurate and undermining for students of all backgrounds to be indoctrinated in the belief that the heterosexual nuclear family is the only possible model for family life. One quarter of London families, for example, are single parented. Many children from ethnic minority communities do not live in nuclear families for historical, social and cultural reasons – as well as because of racist immigration laws – so it is racist as well as heterosexist to assume that all children do.

For the children of lesbian and gay parents it is particularly difficult. Many feel that they have to lie or invent a nuclear family in order to feel accepted at school. As we have seen it is difficult for those parents too, who fear that by being honest with the school about their family structure they will make themselves and their children vulnerable to recrimination and labelling. With some lesbian mothers in particular this may lead to loss of custody of their children as 'unfit' mothers.

The statutory requirement that sex education must encourage children to have 'due regard to moral considerations and the value of family life' (Section 64, Education (No. 2) Act 1986) enables schools to undertake a full evaluation of both positive and negative aspects of heterosexual family life, including domestic violence and sexual violence against women and children. Schools may be reluctant to raise these issues with children in the belief that to do so will be to present too negative a view of family life. Unfortunately, however, a large percentage of children will already be all too familiar with domestic violence, witnessing disputes between their parents/guardians or being on the receiving end of violence and sexual abuse themselves. They do not come to school inexperienced in such matters. It is infinitely preferable to tackle the issues by being honest and supportive to children in their experiences rather than pretending, by our silence, that these things 'don't really happen'. Not only will this alleviate the isolation many children experience, it may also save lives.

Some Specific Recommendations

Despite what Tory propaganda might have us believe, there is genuine support in the community for a balance in what is taught to young people in schools with regard to sexuality:

> 'So, like all concerned parents, I want my children to learn to make good, mature, moral decisions about their sexuality. But they can't do this from a position of ignorance, uninformed gossip or total dependence on my values. So I welcome support from the school, not to reinforce exactly what I think and choose, but to help them reflect carefully . . . so they can choose for themselves.' (Haringey mother, in Haringey Council, 1988)

> 'If my daughter or son were gay, I'd want to know they were being helped at school.' (Hackney parent governor, in Scott, unpubl.)

What follows is a model for attempting to achieve that balance in the whole school curriculum. The recommendations are grouped under four main headings: Sex Education; Whole School Policy; Curriculum – Overt and Hidden) – this refers mainly to secondary school since the primary age range has already been dealt with in some detail; and Teaching Materials.

Sex Education

Any sex education programme will need to educate young people on the legislation relating to sexual practices. Within this context, discussion on the legislation itself, issues of consent, and child protection rights will need to be addressed. We all need to be concerned about children's safety and so need to familiarise ourselves with the research and evidence connected with child sexual abuse.

Contrary to the popular belief that children should not be entrusted to the care of lesbians, we remain the safest group to care for children. It is overwhelmingly heterosexual men who sexually abuse children. Lesbians have been at the

270

forefront of exposing the reality of sexual abuse against children and women by men. Women working with children who have been sexually abused agree that there are many problems with male sexuality, that sexual abuse is a gender-specific crime committed predominantly by trusted hetero-sexual men against girls and young women, and that the heterosexual family unit provides men with easy access to children and women (London Rape Crisis Centre, 1984).

Education for young people on legislation would need to include information on sexual offences. An evaluation of the issues surrounding the age of consent will open up discussion on the value of such legislation. Feminist organisations coun-selling and campaigning against sexual violence are agreed that despite the seemingly ineffectual laws, lowering the age of consent for young women may lead to further abuse of girls.

Many teachers will be uncertain and feel insecure about teaching such issues. It is recommended that schools seek the advice of specific organisations and individuals who may be prepared to talk to staff and students in an informal way and, secondly, that in-service training for staff be given.

Whole School Policy

In delivering a whole school policy – in order to provide a balanced curriculum regarding sexuality – it must be borne in mind that good educational practice means that *all* students receive equal opportunities. If, as a result of lack of positive support, the one in ten of our students who are lesbian/gay do not have their needs met, this will affect their perfor-mance and academic success at school. A young person who is in despair over her/his sexuality is unlikely to fulfil their potential.

'I became attached to one girl and we were "best friends" for 5 years until I told her I was in love with her, or thought I was. I didn't know what I was feeling. In my final year I was a bit of a wreck, cried a lot when we argued, even missed classes because I was crying. It affec-ted my work and teachers used to ask what was the

271

matter. It was terrible.' (Girl, aged 19, in Trenchard, 1984)

In formulating a whole school policy, the following points need to be considered: recognition of the fact that lesbian and gay pupils, staff and parents exist; that the school community needs to inform itself about lesbian/gay issues; that in-service training should be given to teachers in order to increase their understanding and confidence in what they are teaching, and in the use of more appropriate teaching materials; a code of practice and behaviour which effectively welcomes and protects lesbians and gays; the evaluation of all teaching materials and strategies used to challenge heterosexism; that all educational professionals including educational social workers, educational psychologists and careers officers be encouraged to challenge stereotyping, and particularly notions of the 'dysfunctional family'; and finally, that schools should draw up a list of support and advice agencies whose expertise and knowledge they can call on when pupils or parents need particular support.

Curriculum – Overt and Hidden

In the overt curriculum there is no area which cannot address the issues in some way. Subject departments need to evaluate their courses (content and method) to locate areas where it would be most appropriate to develop positive work on lesbian/gay issues and to challenge heterosexism.

Pastoral, personal, social and health education courses provide the obvious vehicle for positive work. Courses should include specific work on relationships, the provision of adequate support for lesbians and gays, and a sensitive approach to lesbian mothers and parents in general. Many schools have devised courses to include sex education presented as more than the biological/reproductive aspects of relationships. Such courses might cover: exploring emotions, an evaluation of family life, the law and sexuality, sexual offences legislation, consent, health, menstruation, masturbation, the sharing of responsibilities, challenging racism and sexism, and encouraging awareness of the needs of the differently abled. Poor self-image and low self-esteem are often part of the reason why young people feel uncomfortable about their own bodies; this may lead young women in particular to lack confidence and assertiveness, and must be addressed in some way in the curriculum. Child sexual abuse and domestic violence as issues for pupils would be best facilitated by long established and experienced counselling agencies which are feminist in their approach, for example rape crisis and incest survivors groups. This work should be done in single-sex groups to enable young women to talk without fear of repercussions from the boys, and for the boys to explore their thoughts and feelings without losing face.

All subject areas are in danger of promoting only one view of sexuality and sexual relations unless particular care is taken to check learning materials and their content. In humanities for example – which considers the human, political and social structures of the past, the present, and across cultures – it is possible to incorporate work on the social construction of sexuality. Maths, languages, business studies, games and PE, the arts in general, all have a role to play in providing a genuinely balanced curriculum and in challenging prejudice, whether through literature, examples of case studies, role play, or enabling students to develop physical and academic skills.

In the hidden curriculum unconscious messages about the school's values are transmitted through the messages on the walls, teaching styles, the way parents and guardians are received, and by uncaring attitudes going unchallenged. The general ethos of the school must encourage a helpful and positive approach to all young people struggling with their sexuality irrespective of whether they are lesbian/gay or heterosexual. It would be appropriate to have counselling helplines and other lesbian and gay information on display throughout the school. Schools must address themselves to the questions of harassment and violence and have ways of supporting and informing lesbian and gay pupils and staff, so that these experiences of young lesbians need never be repeated.

'[My problems at school also included] teasing, harassment, threats of violence, having my bicycle tampered with, having food thrown at me etc.'

'No-one talked to me for a year, I nearly got beaten up, and all the girls thought I'd jump them.'

Teaching Materials

It should already be overwhelmingly clear that learning materials must be very carefully vetted for negative images. There is an infamous science textbook which uses the images of two women to show repulsion and the images of a man and woman to show attraction in magnetism. These crass and inaccurate images must be removed from materials as a first stage. Secondly, a more positive and inclusive approach to lesbian and gay sexuality should be included. It is important, too, not to use materials just because they contain what might appear to be positive images of lesbians and gays: their accessibility, relevance, anti-racist and anti-sexist approaches need also to be assessed. Again there will be a need for teachers to have in-service training in the uses of these materials. Increasingly materials are being produced with thoughtful guidelines and suggestions for how best to use them in the classroom. One example is 'A Different Story', two videos of the lives of young lesbians and gay men, produced by the ILEA 'Relationships and Sexuality' project.

Libraries and resources areas need to have a full range of material, both fiction and non-fiction, available for pupils; this should include works about lesbian/gay lifestyles. Of course, as with learning materials generally, it is important not to go overboard and have just *anything* which has lesbian or gay images in it, for example the much publicised *Jenny Lives With Eric and Martin*, a book telling the story of a young girl living with two gay men. The images in this book, a young girl in bed with two naked men, while seeming to celebrate 'gay' parenthood, are exploitative and extremely distressing to children being subjected to sexual abuse now,

274

as well as for adult survivors. It is also extremely dull and uninteresting as a story book.

These two areas in school can play a vital role in challenging heterosexism. They are often a haven for pupils and present the opportunity for them to find information they may not be able to get elsewhere. Books, videos and displays can present alternatives, and in learning resources areas workers are in the front line of creating alternative images and materials which challenge the heterosexist status quo.

In conclusion I want to acknowledge the women – lesbians, feminists, mothers and children – and gay men whose courage and creativity, energy and enthusiasm have already created the foundations of the struggle we are engaged in. By acknowledging our own power and the collective power we have when we come out and support each other, the possibility of change, of challenging heterosexuality, becomes a reality. Governors in particular must understand the immense responsibility they now have in their role as decision makers on the content of the sex education syllabus in schools.

It would not have been possible to write this chapter if the struggle had not been started. Because of work already done, lesbians and gay men and their pupils coming out at school, the work done by lesbian and gay helplines, lesbian and gay youth workers, incest survivors groups, the ILEA 'Relationships and Sexuality' project, heterosexism awareness workshop facilitators and so on, teachers would not be beginning to understand their responsibility to look at their assumptions and at how and what they teach may be maintaining the heterosexual status quo.

It is because of this grassroots work that when the now infamous Section 28 hit the headlines it was possible to mount an enormous campaign, to raise consciousness, to educate, to encourage schools and colleges to resist it by adding sexuality to their equality policies, and in some places to strengthen their commitment to equality by making statements positively welcoming lesbians and gay men on to their courses. In South London where a school had built a reputation for an excellent equal opportunities policy including sexuality, a local Tory MP wrote to the parent governors enquiring whether they had been consulted on the school's policy on sex education. Because the governors had gone through all the appropriate consultation processes with parents and other interested parties, they were able to respond to the MP that they were angry that such an attempt was being made to influence the teaching of the school, a school, as one parent–governor said, 'which many of us, whether hetero-sexual or homosexual had chosen because of its rigorous and clear policies on Equal Opportunities encompassing approaches to all forms of discrimination, including sexuality.' She goes on to say that

> 'as a heterosexual mother, I want my children to grow up seeing homosexuality and lesbianism as part of a range of choices available to them, and given space by the school they attend. That is my freedom as a parent; I do not want that freedom restricted for me.' (Scott, unpubl.)

Inevitably it will be the work of lesbians and gay men to challenge the status quo in schools, but with support from parents and governors like that offered above, and when heterosexual people start to realise that they have been denied choices, that they have had their sexuality constructed for them, that there are alternatives to the nuclear family and that a great many people are living those alternatives, perhaps they will understand where the 'problem' really lies.

> 'Teachers and pastoral staff should be made to realise that the attitudes of anti-gay pupils/teachers are responsible for the 'problems' concerning being gay or lesbian and that being gay/lesbian is not a problem.' (Lesbian aged 20, in Trenchard, 1984)

> Many heterosexuals claim they were just 'born that way'. Unfortunately this doesn't hold water. All human beings are the result of the interaction of their substance and their environment and heterosexuals, like the rest of us must share in the responsibility for their condition. (Wakeman, 1975)

Notes

1. Twenty per cent of the young people surveyed in *School* (Warren, 1984) had attempted suicide.
2. I use the term 'lesbian mothers' because while gay men may parent children, it is overwhelmingly lesbians who do the parenting and who bear the brunt of the heterosexual world's ignorance.

References

Femi, 'Heterosexism in Haringey – Racism Runs Rife', *GEN, Challenging Heterosexism*, WedG, London, March 1987.

Haringey Council, *Equal Opportunities – The Lesbian and Gay Perspective*, 1988.

London Rape Crisis Centre, *Sexual Violence: The Reality for Women*, The Women's Press, London, 1984.

Scott, Pip, unpublished research and case studies, 1987-88.

Trenchard, Lorraine (ed.), *Talking About Young Lesbians*, London Gay Teenage Group, London, 1984.

Trenchard, Lorraine and Warren, Hugh, *Something To Tell You*, London Gay Teenage Group, London, 1984.

Wakeman, Alan, *What Exactly Is Heterosexuality?*, Gay Sweatshop, London, 1975.

Warren, Hugh, *Talking About School*, London Gay Teenage Group, London, 1984.

Biographical Notes

Davina Cooper

Davina Cooper has been a member of Haringey Borough Council since 1986. She is currently teaching law part-time and engaged in research for a PhD on the local state and sexual politics.

Jane Dixon

Jane Dixon has worked in the Youth Service since 1976, running a youth club and outdoor activities programme at Sobell Sport Centre from 1976-79. From 1979 she was a full-time youth worker at Camden Girls' Centre Project, jointly setting up the North London Young Lesbian Group. From 1985-88 she was Specialist Youth Officer for lesbian and gay young people for the ILEA. Currently she is a Youth Officer in Islington, London; she is a founder member of the National Organisation of Work with Girls and Young Women, and author of 'A short history of the Girls' Club movement 1880-1980'.

Annabel Faraday

Annabel Faraday has been involved in The London Lesbian Archive and Information Centre as a collective member and paid worker since 1984. She is working on a book based on the research for her PhD which is about anti-lesbianism in Britain in the 1920s and 1930s. She is also a potter.

Margaret Jackson

Margaret Jackson has worked for nearly thirty years as a teacher in secondary schools and higher education. She defines herself as a revolutionary feminist lesbian, and her political work has included campaigning against male violence, and analysing the relationship between sexuality and male power. She has recently been involved in developing materials for challenging heterosexism in teacher education.

Liz Kelly

Liz Kelly has been an activist in the Women's Liberation Movement since 1973, in Women's Aid, Rape Crisis, The Rape in Marriage Campaign and other local and national women's groups. She is a member of the editorial collective of *Trouble and Strife* and is currently employed as a researcher at the Child Abuse Studies Unit, Polytechnic of North London. She lives in hope of the emergence of a revitalised (yet changed for the better) activist women's movement in Britain.

Julie Melia

Julie Melia lives in South East London and is in her probationary year of teaching. One of her most pressing concerns is the far reaching effect of the National Curriculum, in particular on equal opportunities in schools.

Gilly Salvat

Gilly Salvat worked in the Youth Service since 1971, as a part-time youth worker in West London. After qualifying in 1976 as a youth and community worker, she set up youth provision in Caxton House, Islington, London. In 1979 she became a full-time youth worker at Islington Girls' Project, jointly setting up the North London Youth Lesbian Group. In 1986 she became a worker at Haringey Lesbian and Gay Unit with a specific brief for outreach and community development work in the lesbian and gay communities. She is a founder member of the Black Lesbian Group and is currently a member of SHAKTI, the South Asian Lesbian and Gay Network. She is founder member of the National Organisation of Work with Girls and Young Women.

Susan Sanders

Susan Sanders was born in 1947, came out as a lesbian when she was twenty and became a feminist a few years later. A teacher of long standing she has worked in schools, prisons, colleges and community centres in England and in Sydney, Australia. She has campaigned against Clause 28 since January 1988, and continues to be an active member of both the Arts Lobby and Education Group. At present she is a supply teacher, assertion trainer and therapist.

Pip Scott

Pip Scott is a lesbian feminist aged 42, who has worked in education as a teacher and Media Resources Officer for over twenty years. She has been actively involved in Women's Aid and a variety of women's and lesbian campaigns for the last fifteen years.

Jane Skeates

Jane Skeates has been a lesbian for 19 years. She loves *Dallas*, cooking, dresses and co-parenting her seven year old daughter. She still thinks that young lesbians are wonderfully brave and heartlifting and hopes that all of us dykes continue to resist enforced heterosexuality (joyfully not hatefully) for as long as it takes. She is not a youth worker any more.

Gill Spraggs

Until recently Gill Spraggs taught English at a sixth form college in Leicester. She is a member of the city of Leicester NUT Lesbian and Gay Rights Working Party, and contributed to their publication, *Outlaws in the Classroom: Lesbians and Gays in the School System*. She has been active in the campaign to raise awareness of lesbian and gay issues within the Union, as well as in the campaign against Clause 28.

Index